The Comprehensive Guide To
# Walleye Patterns

# The Comprehensive Guide To
# **Walleye Patterns**
## by Babe Winkelman

Published by
Babe Winkelman Productions
Brainerd, Minnesota

| | |
|---|---|
| Book Design | Babe Winkelman |
| Cover Photo | Dan Nelson |
| Artwork | Duane Ryks |
| Photography | Jeff Howard/Dan Nelson |
| Layout | Duane Ryks |
| Writing | Babe Winkelman/Dan Nelson |
| Editing | Steve Grooms/Mark Strand |
| Research | Dan Nelson/Jeff Howard |
| Cover Design | Babe Winkelman/Trademark Communications |
| Typesetting | Century Design |
| Printing | Sentinel Printing |

Published by Babe Winkelman Productions
213 NW 4th St., P.O. Box 407, Brainerd, Minnesota 56401

Printed in the United States of America

Reprinted 1986

Reprinted 1987

First Edition, 1985
Library of Congress Catalog
Card Number 85-050200

ISBN 0-915405-01-6

Library of Congress Cataloging in
Publication Data

Winkelman, Babe
The Comprehensive Guide to Walleye Patterns

Brainerd, Minnesota: Babe Winkelman Productions
ISBN 0-915405-01-6

*It is with deepest love and appreciation that I dedicate this book:*
*To my father, for inspiring me to fish walleyes when I was a kid;*
*to my wife, Charlie, for being the strength and purpose to my life*
  *and career;*
*to my children, for all the love that children can give a father;*
*to my first 10 lb. walleye . . . and all the others since;*
*but mostly to my creator, for giving me the right to go fishing.*

# ACKNOWLEDGEMENTS

It would be impossible to acknowledge all the individuals one has occasion to fish with over a twenty year study of walleyes. Each person provided information that helped develop this book.

The information I've gleaned over the years will provide you with some truly new insights, breakthroughs, materials, and approaches to fishing walleye. The final chapter of this book, much of which has never appeared in print before, will improve your walleye fishing tremendously.

Dan Nelson, an excellent walleye angler and longtime friend, worked with me throughout the last year to bring this whole system of fishing walleyes into print. Dan also added a great deal of information on reservoir and river patterns. He is one of the country's finest contributions to the sport fishing industry.

I'm very grateful to angling greats like Bill Binkelman, Spence Petros, Gary Roach, Randy Amenrud, LeRoy Ras, Bud Riser and countless other anglers with whom I've had the occasion to discuss walleyes into the wee hours of many mornings.

I'm grateful also to my brother, Dave, who has shared the boat with me on hundreds of walleye outings, always fishing with an open mind and providing the companionship only a brother can give.

And finally, without a team of professionals: Jeff Howard, Barb Dosh, Kim Peterson, Duane Ryks, Charlie and Dave, this book would not have come to be.

Through the information presented here I hope you come to realize, as I have, that each of us has a personal responsibility to ensure the future of fishing. The information gleaned from these pages of **Walleye Patterns** will help you have not only a more enjoyable time catching fish but a more enjoyable time releasing some of them as well.

# TABLE OF CONTENTS

**Dan Nelson**

Dan Nelson is a professional fisherman from Bismarck, N.D., who specializes in reservoir walleyes. In recent years he's concentrated his efforts on two major river systems—the Missouri in the Dakotas and the Columbia in Washington and Oregon. These two highly productive systems have allowed Dan to indulge in his first love, catching big walleyes. In the last four years he's boated over 100 walleyes each topping eight pounds, including a whopping 15-2 (an I.G.F.A. record), he took in 1984 from the Columbia. He's written a book on fishing reservoirs, **Walleye Fishing on the Missouri River System.** He's also authored numerous magazine and newspaper articles on fishing and done several radio and television shows. Each spring Dan conducts seminars across the Upper Midwest. In addition, he's compiled the best overall tournament record on the Missouri River system during the late 70s and early 80s. We consider Dan an extremely important member of the Babe Winkelman Research Team and a close friend.

# Foreword

Walleyes won't smash a topwater lure like an irate largemouth, nor will they rocket across a water surface like a super-charged small-mouth. They lack the speed of pike and the ferocity of musky. Walleyes are excellent eating, but so are bluegills, crappies, steak and pizza.

Then why do tens of thousands of anglers across the country beam in anticipation of their next walleye outing?

The key word is "CHALLENGE." Quite simply . . . *catching walleyes with consistency in all types of water during all seasons of the year, is one of the toughest challenges in freshwater angling!*

Think about it. Walleyes migrate seasonally, making them more difficult to locate. Walleye may also use a wide variety of depth levels in a lake. You might catch a limit of good-size "glass eyes" out of 30 to 40 feet of water or deeper, then go into the weeds for pike or muskies and catch . . . even bigger walleyes.

Primary walleye forage one day might be newly-hatched mayfly over soft-bottomed flats; or small perch in half-grown weedbeds; or six to eight-inch ciscoes near fast-breaking deep edges. Consider this in addition to the walleye attitude which usually demands a near-pinpoint lure or live bait presentation, and you'll get a good idea of what you're up against.

If fishing skill, determination and love for a particular species counts for anything, than I can't think of a better person than Babe Winkelman to help you hone your walleye skills. A lot of people love to fish wall-eyes, but nobody I know lives, breathes and talks walleye like he does. Besides being an outstanding angler, he is also one of America's fo-remost teachers of this sport through his books, popular television series, video cassettes, seminars, tapes and magazine articles. In what-ever media used, his enthusiasm, vast knowledge and communication skills will entertain and educate the audience.

Babe's approach to walleye-catching consistency is not a magic lure, secret system or never-fail method. He begins by first helping you to understand the quarry; the lifestyle, habits, traits, forage and structure preferences. The information becomes increasingly detailed, citing particular lures and baits, boat control methods, specific equipment, and fishing patterns.

This book presents you with the golden opportunity to become a better walleye angler. Babe offers you the insight and experience that has made him one of the country's most renowned walleye anglers. Take him up on the offer. I know I will!

**Spence Petros**
Managing Editor
Fishing Facts Magazine

# Chapter 1
# Why Walleyes?

## A Brain the Size of a Pea

*"A fish, is a fish, is a fish. He has a pea-sized brain, and never had an original thought in his life."*
**—Buck Perry**

A pair of sparkling eyes break the murky water's surface and focus on an unsuspecting fly perched six inches away.

With fixed stare, the smallish fish studies his target for several seconds. Then, with lightning speed and uncanny accuracy, the fish shoots a droplet of water that strikes the fly and knocks it into the water.

The archer fish of the southeastern Asiatic region has developed a highly specialized method of feeding. Like a BB from an airgun, drops of water are so precisely aimed that the target is rarely missed, sometimes even in flight.

The big Chinook salmon is 3,500 miles from home when she first feels the urge to spawn. Instinctively she begins the long migration that will lead her back to the exact spot where she, herself, was hatched some four years earlier.

Biologists, with all their knowledge and sophisticated equipment, still haven't been able to figure out how she makes the trip with such unerring accuracy. Some scientists contend salmon (and all fish) have a biological compass that leads them through the oceanic portion of their journey. Others believe that salmon leave a trail of pheromones (chemical messengers) on their seaward migration. When they return to the rivers of their youth, the theory goes, they use the pheromones as guideposts. Once under the influence of the river of their origins, the salmon swim in and out of the scent track, poking their noses into every tributary until they sniff out the right one.

No, fish are not the most cerebral of God's creatures. With a pea-sized brain, they do not have the mental powers to reason out their problems. What they do have is a finely tuned instinct for survival and propagation, an instinct polished through generations of evolution.

*Some species of fish, such as the exotic archer fish, have developed highly specialized ways of feeding.*

## Why Walleyes?

I am frequently asked "What's your favorite fish?" My answer is always, "Whatever I have on the end of my line." I get as much kick out of catching crappies on ultra-light tackle as I do from grinding a 25-pound lake trout out of 150 feet.

But there's always been a special spot in my heart for walleyes.

Attribute that to my upbringing. The popularity of different fish species can usually be traced to regional boundaries. In the Pacific Northwest, fishermen wait with anticipation for the salmon and steelhead runs, just like their fathers and their fathers before them. In the deep south, bass and catfish capture the imaginations of young fishermen. I grew up in the Upper Midwest, where the walleye has always reigned the number one gamefish.

In recent years there has been an erosion of these territorial boundaries. Largemouth bass, for instance, were once considered a trash fish in our corner of the world. But today bass are sought after by a great many north country anglers. The salmonoid fisheries are exploding on the Great Lakes and the Missouri River system. Stripers came inland to earn the respect and admiration of a large block of fishermen.

But perhaps no species has been able to transcend regional boundaries like the walleye. While not the country's most preferred species— it was number five the last time we looked—*Stizostedion vitreum* is

13

perhaps the fastest rising star on the fishing scene today. Each year anglers from Oregon to Kansas to Michigan are adding their names to the growing list of walleye zealots.

As the ranks of walleye fishermen swell, there's been an increased demand for information on the species. In the last decade dozens of books and thousands of magazine articles have been consumed by hundreds of thousands of wildly enthusiastic converts, all with a seemingly insatiable appetite for knowledge.

### Why Walleyes?

The actual act of fishing for walleyes is not nearly as action-packed as some other types of angling. Slow trolling a Lindy Rig on a deep water hump is pretty dull stuff compared to pitching a surface buzzer until your wrists ache or deftly setting a Royal Coachman on a riffle.

The walleye isn't shrouded in mystique like the elusive musky. It doesn't require 10,000 casts or a summer's worth of effort to land a single keeper walleye. Walleyes won't follow a lure to the boat, glare at the offering with disdain and swim away, leaving the frustrated angler shaking with excitement.

Walleyes aren't even as abundant as panfish. A school of active crappies will provide enough action to hold the attention of any sportsman. Most walleye fishermen have come to accept one and two-fish days as the norm.

Once hooked, the walleye is not a spectacular fighter . . . certainly not as acrobatic as the largemouth bass, which has been known to hit a plug in mid-air, or blast a bait right out of the water. Unlike bass, pike, muskies, or salmon, walleyes rarely become airborne, tail-walking across the surface in a heartstopping effort to spit the hook.

### Why Walleyes?

What, then, is the appeal of the walleye? One obvious answer is eating quality. Anyone who's ever enjoyed a shore lunch of fresh walleyes . . . who's ever watched those fillets sizzling and spitting to a golden brown . . . tasted the delicious flaky, white meat, knows the walleye takes a back seat to no fish as a taste delight.

But there's more to it than that. Much more. Acquiring food is really low on the list of reasons why people fish. When you weigh the high cost of bait, tackle, gas, lodging, licenses and equipment against the actual number of meals that result, we could all be eating caviar three times a day.

Most of us fish because it's a challenge. There's an incredible gratification that comes with taking a limit of fish or a single trophy fish, regardless of species. And walleyes offer the ultimate challenge.

This has something to do with the mysterious nature of walleyes. Generally thought of as denizens of the deep, walleyes are a cautious fish that hug the bottom and carefully scrutinize every offering. Walleyes are a "catch-me-if-you-can" kind of critter. And anyone who can take a limit of walleyes out of a deep, clear lake in the dead of summer has earned the respect of his peers. He's met the challenge.

The walleye has a unique personality among fishes. Muskies and northern pike have the mentality of Jack the Ripper. They're explosive, unpredictable creatures, capable of slashing your line to ribbons with their razor-sharp teeth. Largemouth bass are muggers, slinking around in dark corners, waiting to ambush an unsuspecting victim that might be passing by. No one has ever ascribed a great deal of sophistication to any member of the salmonoid family, either. The chinook salmon is pure brute force.

But the walleye . . . the walleye is something different. He's a cool, calculating critter who defies the angler to out-wit him on his own terms. How many times have you heard the expression, "wily walleye?" His aura is more scholarly than emotional. He can't be provoked . . . he must be out-smarted. He's not a glutton . . . he's a connoisseur. Seducing a walleye doesn't require brawn . . . it takes patience and skill.

Even the physical appearance of the fish suggests something superior, perhaps a bespectacled college professor in a tweed suit. He's a gentlemen. If the fish ever needed a leader, surely they'd elect the walleye. He rules neither with emotion nor force, but with good sense and discipline.

*Stizostedion vitreum, more commonly known as the walleye, is quickly becoming one of America's most popular gamefish.*

As far as the fighting quality of the species is concerned, I think walleyes are vastly under-rated. No, it's not the most acrobatic of species. Walleyes come to the boat with a steady pull rather than bolting off in several different directions at the same time. But the amount of fight is determined, to a great extent, by how and where the fish is caught.

Most walleyes are taken in deep water with slow-trolling methods. A Lindy Rig, fished slowly, does not often evoke a savage strike, even from a pike or bass.

It's also true that the majority of bigger walleyes are caught in spring and fall, when water temperature is low. And fish don't fight as well in cold water as they do in warmer water.

Most walleyes are caught deep. Again, a fish in deep water won't put up as much of a struggle as one hooked in the shallows.

What kind of accounting would a walleye give of himself if caught with typical bass tactics . . . up shallow with a fast-moving spinner or crankbait?

Dan Nelson knows. "On the Missouri River system, most of the walleyes are caught in June and July in 10 feet of water or less. The most effective methods are speed-trolling a big bladed spinner or crankbait. During peak fishing, it's not uncommon to take a limit that will average six or seven pounds. These shallow fish smack a bait with an elbow-shattering strike and put up a struggle you wouldn't believe if you hadn't experienced it. I'll never forget the first time my buddy, Dave Jenson of Fargo, fished Lake Sakakawea's Van Hook Arm. We took a limit of walleyes that averaged about six pounds on a clear, hot, late July afternoon. The first fish Dave hooked he swore was a 15-pound northern. It fought that hard. When he saw the white tip on the tail of that six-pound walleye, he was absolutely amazed.

"It's pretty much the same on the Columbia River, where we take a lot of our big fish on crankbaits in fairly shallow water. In 1984, I caught a 15-pound, 2-ounce monster below the John Day Dam in about ten feet. I was fishing with Gary Roach, one of the finest and most experienced anglers alive. Watching that big fish strip line off my reel in a mad dash for deep water, Gary insisted I'd hooked a steelhead. I've never battled such a strong, determined fish. Most folks would never believe a walleye could put up a fight like that."

Yup, walleyes can fight. But that's only part of it. The real thrill of catching a big walleye comes from the satisfaction of knowing you outwitted a very crafty opponent.

Dan Nelson (left) and Gary Roach admire Dan's world line-class record walleye. The 15-pound, 2-ounce trophy was caught in July of 1984 on the Columbia River in Oregon.

For a lot of folks, the walleye is the only fish that swims. While walleyes have long been the fishermen's favorite in the north country states of Minnesota, Wisconsin and the Dakotas, their popularity is spreading rapidly thanks to intensive stocking programs.

Walleyes have proven to be an extremely adaptable fish, thriving in a variety of environments. Walleyes were originally a river fish, but they've proven well suited to lake habitats as well. The earliest stocking efforts were in the Upper Midwest. In recent years, the walleye's range has been extended to include rivers, lakes, and reservoirs throughout the United States and Canada. Today it's possible for a walleye enthusiast to practice his trade everywhere from Washington to Texas to Tennessee.

Although commonly referred to as the "walleyed pike," walleyes are actually a member of the perch family. Among the vernacular names for the species include okow, Susquehanna salmon, perch-pike, glasseye, green pike, grass pike, jack, jack salmon, white salmon, doré, blowfish, hornfish, spike and pickerel.

The walleye is the official state fish of Minnesota, accorded that honor in 1965 by a 128 to 1 vote in the House of Representatives (there's at least one crappie fisherman in every bunch).

The world record was a whopping 25-pounder caught in 1960 by Mabry Harper of Hartsville, Tennessee. Harper caught his record fish on Old Hickory Lake, an impoundment on the Cumberland River in Tennessee. The lunker had a 29-inch girth and was 41 inches long.

Some of the southern impoundments have the capacity to grow 20-pound plus walleyes, and many experts agree that the next world record will be caught in the South. Arkansas' Greer's Ferry is believed to hold at least a few fish exceeding the world record.

In most sections of the country, any walleye over eight pounds is considered a trophy and anything over ten is a real lunker. Most anglers go all their lives without ever catching a walleye over ten pounds.

Some of the most productive walleye fishing exists in the river-reservoir systems so common around the country. These bodies of water can hold lots of good-sized fish. The most suitable lake environment is the mesotrophic (medium-fertility) lakes so common in many of the northern states. They also can be found in deep, clear Canadian shield lakes, and shallow, fertile prairie lakes. The adaptable walleye can be found just about anywhere.

You've probably heard the statement, "a walleye is a walleye." It's true . . . the fish has a basic nature that will be somewhat predictable regardless of its surroundings. The seasonal and daily movements of walleyes, however, are dictated by the environment. Water clarity, oxygen levels, available habitat and forage, among other things, all have a great deal to do with where a walleye will be locating.

A cool water fish by nature, walleyes spawn shortly after ice-out in the spring of the year. Movement towards the spawning grounds is prompted partly by water temperature and partly by the amount of sunlight that occurs each day.

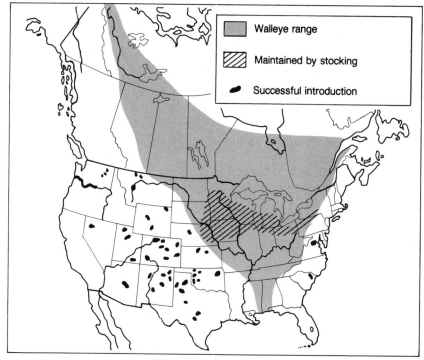

*Map of Walleye Range*

Spawning activity usually begins when the water warms to 42 or 43 degrees and continues until the shallows have warmed up to the mid to upper 50s. Walleyes will move up rivers or streams to spawn. If no moving water exists, they'll opt for a wind-swept shoreline with suitable bottom content.

The preferred substrate consists of gravel-rubble, a clean bottom over which the eggs can roll and be aerated during the incubation period. The fish also could use sand, grass, timber . . . whatever is available. However, the highest degree of spawning success occurs under ideal conditions. The egg-to-fry survival rate on gravel-rubble can be anywhere from 18 to 35 percent. Those figures drop to a meager .6 to 4.5 percent on muck bottom.

Walleyes can be very prolific. A big female will deposit anywhere from 200,000 to 600,000 eggs. The more suitable of habitats require no stocking, even if the system receives intense fishing pressure.

Weather is one of the biggest threats to walleye reproduction. A series of severe cold fronts during incubation can dramatically effect the success of the spawn. In some years, temperatures will fluctuate eight to ten degrees or more during the time the females are trying to deposit their eggs, and eventually many of the fish will be forced to give up and re-absorb their eggs. In the years when the fish are re-absorbing their eggs, fishing success is poor.

On rivers and reservoirs, fluctuating water levels can wipe out an entire year class of fish. A drop of several feet, which is not uncommon, leaves the eggs high and dry.

Some walleye lakes are strictly "put-and-take." Very limited, if any, natural reproduction takes place, and the number of walleyes present is dependent on the annual stocking efforts by fisheries managers.

The walleye is extremely flexible in its diet from season to season, and from one environment to the next. On many natural lakes, walleyes may feed heavily on insects during the spring, shift to perch and shiners during the summer months, and switch to cisco and tullibee in fall.

In some waters, perch, cisco, and tullibees don't occur. On the Missouri River system, walleyes use rainbow smelt as their primary forage. On Lake Erie, smelt and alewives constitute a major portion of the walleye's summertime diet. On the Columbia River, sculpins and squawfish are the most popular items on the walleye's menu. And on most southern impoundments, threadfin and gizzard shad are the primary forage fish.

At certain times of year, bullheads, frogs, white bass, or even carp spawn will be used to fill the walleye's stomach.

The ability of a given body of water to grow big fish is largely dependent on the forage availability. Without adequate forage, survival rates and growth rates will be low.

Any given body of water has a limited carrying capacity, or biomass. The bio-mass includes all living things—from micro-organisms to invertebrates, to forage to gamefish—that exist within that system. Depending on the fertility of the water, the system can carry only so many pounds of fish per surface acre of water.

To some extent, that bio-mass determines the maximum size walleyes can attain. The deep, clear pre-Cambrian lakes of Canada do not generally contain a saturated bio-mass and thus have the ability to produce some very large fish. In shallow, fertile lakes, the bio-mass may have reached its carrying capacity and trophy fish are rare. Yet the total population of fish will be quite high.

A complete food chain is necessary to promote growth. If one link in that chain is missing, growth rates suffer. The fish not only require a high-protein forage like cisco, tullibee, shad or smelt to achieve maximum size, but they need a starter forage to sustain them until they can convert to the larger food stuffs. Walleye fry don't become meat eaters until they reach two inches in length, and need a solid diet of zooplankton and phytoplankton to sustain them until they attain that size.

Of course, there are other factors that dictate growth rates. Water temperature is an all-important consideration. A southern impoundment, with its year-round growing season, has the capacity to kick out 15 to 20 pound (or bigger) walleyes. Fish of those proportions are rare on northern lakes with their limited growing season.

Water temperature initiates growth. Walleyes will not start putting on weight until the water warms to 55 to 57 degrees in the spring. They'll beef up during the summer months, then taper off as the water cools again in fall. During the winter months, under a layer of ice, walleyes will maintain their size but not grow.

Harvest also dictates, to some extent, how big the fish will become in a given body of water. Many Canadian lakes contain trophy walleyes, mostly because of a limited harvest. The lake may not have a strong walleye population, but those fish that do exist can often reach trophy proportions thanks to lack of fishing pressure.

Then, too, some bodies of water seem to have the ability to grow bigger fish. On most lakes, the walleye's life span is eight to ten years. But, there are some lakes in which, for unknown reasons, walleyes will live 16, 17 or even 18 years. Obviously, the longer that fish is alive, the bigger it's going to get.

As a rule, faster-growing fish don't live as long. In southern impoundments, the walleye's life expectancy may be five to seven years. In the northern limits of the walleye's range, the fish may live to 12 or 15 years on the average. Southern female walleyes reach sexual maturity in their third year, while way up north, a female may not participate in the spawn until her eighth year.

If big fish are your goal, it would be wise to select a body of water with a track record for producing trophies. One or two 10-pounders caught each spring does not mean a lake will be a consistent producer of wall-hangers. We'll provide a list of trophy waters later in this book.

For most anglers, a nice batch of "eating size" walleyes is sufficient. But I can recall back in my formative years when catching a single walleye was an event to be cherished. I got my first real taste of walleye fishing, back in the late '50s and early '60s, when my dad bought a cabin on Hay Lake in northern Minnesota.

The extent of our walleye knowledge, at that time, was that you could catch a few fish around the feeder streams in the spring of the year. During summer, according to the wisdom of the day, walleyes lost their teeth and were not catchable. Early in the summer, you might catch one or two fish a day, but no fish was more often a reality. By fall, oldtimers said, the teeth grew back and you could once again catch a few fish. In those days, most anglers fished the shoreline or mouths of feeder streams with little regard to bottom content. Some trolled or drifted across the middle of the lake, never dreaming there was a way to pinpoint walleye location.

The introduction of sonar devices by Carl Lowrance in 1957 changed the way we looked at walleye fishing. Buck Perry came along and described a thing called "structure." By combining Perry's concepts and Lowrance's electronic miracle, we slowly began to unravel the mysterious nature of the walleye.

It was during this renaissance period that I became friends with a gentleman on Hay Lake who seemed to have unearthed some important facts about walleye location. He told me the secret to consistently catching walleyes was "finding the edges."

He liked to fish the edge of drop-offs, the edge of points, the edge of weedlines . . . any kind of edge. He didn't know why, but he was convinced that under different conditions the fish would be located on various kinds of edges.

This was back in the days before I owned a depth-finder, so I'd take bleach bottles, tied up with 15 to 17 feet of twine and weighted with a bolt, toss them into the water as we trolled along, and let them drift with the wind. As the bottles washed towards shore, they'd hang up on the bottom and mark the edges.

By trolling or drifting along these edges with a jig and a minnow, I found it possible to catch walleyes with some degree of consistency. To me, that was a major breakthrough.

Along about 1965, I obtained copies of Bill Binkelman's books, *Walleyes Love Nightcrawlers* and *Nightcrawler Secrets*, which opened up a whole new world to me. I swung around to light line, thin wire hooks tipped with nightcrawlers and buggy-whip rods . . . the whole *Nightcrawler Secrets* approach.

Within a year I'd saved up enough money to purchase a Locator, a 12-foot cartopper, and a used 7½ horse outboard. With the help of this new-found mobility and electronic gadgetry, I began to gain an understanding of the fish and how it relates to its environment.

My love of the sport and a burning desire to learn more about those elusive creatures just naturally led me into a career in fishing. Over the years, I've been fortunate enough to have travelled throughout the country, picking the brains of local experts and fisheries personnel. I've been able to practice what I've learned on a variety of waters, from southern impoundments, to wilderness lakes.

Unlike early fishermen, who guarded their secret holes like protective mother hens, I've always enjoyed sharing the knowledge I've acquired with others. Perhaps the most gratifying experience a professional fisherman can have, is when someone says to you, "I tried what you told me and it really worked. I've never caught so many fish."

Yup, we've come a long way the last couple decades. We understand more about walleyes today than ever before. But in many ways, they remain an unsolved mystery.

For instance, what do we really know about the effects of weather and moon phases on fish movements? There are a few things that have become obvious to us, but for the most part these subjects remain on the gray side, even to the most skilled anglers and the most studied biologists.

And how much do we understand about suspension? I can tell you that walleyes suspend a whole lot more than we ever suspected. I know of some isolated cases where incredible catches are being made on suspended fish. How much walleyes suspend . . . and why . . . is something we simply don't know.

*Walleye fishing is a challenge, often taking years to truly master. This shot of Babe in his younger days shows that he began learning the tricks of the walleye trade a long time ago.*

When you boil it down, we're really just getting started in our understanding of walleyes. We know some of the things that make them tick . . . we understand why they do certain things at certain times of year . . . we've tracked their movements in certain bodies of water . . . studied them with scuba gear. Yet, in a very real sense, our knowledge of walleyes and the ability to catch them are still at a very primitive level. I fully expect that in the next decade we'll make some mind-boggling discoveries that will enable us to become more efficient fishermen.

Babe Winkelman Productions is dedicated to learning everything they can about walleyes, and in the coming years, will be working to uncover as many new discoveries as possible. I think Babe Winkelman Productions is on the verge of some major breakthroughs right now, especially in the area of suspension.

I don't pretend to have all the answers. I do know a great deal more than I did a few short years ago. In this book, I intend to lay down a set of guidelines that will help anyone catch more fish. More important, I want to emphasize the thought process that makes for a successful fisherman.

There really are no hard-and-fast rules that govern fishing. Only these guidelines. It is simply not possible to say that under a given set of conditions *this* is where the fish *will be* and *this* is what they *will hit.*

There's been a lot of misinformation and half-truths disseminated through the fishing information pipeline over the years. Ambitious writers pick up on one aspect of the sport and crank out articles that are nothing short of misleading.

I ran across one such article the other day that left me in a state of shock. It said, in essence, that to catch summertime walleyes you must fish the deep holes using the slowest possible presentation. This, according to the author, was the gospel on walleyes regardless of habitat or conditions. I have no doubt that for the day, lake and conditions that inspired that article, everything he wrote was fact. Walleye fishing, to this guy, meant that in summer months the fish are "always" in deep holes and "always" require a slow presentation.

Tell that to the bass fisherman who hooked a five-pound walleye tossing a spinnerbait into a clump of cabbage weed in the middle of July . . . or the river fisherman who filled out on chunky fish trolling a crankbait through a submerged cottonwood forest . . . or the reservoir angler who tied into his first ten-pounder speed-trolling a No. 5 spinner in six feet of water the first week in August.

This book will contain its share of disclaimers. I'm not going to tell you that anything works all the time. I won't pass along any rules that always hold true. That would simply be a misrepresentation of the facts.

The guidelines I've developed over the years are fairly consistent, if you understand the individual environment in which the fish lives and how it relates to that environment on a day-to-day and season-to-season basis.

24

The guidelines are part of a thought process. And right at the core of that thought process is *patterns*. I'm going to talk a lot about patterns in this book, because understanding pattern fishing will all but guarantee a successful outing, no matter where you fish.

# Chapter 2
# Clayface

## Life Cycle of a Walleye

*"Somehow that river seems awful*
*important today, whether there's a fish in*
*it or not."*

**—Gordon MacQuarrie**
**"Stories of the Old Duck Hunters"**

Every living creature has within it a biological clock, and old Clayface is marking time. The sprawling north country lake she calls home is still wearing two feet of ice, but the countdown has begun. Soon the female walleye will be overcome by an irresistable urge to return to the place of her origin.

Clayface is not the most intelligent living creature. Her life is governed by two basic instincts, survival and proliferation of her kind. For the next few weeks, the need to reproduce will dictate every move the old fish makes.

There's no calendar to herald the coming event, no road signs to show her the way home. But Mother Nature has provided for those needs. Spring will be late this year. It's dark and still under the snow-covered ice. But as a dreary March gives way to April, the days become longer. The alarm sounds. Clayface's instincts tell her it's time to move . . . time to start feeding . . . time to hasten the egg-ripening process.

Those eggs have been growing in her belly ever since her last trip upstream. She senses, from many previous trips, that she'll need every ounce of energy she can muster just to survive the ordeal that lies ahead. Periodic trips to the shallows provide nourishment for the more than 350,000 eggs she's carrying.

Days pass and the spring sun slowly dissolves the ice sheet. Clayface moves to the mouth of the river, but there she loses her sense of direction. She stages off the tip of a rocky point, waiting.

Then it happens. Warm spring rains melt the last of the ice. Runoff washes over rocks, gravel, soil, decomposed vegetation and fecal droppings as it rushes downriver and into the lake. Incoming water draws her to the mouth of the river and the scent track leads her home.

Each section of water has its own chemical makeup. Clayface has been imprinted on the water chemistry of a particular area. Her homing instincts are strong and the scent track draws her, like a magnet, up the river, through two smaller lakes and further up the river. In a little more than a day she's travelled 50 miles, and that evening she's resting within 100 yards of the place where she was spawned some 11 years earlier.

Once, earlier in her life, the rains failed to come. Without runoff to point the way, she became confused. Warm weather came early that spring, pushing water temperatures into the 60s shortly after iceout. By the time she found a suitable place to deposit her eggs, the shallows were too warm. Her belly turned to mush and she was forced to reabsorb her eggs. Reabsorption wasn't complete until fall, too late in the season to start developing a new batch. So she missed two years of spawning.

This year she's made it home. And she's ready to fulfill the most powerful instinct in any fish's life—the urge to spawn.

She's a classic example of *Stizostedion vitreum*. Her elongated body stretches to over 30 inches, and with a belly swollen with eggs, her girth has grown to almost 17 inches. She weighs nearly 13 pounds.

A large lump has formed just below the dorsal fin on the left side of her body. She pays no attention to the cancerous growth. Near her tail is a long scar, evidence of a close encounter with a toothy musky when she was younger. The large opaque eyes from which her kind draws its name have become extremely light-sensitive over the years. Because of this, she's been forced to spend more time prowling the depths or tucked into dense weeds. Age also has bred caution. She doesn't feed as recklessly as she once did. She doesn't have to. She's at the upper levels of the food chain now, and has very little competition for forage.

The smaller fish give her a wide berth. She's become more skittish, retreating to the sanctuary of deep water at the first unfamiliar sound or scent. Her survival instincts are honed to a razor edge.

She's very special, this old lady. Of the millions of walleyes that emerged from the egg sac the spring of her birth, only a handful survived. Disease, predation and fishing pressure took the rest. She once roamed in a large school . . . now there are just a few.

Little males are already responding to the warming surface water by cruising the shallows. Clayface spends most of her time in deep water, moving towards shore only after dark to feed.

As the water warms to the mid-30s, the courtship ritual begins. Clayface is pursued by several small males, their dorsal fins alternately erected and flattened as they circle and bump the big female. Each evening she's courted by a different group of bucks, some nights as many as a dozen fish vying for her attentions.

In a few days the water climbs into the 40s and the courtship becomes more serious. All thoughts of feeding are temporarily set aside. Clayface is carrying nearly three quarts of eggs, and those eggs are getting soft. It's time.

*Several smaller males come to call on Clayface.*

The setting is romantic. A full moon and a sky full of stars light up the warm, early May evening. The fish's aquatic home is 46 degrees. Half a dozen males come to get Clayface, but only two actually escort her to the shallows. The rest wait in the wings.

Dorsals erect, they approach Clayface from behind, circle around and nudge her bloated belly. Suddenly they rush forward to the shallows, boiling the surface of the water. The trio swims frantically, the males knocking Clayface on her side until the moment of orgasm.

Clayface broadcasts the eggs across the rock-rubble bottom and the males randomly fertilize the scattered eggs with sperm. The ritual is repeated at five-minute intervals, and by dawn the old fish is spawned out. At best, only about ten percent of the eggs will be fertilized.

*The big female broadcasts her eggs over the rock-rubble bottom, where they're randomly fertilized by the males.*

At first, the adhesive eggs cling to the bottom. After several hours they begin to harden. They'll roll down the shoreline with the current for one to three weeks before hatching. A hard bottom is necessary for the eggs to remain aerated, while rolling down the shore. On a soft bottom, they'd likely suffocate.

The tiny fry will live off the yolk sac for several days as they drift down the river. After that, they'll survive on the zooplankton and phytoplankton that begin to bloom on the surface. At this point, their movements will be restricted to vertical swimming. They'll sink, then push to the surface with a vigorous motion of their tail muscles. Only a handful will survive. Some will starve and many will be eaten.

None of this is of any concern to Clayface. Her obligation to nature complete, she slips downstream to a small lake where she'll spend the next week lying on the bottom recuperating . . . completely dormant.

The big fish has participated in the spawning ritual since her third year, but the last couple trips have been particularly troublesome. The years are taking their toll.

*After the difficult spawning ordeal, Clayface retreats to the bottom where she spends several days recuperating.*

On the eighth day she begins to move around for a short time, but it's not until the tenth day that she feels like eating. The sun's warmth has not yet penetrated the depths, and in this cold water her metabolic rate is slow. She doesn't require a great deal of food.

Two weeks have passed since she spawned and now it's time to move again. She travels further down-river to another lake with a large, shallow bay, stopping to feed periodically along the way. The bay's dark water absorbs more of the sun's rays and is warm. Insect hatches are coming off and her appetite is starting to return.

*When insect hatches come off in the shallows, Clayface is there and feeds ravenously.*

Along the way she eats a few fry, perhaps some young wall-eye . . . some perhaps her own offspring. Her color has turned to a washed-out shade of gray, the result of a lengthy stay in the murky depths.

After building up her strength, feeding on insect larvae, she resumes her journey and by evening she's back to the 60,000 acre lake that will be home for the remainder of the year.

**Spring Transition—Coming Alive**

Clayface's underwater world is undergoing rapid changes. As water temperatures push into the 60s, the food chain comes alive. The aging but sturdy walleye is confronted with a literal smorgasbord . . . insects, minnows and young-of-the-year fishes abound.

The banquet being spread out by Mother Nature came just in time. Clayface has withered away to a mere ten pounds the past few weeks. Most of the weight loss was the result of losing her eggs. In the deep, cold water her metabolism was low and she really didn't require a great deal of food to survive. For the last six months, under the ice, she has eaten only to sustain life. As spring approached, nutrition was necessary for development of the eggs. But now, after spawning, she is feeding to grow.

Her first stop, back at the big lake, is a shallow rock pile. The big lake is slower to accept seasonal change than the river and smaller lakes, and the water here is still on the cool side. But the rock pile absorbs and holds the sun's warmth. Like a radiator, it draws large schools of shiners. Twice a day she moves to the rocks to feed on the baitfish concentrated there.

She's joined by other fish, most of them big, with the same idea. Through the spawning ordeal, she was pretty much a loner. But, now she'll start to bunch up in loosely formed schools with other fish her size. When not prowling around the rock pile, she occasionally drops to deep water and chases young-of-the-year eelpout. At other times she heads to the shallow bays to feed on perch fry.

She roams a lot. This is one of the few times of the year when a big fish has the run of the lake. The lake hasn't yet stratified . . . oxygen is abundant . . . food is readily available . . . sunlight isn't yet a real factor. In short, she can be just about anyplace she wants in the entire complicated system.

Clayface's home reaches a maximum depth of 100 feet and actually is several different environments combined into one. The water in the main lake is of medium-fertility with lots of rock and gravel points and some islands. Weeds grow to 18 or 20 feet. The back bays are eutrophic in nature, with very fertile water and dense vegetation. The river is yet another environment altogether. The lake contains pike, a few musky, bass, perch, bluegills, crappies and lots of walleyes. It's just about a perfect habitat for a walleye.

*Spring transition finds some of the bigger fish working shallow rock piles.*

And this is the perfect time to be a walleye. Not only can Clayface move about freely, but she has a variety of choices of food.

At times, she'll be up in two feet of water where the wind is crashing in on a soft-bottomed shoreline. Later, she may find a rock island and chase shiners. She spends quite a bit of time back in the organic bays, feeding on insect hatches and young-of-the-year perch.

When moving from deep water into the shallow bays, she undergoes a type of temperature shock. It's quite a bit warmer in the bays than in the deep water, and she needs some time to adjust to the change.

More and more she groups with other fish. Most of the fish in her school are large. Since large fish are rare, such schools are usually not big.

The sun's rays are hitting the lake more directly now, somewhat limiting her movements. She feeds most actively in the low-light hours of dawn and dusk. Occasionally she visits the turbid, soft-bottomed flats at mid-day. The water's murky here, and sunlight is not a problem.

Soon Clayface's world will undergo more changes, affecting the way she lives.

## Summer—A Time to Grow

The sun has burned through the upper layer of water, promoting lush weed growth down to 20 feet. A thermocline is starting to set up on the lake. The upper layer of the water is warm . . . the lower layer is cold . . . the thermocline is the dividing line between the two.

Some of Clayface's peers set up residence in deep water. Others set up housekeeping in the dense vegetation that's developed. Here, during the daylight hours, she finds protection from the sun's rays, ample oxygen and a wealth of forage. The weeds will be home . . . at least for a while.

In morning, and evening she prowls the outside edge of the weedline looking for food. After dark, she may cruise the tops of the weeds in search of a meal. During the day she travels through tunnels in the vegetation. Life is at its best. It feels good to be a walleye.

But, summer wears on and things change. The smallish baitfish can hide almost too well in the underwater jungle. Besides, she's usually still hungry after running down a few. A meal would do better than a snack.

One late June afternoon, Clayface decides to move on. Satisfying her ever increasing appetite is foremost on her mind. She slides down the edge of the weedline to the side of the long point, that eventually leads to the deep water section of the lake. She spends a few days hanging around the clam bed near the end of the point, dropping down to 30 feet or even slightly deeper during the day. As light intensities and other factors change, she moves up and down the point, usually on the lookout for an easy meal.

*Clayface's constant need for food keeps her moving, always on the lookout for a healthy meal.*

In a few days, Clayface again is on the move, drifting out across open water to a big rocky island that she remembers lies a few hundred yards from the point. It's time for a change. She arrives at the rock hump, only to find a number of other large female walleyes already there. For the time being, at least, she joins the others, working the top and sides of their boulder-covered dinner table.

Some days, usually when it's brighter, the schools of cisco move out from the island to feed on small critters suspended in the open water areas. Clayface and her comrades often follow, staying slightly deeper than the silver bait fish. When it's time to feed, it's normally a simple task of moving up and chomping down a few.

One day Clayface decides to stop off at still another island, this one a bit different than the last. She leaves one group of walleyes, only to join up with another bunch. A few others from the group follow. There are rocks, but only on one side. The rest is primarily sand and clay with a sparse growth of sand grass on top.

*A portion of Clayface's year is spent in open water . . . suspended . . . chasing cisco and tullibee.*

And so goes her summer, always changing, but always with the same purpose . . . food. Eventually, she finds herself back on the same weedbed where she started the summer. The forage is now better developed; she decides to stay for awhile.

During one of her late afternoon swims along the outside edge of the weeds, she senses danger. There's a scent in the water, but she's too slow. A giant musky sinks its teeth into her flesh. The toothy predator quickly releases its grip, thinking his prey will be too stunned to move. But old Clayface is a sturdy creature, and with a powerful burst she vanishes into the weeds.

*Encounters with toothy predators like the musky are a way of life in Clayface's underwater world.*

Attacks like this have been rare since she attained her present size. Yet, the scales that have been ripped from her side are a painful reminder that she's not yet at the top of the food chain. There's a pecking order in any body of water. From the tiniest invertebrates to the baitfish, to perch, to walleyes, to the giant musky, who knows no natural enemy once he reaches a certain size.

She doesn't school much while roaming the tunnels beneath the cabbage weed. Other fish of her kind, the ones that still inhabit a deepwater summer home, are more tightly schooled. In open water they use their numbers for protection and to herd baitfish. Inside the weeds, there's little need for companionship.

At times, while cruising the tops of the weedbed after dark, she's joined by other fish, and they make an impressive team. They surround their prey, pushing it toward the surface until it becomes completely vulnerable.

One afternoon in late July, Clayface gets the urge to roam. She heads out across the lake, moving at an incredible rate of speed. She's really a powerful swimmer, able to overtake a largemouth bass if she has the notion.

She crosses the lake and winds up on a rock point some three miles away. Maybe she just needed a change of scenery . . . maybe she got the urge to travel. Whatever the reason, her stay lasts only two days before she returns to home base.

The seasonal changes that occurred in Clayface's world are quite dramatic. Daily changes are more subtle, but they nonetheless affect her movements.

Early in August the weather turns hot and calm. For several days, the bright sun burns into the lake without so much as a breeze. Moisture and dust particles collect in the upper atmospheres. Algae blooms thicken on the surface of the lake. Oxygen levels are depleted in the upper third of the system, forcing the bulk of the aquatic life into the weeds. Through the process of photosynthesis, weeds give off life-supporting oxygen that attracts fish.

The moisture and dust particles in the air and algae on the surface serve as a protective umbrella to filter out the sun's rays. Clayface finds it comfortable to cruise the edge of the weeds in the middle of the day. She even spends some time hovering over the tops of the weeds, just a few feet below the surface, under a blazing sun. She feeds ravenously.

During the fifth day of unchanged weather, she's on patrol atop the weed bed, when her attention is drawn to what looks like an injured minnow fluttering a few feet away. Instinctively, she spins to attack the "helpless" prey.

There's nothing helpless about this morsel. As she sinks her teeth into the potential meal, it fights back. She dives into the weeds, only to be pulled back to the surface by an invisible force. Still uncertain of what's happening, she slides off to the side, but finds it difficult to swim.

It's not until she sees a net in the water, that the old fish becomes panic-stricken. Mustering every ounce of strength in her body, she dives straight toward the bottom. The invisible force releases with a "snap" and suddenly she's free. But something remains lodged in her lip. Clayface buries herself in the weeds for several hours and soon forgets about the traumatic experience. By the next day, acid from her body has dissolved the hook and it falls away.

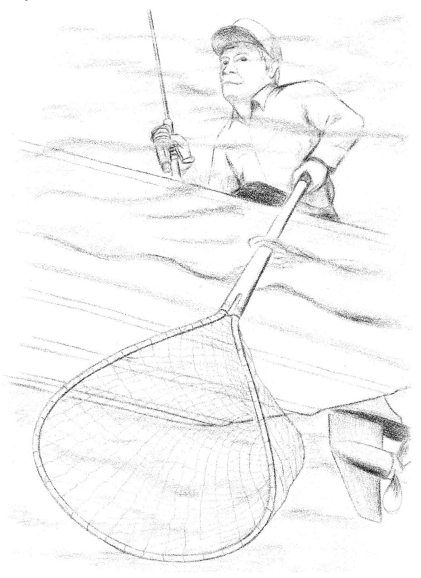

*Clayface was overcome with terror when she saw the landing net enter the water.*

That night a severe storm blows across the lake. The rain, cold temperatures, and wind will alter life in Clayface's underwater world. The rain washes dust and moisture particles from the air. The wind drifts algae across the lake, stacking it on the windy shore. The warm surface water also is pushed across the lake, being displaced by cooler water on the lee side. The thermocline is actually bent.

Next morning, the water above Clayface's weed patch is several degrees cooler and the sun's rays penetrate deep into the lake. All activity comes to a standstill. Clayface remains buried in the weeds, her belly flat to the bottom. She doesn't move for most of the day.

A week later, Clayface gets the urge to roam again . . . to do something irresponsible, if you will. She swims out to open water where she spends a few days chasing whitefish.

Most of her life is spent relating to something—points, weeds, river channels or even the thermocline. Now she's relating to nothing but open water. Perhaps she enjoys the feeling of freedom or perhaps she needs some variety in her diet. Whatever the reason, she roams the open water.

Eventually she returns to the weed bed. Instead of spending her time under the weeds, she suspends over the thermocline, several yards off the deep-water edge of the weeds. Here she lays for hours on end, not making a move.

When she gets the urge to feed, which is usually early in the morning or very late in the afternoon, she follows the thermocline to the edge of the weedline to herd baitfish. She's feeding mostly on perch, but also picks up the occasional crayfish, leech or minnow. When suspended, she's usually in the company of several other fish.

Clayface seems to be afflicted with wanderlust. After a couple weeks of hanging around the thermocline, she decides to make a visit to deep water. She finds a long, tapering rock point and follows it down to 60 feet. When it's feeding time, she'll follow the point up to 30 feet, take a quick meal and drop back down to deep water.

She's very adaptable, this old gal. A cold-blooded creature, she really doesn't have a comfort zone. She can go wherever she likes. Almost every move she makes is dictated by the availability of forage, because during the short summer period, her main objective is to grow.

She can, and will, go into water that's very warm, very cold, low in oxygen and exposed to bright light . . . but only if that's what it takes to find a meal.

Right now she's getting ready to return to the weeds, because Mother Nature is signalling another change.

*During the hot summer months, Clayface spends a lot of time prowling the weeds.*

## Fall—Completing the Cycle

The days are getting shorter and Clayface senses life in her under-water world is about to undergo another change. She's already seeing a reduction in the available forage. The perch population has been hit hard all year and has dwindled down to almost nothing. Surface water is beginning to cool and some of the weeds are starting to die. As the vegetation dies, it ceases to give off oxygen and starts releasing carbon dioxide.

Clayface is forced out of her home on the south end of the lake to travel to a similar environment on the north side. The prevailing north-west wind is pushing the cooler surface water south, the result being a rapid die-off of weeds on that side of the lake. The water's slightly warmer across the lake and there are still a few patches of green vegetation for her to prowl.

Before long the top layer of water becomes heavy and begins to sink. The process doesn't happen overnight, but eventually the lake has flip-flopped. The surface became more dense than the water beneath it until it could no longer float. As it dropped, it displaced the water on the bottom. The thermal barriers have disappeared and the lake is homogenized. The whole system is in a state of turmoil. Organic matter that has been collecting on the bottom floats towards the surface. The lake looks and smells bad.

At first, Clayface's reaction is to drop out of the weeds and get into deeper water, becoming dormant. But after a few days, she begins to move.

Her first stop is the mouth of an incoming river. The current that flows into the lake at that point has attracted some shiners, which have left open water and moved towards the shallows.

A week has passed since the lake "turned over." Water temperatures are fairly constant from top to bottom. So are oxygen and pH levels. Unlike summer, when she was confined by thermal barriers, Clayface now finds it possible to make very dramatic vertical movement.

As the water cools, her metabolism slows down. She's not nearly as aggressive as she was a month ago. But she has the powerful urge to feed. She senses that soon the lake will again be coated with a layer of ice and she will become almost dormant. It's time to add a layer of fat to carry her through the long, cold winter that lies ahead.

With temperature and oxygen levels fairly constant and the sun's rays striking the surface at a less direct angle, she can go just about anywhere in the lake in search of a meal.

Mostly, she hangs around a rocky point that dumps sharply into the deepest water in the lake. She may rest in 80 feet during the day, then hop the elevator and ascend to the tip of the point in 20 feet to feed.

She shows an obvious preference for rocky bottoms, probably because the rock absorbs and holds warmth which attracts baitfish. She's looking for big, easy meals right now. And the lake is full of them.

The ciscoes and tullibee are moving to the shallows to spawn, and towards evening she likes to slide into the extreme shallows to chase the protein-rich baitfish.

The frog run is coming into the lake, and she spends some time poking around sloughs and feeder streams, dining on frog legs. She can be anywhere from 2 to 80 feet and feeding on anything from cisco to whitefish to salamanders. But the bulk of her diet consists of shiners, big perch and tullibees. Most of her time is spent on the sharp drops.

*In fall, big fish hang on sharp, rock breaks.*

With each passing day, she feeds more intensely. Her eggs are very well developed by now and she's trying to put on a layer of protective fat, a buffer that will see her through the lean times ahead.

As a crust of ice begins to form on the lake, she goes on a real binge. She's moving almost constantly now, seeking out whatever food is available.

As the ice gets thicker, she slips into deep water, settles to the bottom and becomes almost dormant. She won't feed for days at a time. She remains that way for the better part of the winter.

She really doesn't require a great deal of food now. Her metabolism is so low that she burns up very few calories. One perch can sustain her for days.

The cycle repeats itself. As the days grow longer the ice begins to melt. Soon Clayface feels the urge to return to the spawning grounds. The ritual of procreation is repeated, as it has been for uncounted thousands of years.

Only this time, the ordeal is particularly difficult for old Clayface. She deposits about two-thirds of her eggs and only with considerable prodding from the aggressive young males, who slash and jab at her midsection. The rest of the eggs don't want to drop.

She retreats to the murky depths with her last ounce of strength. There she remains for several days, barely able to keep herself upright. It's been tough before, but this year the water feels colder and darker.

She slips over on her side and struggles to get upright. Her color turns from gold, to brown, to a pale gray. Her instincts tell her to return to the shallows and rid herself of the remaining eggs. But she hasn't the strength.

Slowly fanning her tail, she starts to move in a circular path, her body tipped sideways. With her last burst of energy, she swims vertically several feet, where she remains suspended for a few moments. Then her arched body spirals to the bottom, nose-first.

There she lies, her tail fanning little clouds of mud. Her gills pump frantically trying to collect oxygen. Within minutes, this regal denizen of the deep is dead.

*Unable to recuperate this time, the majestic old female finally dies.*

# Chapter 3
# Location

### First You Gotta Find 'Em

*"At the top, At the bottom, and in the middle."*
**—Izaak Walton, 1577**

*"The fish will be deep, shallow, or somewhere in between."*
**—Numerous 20th Century anglers**

August. A stifling heat wave has blanketed the country. Years ago these were called the dog days of summer. According to the wisdom of the time, fish lost their teeth and didn't feed.

Phooey. Even Izaak Walton knew better than that when, more than 400 years ago, he authored *The Compleat Angler*. Still, a lot of modern fishermen fall back on the old axiom about sore gums and sulking fish to explain their inability to catch walleyes during the hot summer months.

Let's make a coast-to-coast tour and see if anyone's catching any walleyes.

— Out near Portland, Oregon, it's 115 in the shade, below the Dalles Dam, but Ed Iman is picking up big walleyes on crankbaits, trolled over the tops of shallow, rocky shelves on the Columbia River.

— Further east, we find Dan Nelson cashing in on some fast reservoir action on North Dakota's Lake Sakakawea. The mercury's bumping 102 in New Town, but Dan's finding fish in less than 15 feet of water. And they're hitting spinners, trolled near the speed of light. No dog days here.

— Up near my stomping grounds, Marv Koep has taken a few days off from his successful tackle shop at Nisswa, Minnesota to practice his favorite past time—chasing big walleyes. Marv's coaxing fish out of 45 feet of water, with a Lindy Rig and jumbo leech, on a couple nearby lakes that are deep and clear.

— On Wisconsin Prairie Lake, Brian Ferrantz has been taking fish the last three days, pitching plugs to the inside edge of a dense weed growth, in less than six feet of water.

— Out on the western basin of Lake Erie, Jim Fofrich is fishing a tournament and banging a lot of nice-sized walleyes, drifting and casting a weight-forward spinner. Jim's finding fish suspended in ten feet to over 25 feet of water.

— On the eastern basin of Lake Erie, Bud Riser and his *Walleye Magazine* research team have been working out of Barcelona, New York, catching walleyes in 70 to 100 feet, on downriggers.

I've probably heard the expression "a walleye is a walleye." But I've just examined half a dozen different bodies of water, and in each case the fish are doing totally different things.

In this chapter, we'll be studying the various stimuli that cause fish to react differently within different bodies of water. I'll be talking about things like lake types, pH, predator/prey relations, activity levels, schooling tendencies, rivers, reservoirs, super-structure, mini-structure . . . and much more.

It's all part of the thing I call location.

Location, is a multi-faceted subject. When most of us think about location, we picture sunken islands, rocky points of dense weed beds . . . some type of physical structure we can locate with the help of a hydrographic map or a depth finder.

But location is more complex than that. Far more complex. Because despite what you've read or heard, fish don't always adhere to the classic structures.

My best definition of "location" would be, "those factors that motivate walleyes to be in a particular place at a given time".

There are reasons that Ed Iman's Columbia River fish are working a 10-foot shelf, while at the same time, Bud Riser's finding walleyes down to 100 feet. Wherever walleyes, or any species of fish choose to locate, you can bet there's a reason or motivation. And, often as not, that motivation is the availability of forage. At least that's true if we're talking about *catchable* walleyes. Catchable walleyes, nearly always, locate because of food.

No one understands all the variables that motivate fish movements. And no one ever will. In the coming pages, I'll be taking a step-by-step look at the all-important food chain and how it affects walleye movements. Keep in mind, however, that every body of water has its own distinct personality . . . every day brings changes in the fish's underwater world . . . every situation offers new challenges for both fish and fishermen.

I hope in this section of the book to unveil the "thought process" that results in successful fishing. There's no way to predict all of the influences that alter fish behavior. But, by understanding that those influences do exist and learning to look for and recognize them, you'll be able to unlock the mysteries of walleye location. Not all the time, but most or some of the time.

## Predator/Prey Relations

Any body of water, whether it's a 500-acre dishpan lake, in the late stages of eutrophication, or the massive 800,000-acre western basin of Lake Erie, has a food chain, each one unique (see Figure 1).

The most basic element in that food chain is the water itself. Add to water a variety of elements like nitrogen, phosophorus, carbon, sodium and others, and you have the beginnings of a food chain. When these elements exist in proper balance, they produce food.

The most basic of these foods is phytoplankton, a form of plant life that assimilates the various nutrients from the water. Algae is an example of phytoplankton.

Phytoplankton, in turn, provides food for zooplankton, a microscopic form of animal life, like daphnia.

The various kinds of phytoplankton and zooplankton provide nourishment for those creatures that are on the next step of the food chain, like small fishes and minnows. In the early stages of their development, walleye fry depend heavily on these micro- organisms for survival.

Another vital member of the aquatic community are the invertebrates like caddisflies, mayflies and numerous other insects. Insects provide food for fish of all sizes, even jumbo walleyes at certain times of the year.

When one thinks of minnows, suckers, shiners and fatheads come to mind. But most bodies of water contain dozens, maybe hundreds, of different minnows that are rarely seen by people.These little fish provide food for larger forage species, like perch and crappies.

Finally we arrive at the top of the food chain, the predators. These include walleyes, bass, northern pike and muskies.

Some bodies of water have a well balanced food chain, and the result is a strong population of fish and generally good fishing. But lakes can be thrown out of balance very easily. To understand how this happens, we go right back to those basic elements dissolved in the water.

If a lake contains too much nitrogen, phosophorus or carbon, an over-population of blue-green algae can occur. With an over-abundance of nutrients at their disposal, the blue-greens eventually become so dense that they become light-limiting. The thickest growth occurs within the top foot of the water column.

As the surface temperatures warm, the blue-green's metabolism increases to the point where it starts to use up all the available nutrients in the water. When that happens, some of the cells start to die and sink through the water column. The decomposition of organic material consumes oxygen. As wave action forces this water into the deeper zones of the lake, oxygen levels drop and a fish kill becomes a very real possibility.

On the other side of the spectrum are sterile environments. Some lakes, especially those along the east coast and up in Canada, have been subjected to excessive amounts of acid rain. The extreme acidity of the rain kills many of the nutrients so essential to the development

ENERGY FROM SUN

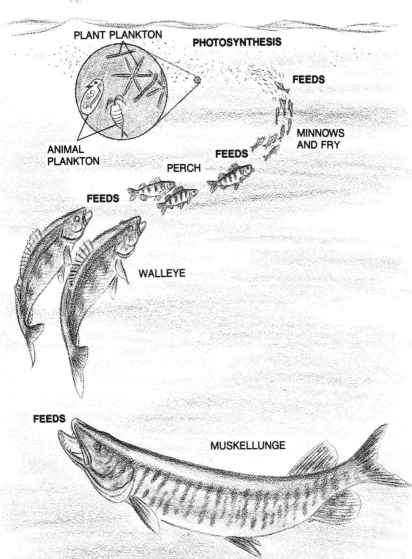

PLANT PLANKTON

PHOTOSYNTHESIS

FEEDS

MINNOWS AND FRY

ANIMAL PLANKTON

FEEDS

PERCH

FEEDS

FEEDS

WALLEYE

FEEDS

MUSKELLUNGE

*Figure 1.* A healthy food chain starts with the tiniest micro-organisms like phytoplankton and zooplankton and ends with the largest predators like muskies and northern pike. A complete food chain is essential to a productive fishery. If one or two links are missing, the entire system suffers.

of life. Eventually, the life-giving planktons disappear, and with them goes the future of the environment.

At this point, you're probably beginning to wonder what all this has to do with fishing. Plenty, my friends, plenty. Perhaps, your area experiences an unusually cold spring and daphnia are slow to develop. If that daphnia isn't available for young-of-the-year fish, an entire year class of walleye fry could be wiped out because they lack the proper starter forage.

Arkansas' Greer's Ferry has attained a reputation as a trophy walleye water, and rightfully so. Yet, most anglers who venture to Greer's Ferry don't come home with enough to stink up the frying pan. Yes, Greer's Ferry has some huge walleyes. But it doesn't have very many. The primary forage on Greer's Ferry is shad, and the shad don't spawn early enough to provide walleye fry with forage during that critical stage of their life when they become meat-eaters.

The availability of forage affects the seasonal location of walleyes. Let's say that the previous fall ciscoes had perfect spawning conditions and produced a higher than normal amount of young. Let's also assume that the same lake had poor reproductive conditions for shiners. Those two factors could force walleyes to feed in much deeper water than they would in a normal year.

The food chain also dictates, to some extent, activity levels of fish. Feeding activity increases with the density of forage. Well fed fish have higher energy levels, better health and condition factors, enjoy higher reproductive success and do not have to expend as much energy finding and taking food.

Perhaps you've caught a really thick-bodied walleye, one that looks like a football. That fish isn't a freak of nature; he got that way by stuffing his face with a lot of high-protein food. The walleye that looks like a wet sock with teeth probably came from a system that lacked a complete food chain.

The more sterile the environment, the less likely a body of water is to have a strong fish population (see Figure 2). An oligotrophic lake, for instance, is a very sterile environment. As a result, it doesn't have the capacity to produce many pounds of fish per acre. But, for a number of reasons, lack of fishing pressure being just one, these lakes can produce some extremely large walleyes.

A eutrophic lake, on the other hand, is a very fertile system and has the ability to support an abundance of aquatic life. These lakes support lots and lots of fish, but not near as many "big" fish. Let me explain why.

A lake is a lot like a piece of farmland. Some nutrient-rich areas of the country have the ability to yield 100 bushels of wheat per acre. But only 100 miles away, the land might be so void of nutrients that 30 bushels per acre would be considered a good yield. Most mesotrophic lakes tend to be clear environments with a sand-gravel substrate. Such a lake has a somewhat limited carrying capacity, perhaps 25 to 40 pounds of fish per acre.

## LAKE TYPE VARIATION WITHIN BROAD CATEGORIES

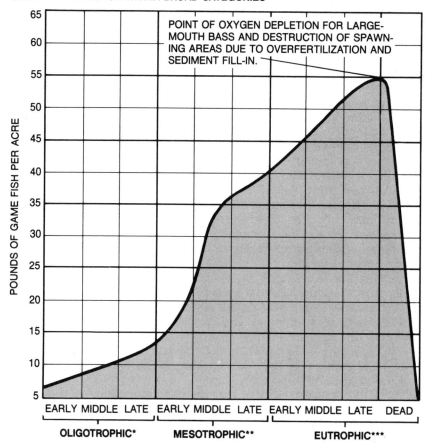

**Figure 2.** Fish population of different lake types.

Some reservoirs, on the other hand, have much higher carrying capacities. Impoundments, which flooded nutrient-rich farmland, contain a high amount of organic material. Water leaches these nutrients from the soil creating a very fertile environment. As a result, the system may have a carrying capacity as high as 250 pounds of fish per acre.

Any body of water can be thrown out of balance. On some natural lakes, for example, there may be an over-population of bluegills. These bluegills occupy more than their share of the bio-mass and consume a disportionate amount of food. As a result, the lake is thrown out of balance and a population of mostly stunted fish occurs.

That situation creates a real dilemma for fishery managers. In a reservoir situation, it's often possible to "draw down" the lake, forcing the stunted baitfish out of their protective cover and exposing them to predators. The predators will quickly deplete the baitfish population, creating a void in the bio-mass. Hopefully, the void will be filled by faster-growing, healthier gamefish.

Problems also can occur at the other end of the food chain. A number of years back, Nebraska fisheries personnel decided to stock stripers into Lake McConaughy. "Mac" once had been a very productive walleye lake which also contained a good number of rainbow trout. The primary forage for all species was shad.

But stripers are very efficient predators, and they quickly decimated the shad population. After that, they turned their attentions to small walleyes and trout. Before long, nothing remained but trophy-sized stripers. The lake was out of balance.

Fortunately, McConaughy is primarily a put-and-take fishery, and striper numbers can be controlled by cutting back on stocking efforts. Nebraska officials are now seeing a comeback of the gamefish that are bigger and healthier.

Oligotrophic lakes, with their sterile environments, have limited areas with elements necessary for young fish to survive and thrive. Those fish that do make it through the first few years of life don't have a lot of competition for forage, and that—coupled with minimal fishing pressure–can result in some very large walleyes.

Prairie or carp lakes have complete food chains, and as a result will hold large numbers of fish. But, because the bio-mass is full, fish in these systems tend to be more stunted.

Biologists can keep track of the bio-mass by monitoring the forage base. For instance, a lake with stunted perch obviously has a niche in the bio-mass that's reached it's capacity. But, if over a period of a few years, those perch run at a larger average size, a change has occurred in the bio-mass. Such a change might result if northern pike bring off a strong year-class. As those pike attain a certain size, they might take a big bite out of the perch population creating a void in the bio-mass and allowing all species of fish to grow into that void.

Some lakes have only a small overall population, but lots of big fish . . . some have good numbers of fish, but few of any size . . . and a few well balanced lakes have substantial numbers of fish in all age classes.

Fish also occupy different niches within the ecosystem. For instance, salmonoids and lake trout thrive in cold, deep oxygenated water. But just because you have a clear, deep lake doesn't mean you'll have lake trout. Those lakers still need an adequate forage for the niche they occupy.

Take for example Fort Peck in Montana, the first and western-most of the six mainstream reservoirs on the Missouri River system. Montana has a good population of lake trout. Fed by mountain runoff, Fort Peck is a natural environment for lakers. But the big reservoir has a forage imbalance. As a result, lake trout have been feeding on walleyes. Now, normally walleyes and lake trout occupy different niches in the system. But a fish has to eat. And when they can't find food within their niche, they'll adapt as necessary.

An even more dramatic example of this has been noted on Lake Sakakawea, Fort Peck's sister to the east. Sauger normally are found in very turbid environments, like rivers. But on Sakakawea, a large percentage of the sauger population has, in just a few years, evolved to occupy an entirely different niche in the system. Presumably because they were forced out of their natural environment, sauger now are inhabiting the lower end of the reservoir, which is a deep, clear section of water. They've just dropped down and are in 75 to 100 feet, utilizing a previously unoccupied niche in the system. Typically a very early, shallow spawner, the sauger now are spawning in July in 35 feet of water. Four distinct schools, as big as a mile and a half long and a quarter-mile wide, have been observed by biologists working Sakakawea. Why did this happen? Because the fish found a niche in the environment that offered an adequate forage base, in this case, smelt, while at the same time meeting all their other needs.

Anything that alters the forage base from year to year can have a dramatic effect on fish success.

In some lakes, walleyes use the weeds during most of the summer period. That's a cause-and-effect relationship that results mostly from the fact that chlorophyll-bearing plants give off oxygen and absorb carbon dioxide. Fish need oxygen to live. Weeds not only provide life-supporting oxygen, they also offer protection for baitfish that would quickly be gobbled up swimming around in open water.

With a substantial portion of the baitfish utilizing the weeds, a certain percentage of the walleye population will follow. Remember, a fish has only three functions in its life. The first, and most urgent, is to reproduce. The other two are to eat and to avoid being eaten.

For that reason neither walleyes, nor any predator for that matter, will ever be far from their forage. They may not follow the baitfish 24 hours a day, but you can bet they're always close by, especially during the summer months when the walleyes' increased metabolism dictates that he feed more heavily than during the cold-water period.

Early in the season, the walleye's diet may consist largely of insects. By the time the insect hatches have come off, the walleye will turn its attentions to young-of-the-year fishes, like perch.

In most waters across the country, the yellow perch is the number one food choice of walleyes. Among other popular foods are lake emerald shiners, suckers, alewives, cisco, fatheads, tullibee and smelt. In some of the southern impoundments, gizzard shad and threadfin shad are the main source of nourishment for the walleye.

Studies indicate that perch are probably the preferred forage because perch tend to be available in a suitable size for the longest period of time. Walleyes show a definite size preference when it comes to forage. If several forage species are available at the preferred length, the walleye will likely select the most abundant species. Walleyes can, without a doubt, thrive in waters where perch are in short supply or even non-existent.

The preferred length of forage for a walleye, apparently, ranges from 25 to 40 percent of the walleye's total length. One study showed that a seven-inch fish preferred a food that was two inches long, 14-inch fish preferred a bait that was 3.5 inches long, and a 17-inch fish went after a meal that was 4 inches long.

When you think in terms of a trophy-class fish, you're talking about a walleye that's anywhere from 28 inches on up. A fish that size is going to be looking for a meal that's seven to 12 inches in length. I know fishermen who are reluctant to tie on a four-inch crankbait because they think it's too big for the walleyes to handle. Well, that big old sow down there not only isn't going to be reluctant to hit a big bait; it's actually her preferred size.

Big baits catch big fish? In many cases, that's exactly right. A big bait is just what that old mama is looking for . . . at least when she is feeding to grow or fatten.

Any imbalance that results in a reduction of available food of preferred size can have a direct effect on the quality of fishing. As we said, activity levels are affected by the density of available forage. The more forage that's available, the more those walleyes are going to eat. They don't have to be picky eaters or worry about the amount of energy they're expending in the process. As their condition factor improves, they become almost ravenous. But with lack of proper forage, the fish will become more lethargic.

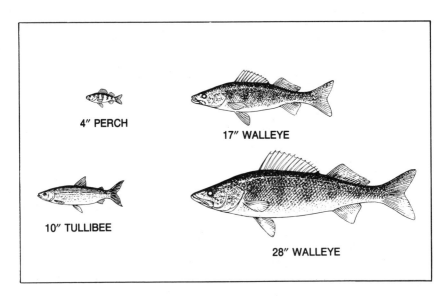

**Figure 3.** *The preferred length of forage fish for a walleye is approximately 25 to 40 percent of the walleye's total length.*

As we've seen, the delicate balance can be toppled by numerous natural causes. But often as not, man is the culprit.

Acid rain is a good example. High acidity in water destroys the life-giving nutrients that are so basic to a balanced food chain. Unless the problem of acid rain is corrected soon, hundreds of lakes in Canada, along the east coast and in Europe will be dying off in the years to come. Unfortunately, right now the demands for energy overshadow the necessity to protect the environment. That's typical for man! In many areas of the country, especially the more popular resort states like Michigan, Minnesota, and Wisconsin, the opposite problem exists. Some of these lakes have become over-developed and excessive nutrient levels have resulted. One of the offshoots of this development is sewage that's dumped either directly into the lake or enters the water through seepage. In agricultural areas, animal wastes pose the same threat. Runoff washes fertilizers through the watershed and into the lake. The result is a buildup of nutrients which promote the growth of blue-green algae and create oxygen shortages.

Another example is when cabin-owners clear the shoreline of unwanted vegetation. In their desire to have a clean, sugar-sand beach for swimming, they're actually helping to destroy a vital part of the lake's environment.

There are other ways man contributes to the problem. Commercial fishing has all but wiped out many vital, healthy fisheries. A prime example was Lake Erie; fishermen practically ruined Lake Erie. Happily, a few concerned sportsmen tackled the problem and, in this case, man was part of the solution.

By putting limitation on the commercial harvest, and stopping the flow of pollutants, man started the process that turned Lake Erie around, and today it's one of the best walleye waters in the world with a very bright future. I hope what happened on Lake Erie will serve as a lesson man can learn from.

On many rivers and reservoirs around the country, manipulation of water levels has a lot to do with the quality of the fishery. A sudden drop in water levels at spawning time could leave billions of walleye eggs high and dry, wiping out an entire year-class of fish.

In the absence of that year-class, a void is created in the bio-mass. That void could be filled by rough fish, altering the very nature of the system.

From a more practical point of view, at least as far as fishermen are concerned, fluctuating water levels have a lot to do with where the fish will locate on a reservoir or river system.

If high volumes of water are being moved through the power-generating dams, fish will tend to move upstream. The fish will migrate right into the tailwater areas to feed on all the food items that are being ground up and washed through the turbines. A similar thing is occuring above the dam on the reservoir. If water levels are dropping, the fish tend to move downstream. With rising water, fish instinctively move upstream.

True to their nature, river and reservoir fish are migratory creatures that think nothing of moving 20 or 30 miles in a very short period of time.

Nature and man. Each can contribute to changes in the ecosystem and effect the way fish locate. Understanding how fish relate to the food chain can go a long way towards helping you understand how to fish a particular body of water.

The information we've just covered may not seem important now, but as we continue our look at location, I think it will all fall into place. And, hopefully, you'll come away with a better understanding of the delicate balance of nature that's such an all-important part of the total angling experience.

## Moods/Schooling Tendencies

Generally speaking, walleyes are school fish.

That's not a traffic-stopping bit of information we just dropped on you . . . every fisherman alive knows that during most times of the year, the walleyes travel in schools. But only a handful of fishermen really know how to use that information to their advantage. And some commit very serious errors by overlooking the schooling tendencies of their favorite gamefish.

Here's one classic example. Two guys are working the 17-foot contour off the edge of a classic rock point. They're seeing fish on the flasher and have missed a couple hard strikes. Finally, the angler seated in the bow gets a solid set into a real brute . . . a fish so big there'll be no need to lie about it later.

Instinctively, the boat operator swings the motor around and moves out over 35 feet to do battle. The rationale is that getting that big fish out of the school quickly will avoid spooking the rest of the fish.

In most cases, that's the worst mistake possible. Fish are curious, competitive creatures. When one walleye out of a school hits a bait, the others are likely to follow for a short distance, hoping to pick up some scraps or maybe just checking things out. Swinging out over deep water, often as not, pulls the entire school out over deep water. The other fish might not follow the hooked walleye all the way to the landing net, but they could move well off the contour and wind up suspended over deep water. Eventually they'll return to the shallows . . . maybe. But, for the time being, they've been moved off the structure.

Depending on weather conditions, you have several options when fighting a big fish. If the water's calm, shut down the engine and play the fish right where you sit. Get that fish up as quickly as you can without putting undue stress on your line.

If there's a wind, you'll be forced to keep the boat moving along the exact same depth. That way if you do move the school, you'll be moving it laterally along the same contour. After you've landed the fish, you can resume trolling along that contour and once again contact the school. They may be 50 feet away, but at least they'll be at the same depth.

I've seen days when understanding *how* the fish are schooling can increase your catch by as much as 50 percent. For example, let's say you're drifting and trolling over a point that has direct exposure to a strong wind. The water's churned up and those walleyes have moved in fairly shallow and are extremely active. As you drift the edge of that point with the wind, you pick up two or three fish per pass. Then, efficient angler that you are, you troll back over the same water, but catch nothing. Drifting back, you pick up a couple fish. Trolling against the wind produces nothing. After three passes, your engine eventually spooks the school. Or maybe the fish just filled their stomachs and retreated back to deep water. Whatever the case, they're gone.

See the mistake? Usually, fish will lie facing one direction. And, often as not, they'll be facing the incoming waves. Wave action is what pushes food toward the structure, and those walleyes will be lying with their mouths open, waiting for an easy meal to come along. Drifting with the wind works well under these conditions, because the bait is moving towards the fish's face. But when back-trolling against the wind, the angler is bringing the bait past the fish's tail . . . an unnatural presentation. It may be possible to take an occasional fish that way, but the majority of the action will come on the drift.

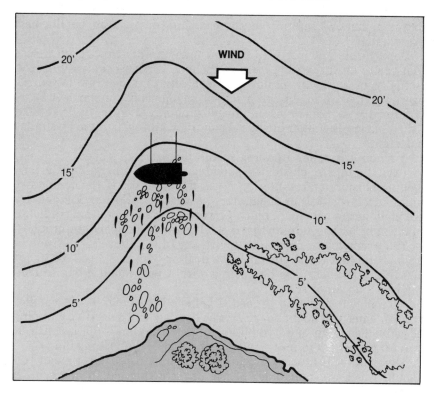

**Figure 4.** *Usually walleyes will lay facing into the oncoming waves, waiting for an easy meal to be washed their way. So it makes sense to troll or drift your bait with the wind for a natural, effective presentation.*

These walleyes aren't going to be active all day. Feeding sprees usually only last 10 to 15 minutes, maybe a lot less. You want to capitalize on the situation by taking as many fish as you can as quickly as you can. The best way to accomplish that is to dispense with the trolling pass and just drift. In some cases, it's possible to double your catch just by understanding which direction the fish are facing.

Under normal conditions, river fish will always lay facing the current. Again, the moving water is delivering a meal right to their mouth. Also, it's easier for a fish to swim facing the current than with it's back to the current. That's why it's usually more effective to drift with the current than to troll against it.

Even if there's no wind, the bulk of the school likely will be facing in one direction or the other. Discovering which direction they're facing can increase your overall catch tremendously.

In some cases, especially on turbid waters like reservoirs or smaller, fertile, natural lakes, the fish might move into the extreme shallows in a big wind. I've caught walleyes on a point or food shelf in a foot of water. When they're that close to the shore, the fish usually will be positioned with their backs to the wind. That's because the waves are crashing against the shore and washing back, carrying insects, grubs or stunned baitfish against the waves. If the fish are working the extreme shallows, casting to shore and retrieving can be the best presentation.

Don't think that just because you take one or two fish off a spot that you're dealing with a massive "school." Schools can vary in size. Actually, biologists break down concentrations of fish into three categories. What we might call a school, scientists call a shoal. A shoal is defined as "a more or less prolonged grouping of mutually orientated fishes, of closely similar biological condition and age, united by similar behavior."

A school is smaller grouping within the limits of a shoal.

Then there are clusters—spawning clusters, migrating clusters, feeding clusters and wintering clusters. A cluster is the temporary union of a few shoals or elementary populations of fishes. Elementary populations are usually of one age, frequently a life grouping of fishes in the same basic condition that is established at the spawning grounds.

You needn't concern yourself with any of the above terms. Merely understand that while you could be dealing with a "school" of 200 or 300 fish, you might also be dealing with a very small group of fish, say half a dozen or so.

As walleyes move up to feed, I believe they break off in smaller groups. Thus, you might not always be dealing with a massive grouping of active fish. And often you'll encounter stragglers—the last fish or two from a school to move away at the end of the feeding binge.

The point is, just because you take a couple fish doesn't mean you should waste the remainder of the day growing old in one spot. If several other passes with different presentations don't produce any action, the school is likely gone. Or perhaps you were only dealing with a very small group of fish in the first place. At that point, I'll review the information about bottom content, depth, availability to deep water and all the other factors that go into the building of a pattern and I'll *move to another, similar area.*

Under certain conditions, it may actually be possible to follow a school as it moves up and down to feed. This is perhaps the exception rather than the rule, but it can happen.

Let's say you're catching fish off the tip of a rocky point in 22 feet of water. As clouds block out the sun and the wind picks up, the action stops. It could well be that with reduced light penetration, those fish made a move towards shallower water. Now they're working the top of the point in 15 feet.

As the sky turns to heavy overcast and the wind really starts howling, the fish move again, all the way to seven or eight feet. Eventually, they'll fill their stomachs and will drop back towards deep water.

It's been my experience, that as the walleyes move shallower, they'll break off into smaller groups. And when they start dropping back to deeper water, they'll stage and re-group, probably off the tip of the point where they started to feed initially.

By paying close attention to weather conditions and fish activity, it may be possible to actually follow the school all the way up and back down again. Even though the fishes' stomachs are full, they are still in an active mood. Their adrenalin is pumping, if you will. So, as they stage on the top of the point in 22 feet, it will often be possible to milk one or two bonus fish before they disappear to deep water.

The last few years I've found myself relying more and more on my graph recorder to locate and relocate active fish. If I make contact with a school but lose that school, I'll pole around in the surrounding water, with the graph, in an attempt to find those fish. More often than not I can, but that doesn't mean they will still be feeding. Don't forget, your goal is to find "catchable" fish, not just walleyes.

Graphs are an excellent tool to use in determining the activity level of the fish you encounter. As a rule, the more active the walleye, the further it will be off the bottom . . . to a point. Neutral fish will often be lying right on the bottom, slightly active fish will ride up a foot or two and very active fish may be three, four or five feet off the bottom.

This information may dictate a change in presentation. For instance, if you've been dragging a jig, it may be necessary to start giving that jig big hops. If you're working a short-snelled Lindy Rig, you may have to switch to a floating rig or floating jighead, and get that bait up to where the fish are feeding. If they become active enough, you may even change to an attractor bait like a spinner or crankbait.

When you encounter a school of extremely active fish, don't waste time. Those fish aren't going to make themselves available to you all day. Catch 'em as fast as you can. When I get into a "big bite," I may not even take the time to put the fish in the live well.

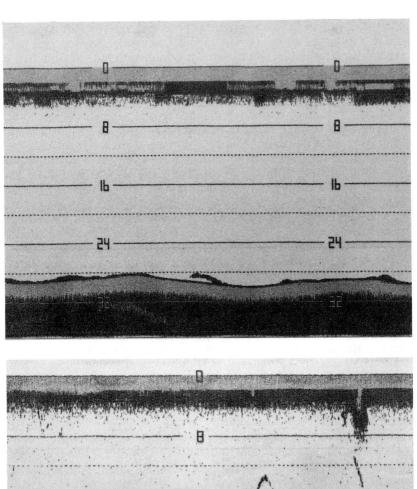

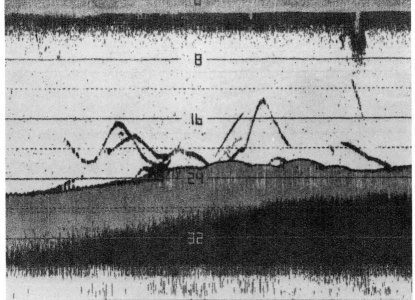

Graphs are an excellent tool to help determine the activity level of a walleye school. Active fish will generally be up off the bottom and moving (bottom photo). A neutral or negative school is often "belly to the bottom" (top photo).

There are ways to determine the activity levels of fish without using a graph. Often, if you have a large school of extremely active fish they grab a bait and make a mad dash to excape their greedy schoolmates. I've seen times when a big walleye would pick up a crawler and run 20 feet before stopping, getting out of the crowd before attempting to swallow the meal. That's an indication you're dealing with a sizeable school of active fish. Conversely, if a walleye just nibbles at the bait, picking it up and spitting it back out, chances are there aren't many fish in the school.

It is extremely important to know how many fish you're dealing with in a particular area. I can't tell you how many times I've seen a group of fishermen waste a whole day working an area that simply didn't have many walleyes. Just because they took one or two fish upon arriving, they'll sit there all day waiting for one more fish . . . that never comes.

So, how long do you stay in one spot? I like to move from spot to spot until I encounter active fish. Make a couple quick passes, working different depths with different lures. If you don't get some indication that fish are working that structure . . . move. How long you actually devote to each section of water depends on the size and diversity of the structure itself. Some can be thoroughly checked in a matter of minutes . . . others require a lot more time.

It's possible to encounter more than one school working an area, especially if you're dealing with a "super-structure," which we'll be talking about later in this chapter. Granted, this is a rarity, but it happens. And it's important that you recognize it when it does.

Fish generally school according to age class. I've noted exceptions to this rule. Once I saw a walleye about 13 pounds and another one that made the 13-pounder look like a dwarf. These two monsters were swimming along side a school of 2-pounders. But that's not going to happen very often. Usually, fish within a given school will run about the same size.

Maybe you're working the top of a point and catching some eating sized walleyes. As you slip off the deep tip of the point, you bang a 6-pounder. There's a very good chance you're dealing with two distinct schools of fish here. The smaller fish are on top of the point, the bigger ones are lying off the tip.

If you're after numbers, stay with the school of smaller fish, which likely will have a whole lot more walleyes. If you're after something to hang on the wall, concentrate on the bigger fish.

I recall one instance, where I had four different schools of fish working a relatively small section of water at the same time. There were two points in conjunction with one another, one rocky and the other soft-bottomed. Between the two was a nice food shelf with a rock pile. We encountered one school of fish on the tip of each of the points, another on the rock pile between the points and a fourth school lying in deep water off the tip of the rocky point in about 22 feet. The biggest fish were in the deeper water and, by concentrating on that school, we were able to take a nice mess of six to eight-pound walleyes.

By being observant and making a mental note of each seemingly minute detail, you can often gain that all-important understanding of what the fish are doing under the surface. Each little clue leads you one step closer to solving the puzzle.

Once in awhile you'll be into a school of walleyes and suddenly the action stops like someone slammed a door in your face. Seconds later you get an elbow-shattering strike and a bite-off from what felt like a big northern or musky.

"Toothies" and walleyes don't mix. Since they were fry, those walleyes learned to associate the smell of a pike or musky with danger, and they'll retreat at the first whiff of danger.

I like to carry an extra rod rigged up with a jerk bait or other northern pike lure for just such an occasion. As soon as the bite-off occurs, I'll toss that big bait up to the fish and, often as not, will hook that aggressive predator within a few casts.

When the northern or musky invaded their dining room, the walleyes probably did one of two things. They either dumped into deeper water or they snuggled to the bottom where they lay totally motionless. They will not be moving around actively feeding when that big toothy's on the prowl. Once you eliminate the danger, the walleyes may well resume feeding. But as long as that toothy torpedo is in the vicinity, your walleye fishing is dead.

On the other end of the spectrum is the relationship between perch and walleyes. If you're picking up lots of perch or experiencing a bunch of perch nibbles, you can just about bet there are no walleyes around. Those perch wouldn't be feeding at the risk of becoming a meal themselves. You might as well hit the road and check another spot. Then, too, the presence of those perch likely will attract a school of walleye, sometime, so don't write the spot off entirely. Check back periodically and sooner or later you'll probably find walleyes on that spot.

## Activity Levels/Moods

Like people, fish have moods. Those moods can be affected by a number of factors, like weather conditions, seasonal change, fishing pressure, environmental conditions and availability of forage. Being able to recognize the mood of the fish is an integral part of successful fishing.

Fish will exhibit different activity levels by the seasons. In cold water, the fish's metabolism will be low. They'll not be in a chasing mood. The fish simply will burn up more calories racing around after baitfish than can be replaced in that taking of the meal. It's a no-win proposition. For that reason, a slow presentation is almost always most effective in cold-water situations.

Pre-spawn and late fall are two of the best times to catch walleyes, especially big walleyes. Big fish are busy "larding up" during these two periods.

Wait a minute, this is getting confusing. The fish are feeding heavily, but are inactive at the same time?

Nope, that's not what we said! The fish are slow, lethargic, not willing to "chase" a meal. But, they are feeding as often as possible. Speed is the critical factor here. If you can move a bait right past the fish's nose so the walleye can feed without expending a great deal of energy, chances are that old fish is going to accept your offer. Run that bait by too quickly, and the walleye probably won't give the bait a second look.

During the winter months, those fish feed only to maintain. They can go for days without taking a meal. Under the ice, they're just lying around all day in a sleep-like state. They simply don't have to feed very often.

In the warm-water period, it's a different story. From the time water temperatures reach 55 to 57 degrees until shortly after ice-up, those fish are feeding to grow. The warmer the water gets, the more active the walleyes become. Now they're getting aggressive and might well chase a bait ten feet. In fact, I've seen graph paper where big walleyes streaked as much as 30 feet vertically to hit a big crankbait.

Weather conditions, also, can have a dramatic effect on walleye activity. One of the most important considerations is light penetration.

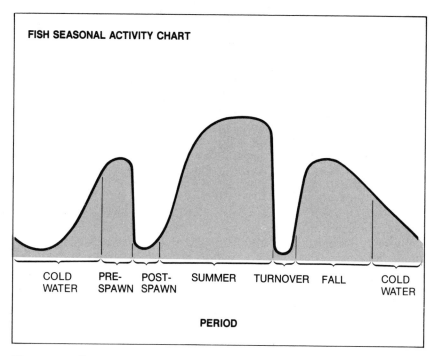

**Figure 5.** *Walleye activity changes throughout the year. Pre-spawn, the summer period, and early fall are three of the best times to consistently take fish.*

This is a very complex subject and one that's been kicked around and argued about to the point where almost no one can separate fact from fiction.

First, walleyes do have extremely light-sensitive eyes. Those big eyes allow them to feed under the most subdued light conditions. As a rule, the best walleye fishing occurs during the low-light hours of early morning, late afternoon and during the night.

But, there's a whole lot more to it than that. Consider, for example, the angle of the sun's rays. In spring and fall, the sun's rays are striking the earth at a very indirect angle. As a result, fish can be up in very shallow water at mid-day and not be bothered by light penetration. Even in ultra-clear water, those fish can be prowling the shallows at will.

Each spring I fish some excellent Canadian shield lakes that have gin-clear water. I locate walleyes visually, using a pair of polaroid sunglasses to block out glare and enable me to see under the surface.

That wouldn't be the case in mid-July, when the sun's rays are hitting the earth from straight overhead. By July, the walleyes would be forced into deeper water.

Water clarity, also, is an important factor. In a turbid system, fish can move very shallow on a hot, calm, clear day if there's enough material suspended in the water to block out sunlight.

A build-up of sun-filtering particles in the upper atmosphere also can allow those walleyes to move about more freely. If several days pass without a cold front moving through an area, there will be an accumulation of dust particles and moisture in the upper atmosphere. These will help filter out the ultra-violet rays. The screen of dust and moisture will promote the growth of algae on the surface, and that in turn will reduce sunlight penetration into the water.

But look out . . . here comes the dreaded cold front. A storm blows through, washing the dust and moisture particles from the air. The wind pushes algae across the lake stacking it against the shoreline in clumps. Now, in the main basin of the lake the sun's rays penetrate deep into the water. The fish dump into deep water, lying in a state of dormancy with their bellies in the mud. Or they tuck into dense weeds, reluctant to move.

As a scuba diver, I've seen post cold-front walleyes lying on the bottom and absolutely refusing to move. You sometimes have to actually grab these fish by the tail to get them to move. Imagine how impressed a fish like that is going to be if you run a bait past its face. Forget it! I'm not entirely sure why fish become so lethargic following a cold front. The best bet is that either light penetration or barometric change is the main factor . . . but more probably, it's a combination of factors. The research staff at Babe Winkelman Productions is looking into the question and hopefully will have some answers in the years ahead. Right now, it's open to speculation.

One effect of a cold front, especially if there's a good rainfall, could be a drastic change in the pH levels of the water. Sudden changes in pH affects the fish's ability to utilize oxygen and results in lethargy.

However, we suspect light penetration is the most important factor. We say that because cold fronts don't really have as much effect on river fish or fish in very turbid systems.

In fact, on some reservoir systems, fishing actually *improves* following a cold front. The passing of the front stirs up the water in these big impoundments, and fish go on a feeding binge in extremely shallow water the following day. Of course, like other rules, this doesn't always hold true.

River walleyes may remain semi-active following the passage of a front as well. And walleyes in shallow, dishpan lakes often are not as affected by the storm system.

A number of years ago, I spent three days hammering big fish on a lake near my home. The weather was steady and each day those walleyes got a little more active. Then a cold front moved through and I knew the clear-water lake would be reluctant to yield any fish. Word had leaked out about my success, and the morning after the front passed through, two dozen boats were bunched up on the area I'd been fishing. They didn't get so much as a nibble.

The same day, I launched my boat on the Mississippi River and continued catching fish.

There are ways of coping with cold fronts, even on clear-water lakes. But to do that, you must understand what's happening in the walleye's underwater world.

As the storm moves through, the wind will push warm water and algae to one side of the lake. Wave action also will oxygenate that section of the lake that had the most direct exposure to the wind. As the warm surface water moves in one direction, it will be displaced by colder water on the lee side.

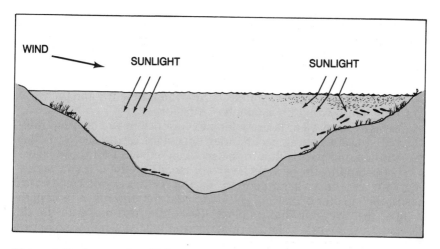

**Figure 6.** During tough cold front conditions, fish the windy side of a body of water. The wave action cuts down on light penetration, and the wind blows all the phytoplankton and algae to one side, attracting baitfish and any active walleyes to feed.

Your best bet under these conditions will be to fish the windy side of the lake. The water will be warmer here, possibly attracting some baitfish. The algae will provide an umbrella to block out the sun's rays. And oxygen also will be more abundant on the windy side.

I've had my best luck under these conditions, using a small bait, light line and fishing extremely slow. Even fish on the windy side of the lake are likely to be in a negative mood.

As a rule, the best fishing occurs during those periods when no fronts are moving through the area. If you experience four or five days of steady weather, the fish are going to become more and more active each day.

Activity levels can really peak just prior to the arrival of the front. How do these fish know a front is on the way? Fish have the ability to detect very slight changes in barometric pressure through their swim bladder. They instinctively know when a major front is coming, and they know that for several days, they're going to be inactive. So, they compensate by stuffing themselves prior to the arrival of the front and while the front is moving through. Of course, I am not suggesting you sit out on the lake during an electrical storm. I don't want any of my friends getting fried. But, when I felt compelled by a tournament to take a few risks, I have had some excellent fishing during storms.

Mother Nature isn't the only thing that affects fish activity. Fishermen can do the same thing.

Understand this: big fish are not like little fish. Big walleyes have a very highly developed instinct for survival. You may be able to catch 1½ pound walleyes all day with 50 boats messing around right over the top of the school. But that 10-pounder? She'll scat for deep water at the first sign of commotion. She didn't live to reach 10 pounds by accident.

I would guess that 90 percent—maybe more—of the really big fish I've caught were taken on the first pass through a stretch of water. If you suspect a structure might be holding a lunker, it's advisable to sneak into the area at idle speed or using the electric motor. By the second pass, the big fish are likely to have spooked. And it's very rare, indeed, when you'll see many trophy fish caught in a crowd.

There are exceptions, of course. If the wind is howling and the waves crashing, noise won't be as much of a factor.

On many ultra-clear lakes, which experience heavy boating traffic, the only decent fishing occurs after dark. Part of the reason is light penetration and part is due to the spooking effect of all those boats.

Understanding the activity level—or mood—of the fish you're dealing with, can be a very important part of setting a pattern. As we'll see in the chapter on setting patterns, often the difference in hopping a jig or just dragging that jig along the bottom can make all the difference in the world. The more active the fish, the more movement and/or speed you might find necessary to trigger a strike.

Activity levels will be determined by a variety of factors, the most important of which seem to be the number of fish in the school, available forage and weather.

It's safe to say that with a large school of walleyes that are up shallow herding baitfish, you can run a crankbait or any kind of attractor lure through the school and enjoy some success. With just two or three fish down deep and no forage in the vicinity, you may not be able to provoke a strike regardless of what you put down there. Larger schools of fish tend to be more competitive and more aggressive. Smaller schools are less competitive.

The condition factor of the fish also dictates, to some extent, what their activity levels will be. With a solid forage base and a healthy population of well conditoned fish, you'll note very high activity levels. The fish will feed more often, more aggressively and longer. With a small population of fish and a weak forage base, walleyes won't be in as good a shape and won't be as aggressive.

Remember, too, not all the fish in a given population or even within the same school will exhibit the same activity levels. Perhaps 75 percent of the fish within a school are very active and want a fast-moving crankbait. There still will be other fish in that same school that will be susceptible to something different. They're less aggressive and want a jig or Lindy Rig. Still other fish from that school might be neutral and not susceptible to anything.

Again, it all comes back to forage, or predator/prey. We know of cases where walleyes are super-active in 100 feet of water. Why? Because they're down there chasing some type of food. Running a crankbait behind a downrigger at four mph, may produce a lot of action, even from fish that are far below the surface.

If you can locate a large school of baitfish on your graph or flasher, there's a pretty good chance that walleyes—catchable walleyes—won't be far away.

Look for the signs . . . pay attention to what Mother Nature's trying to tell you . . . listen to the fish. Predator/prey and activity levels are two of the most important aspects of setting a pattern.


## pH: Another Factor to Consider

A long time ago, I faced the fact that we're in the modern age of fishing technology. Because it's my business, I at least investigate every new-fangled concept that comes along, promising to be **the** answer to helping catch fish.

I know what you're thinking. Flashers...graph recorders...trolling speed indicators...oxygen probes...your boat already looks like an oceanography lab. Where does it all end, you wonder?

Who knows. I'm certainly not done experimenting, and I follow every major breakthrough. That's the way it is with pH and me. I am convinced, after studying the principles and working with the pH Monitor in the field, that alkalinity/acidity levels play an integral role in fish locations.

Do you have to buy one of Dr. Loren Hill's inventions to catch walleyes? Of course not. It's an aid, a tool, like everything else. I am not going to tell you that using a pH Monitor will guarantee you a limit of fish on every outing. Nothing can do that; there are just too many variables involved in catching or not catching fish.

Whether you add pH to the factors you consider in your fishing is a personal decision. If you're a casual fisherman who doesn't want to be bothered by any more complications while you're out there trying to "get away from it all," then it's probably not for you.

But if you do want to consider it?:

Basically, pH is a measurement of the acid-base relationship in water. It is measured on a scale of 0-14, with 0 being the most acidic and 14 the most basic (alkaline). A pH of 7 is **neutral,** meaning that acid and base ions are in equal concentration.

The pH scale is logarithmic; in other words, a pH of 8.0 is 10 times more basic than one of 7.0, and 7.0 is 10 times more basic than 6.0. According to Dr. Hill, a change of two-tenths (say, from 7.2-7.0) on the pH scale corresponds to a 12-degree change in water temperature.

One of the most important things you can use the pH Monitor for is locating the preferred pH range of the species you seek. According to Dr. Hill, the walleye's preferred pH range is 7.3-7.8. But, it is important to note that fish can acclimate to a much wider range of pH. So don't quit fishing walleyes just because none of the water in your lake falls within the range of 7.3-7.8!

The way to use the pH Monitor, then, is to first take a reading of the surface pH, then slowly lower the probe, checking for where the pH reading changes markedly in a short distance. This point of rapid change is called the **pH breakline.** Let's say you find a surface pH of 8.0.

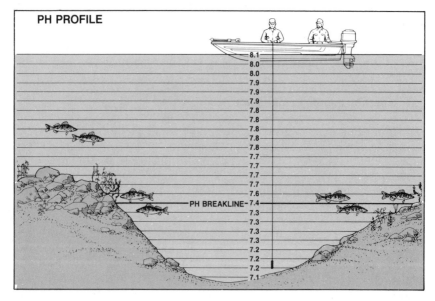

**Figure 7.** *One way to use pH to your advantage is to lower the probe through the water column looking for a pH "breakline." Here the breakline occurs between 15 and 17 feet, and that's where most of the fish are concentrated.*

Then, the pH doesn't change much until, at 19 feet, the pH drops fairly rapidly to 7.3. In this case, a definite pH breakline exists at the 19-foot level, and you would want to concentrate your efforts, at least during the beginning of that day, just above that level (Fig. 7).

This information can be very useful in helping you set a pattern. For instance, if you know of a sunken island that tops off at 25 feet, it might be safe to assume that no fish will be working that island. Another sunken island that tops off at 16 feet could be loaded with active fish.

I am not saying that a pH Monitor is a fishing necessity. Neither is a graph recorder, graphite rods, or a lot of the other equipment so many of us own and use today. Necessary? No. Beneficial? Absolutely.

## Structure—A Matter of Options

Structure. It's the biggest nine-letter word in fishing. It's also one of the most over-used and misunderstood words in the angling vocabulary.

The concept of structure fishing was developed by Buck Perry. The word itself, as defined by Perry in his book Spoonplugging, means "the bottom of the lake with some unusual features that distinguish it from the surrounding bottom area." The fishing world owes a great deal to Buck Perry. Not for inventing a word, but for developing a concept of fishing that literally changed the nature of the sport. Once Perry's message had been delivered to mass audiences, fishermen moved away from the shoreline and began seeking out those bottom areas that were likely to attract and hold fish.

It was at about that same time that Carl Lowrance provided the first sonar devices for fishermen, enabling us to seek out these under-water sanctuaries. Those two developments—Perry's concept of structure and Lowrance's "little red box"—have resulted in more walleyes hitting the skillet than any other discoveries in the history of fishing.

If this book is your introduction to "structure fishing," or even if you consider yourself well versed on the subject, I would strongly recommend two other books as supplemental reading. One is Perry's Spoonplugging and the other is Walleyes Love Nightcrawlers by Bill Binkelman. Walleyes Love Nightcrawlers is out of print, but you may be able to find an old-timer who has a copy. Neither of these books is the last word in fishing, but they were among the original works dealing with the subject of structure and will provide a ground floor look at scientific angling.

During a decade of on-the-water research, I've discovered some things that contradict some of Perry's original teachings and others that go beyond it. For instance, Perry contends that "you can have structure without fish, but you cannot have fish without structure."

We now know that isn't necessarily true. Fish suspend a great deal more than we'd ever anticipated. True, in many cases they are suspending in direct relation to some type of physical structure. But in other cases they are merely following their forage base with no regard to the bottom of the lake. And still other times they're out in the middle of nowhere for reasons we simply don't understand.

I have also seen instances of fish moving onto huge flats that contained no distinguishable features and were a long way from the nearest deep water. I've seen walleyes, and big walleyes, move to the backs of muck bays, apparently relating to nothing in particular. Again, forage is always the key to these seemingly unusual movements. And if the forage should stray from what most of us would consider structure, the walleyes are sure to follow.

Walleyes in systems that contain smelt, alewives, whitefish, cisco or tullibee may, at times, be found doing all sorts of things that you won't find in "the book."

I am not trying to downplay the importance of structures. The vast majority of fish on most lakes, rivers and reservoirs still adhere to structure. It's still true that under most conditions, structure is "where the fish are." But Perry's ideas need to be updated.

So let's take a look at this thing called structure, beginning with the basics and then moving into a more detailed discussion dealing with particular types of waters.

The major misconception about structure is that it is merely a sudden change in depth. The uninitiated angler motors across the lake, a keen eye glued to his depth finder. Suddenly, the bottom reading jumps from 55 feet to 20 feet and Joe Fisherman about jumps out of his seat. "Wow, look at this. What a great spot."

Often as not, he's going to be disappointed and perhaps a bit disenchanted with the theories on structure fishing. A sharp change in depth does not, in itself, constitute structure.

I like to think of structure in terms of two basic ingredients—*edges* and *food shelves*. Change is a vital part of structure, and a sudden change in depth could be the first basic step in locating fish holding structure. But with the possible exception of a dishpan lake, sudden changes in depth—called a drop-off—exists along the entire course of just about every lake. On some of the larger reservoir systems, you may have 3,000 miles or more of river channel alone. Along every inch of that river channel, you'll see a sudden change in depth. To get the whole picture, you must look beyond just quick breaks.

What I try to accomplish is to envision the bottom of the lake as the fish sees it. What options do those fish have? Keep in mind it's not necessarily the structure itself that holds fish . . . it's *something on that structure*.

We're looking for edges. Examples of edges could be the inside or outside edge of a weedbed, a point that breaks up an otherwise straight stretch of shoreline, a mud line, a gravel bed surrounded by sand, a creek channel, the thermocline, a sudden change in the pH reading, a stairstep ledge, a little hook or cut along the drop-off, a rock finger, a neck-down area between two lakes, a river of creek channel . . . and these are just a sampling.

These edges all qualify as changes—something different. Once you locate an edge, you must break it down even further. Let's say you find a rock finger coming off a small point. Now you must examine that finger, looking at inside turns, variations in bottom content, weeds, rocks, or any other factors that might attract fish to a particular section of that finger.

Another very important consideration is the food shelf. The more food shelf that's available to the fish, the more walleyes are likely to be using that food shelf. Very small food shelves may, at times, attract some big fish. But they can't attract large numbers of fish.

It's important to keep in mind that in their movements from deep water to the shallow food shelves where they'll feed, the fish will follow a visible path, called a migration route. Again, we're simply talking about edges. During these vertical movements the fish will relate to something different . . . a change . . . and edge.

Picture a stretch of shoreline a mile long. Along the entire course of that shoreline the bottom drops very gradually from the shallows out to 18 feet. At 18 feet there is a sudden drop-off, called a breakline.

The breakline, in itself, does not constitute structure. Along the entire course of this mile-long shoreline there may exist only two or three areas that have the potential to attract and hold fish. Those areas will have some distinguishing features.

One of the most obvious, and easiest to find, would be a point. Some points may extend a long way out into the lake while others are very small. The important thing to remember is that any point offers *something different* that the fish can relate to in their vertical migrations.

Obviously, structure does not have to be connected to the shoreline. In fact, some of the best producers of fish exist in the middle of the lake. The quickest way to zero in on these structures is by using a contour map and a sonar device. Don't expect that every potential fish-holding area will be displayed on the map—some of the best spots simply aren't there. Finding them requires several trips around the lake with your eyes riveted on the sonar equipment in your boat.

When you see something unusual or distinctive, study it with your "electronic eyes." Make several passes over the top, asking yourself several key questions about the structure. Where's the quickest drop to deep water? What type of bottom content does the structure have? At what depth does it top out? Are there weeds? Inspect the water closely, looking for every possible detail.

You're trying to identify the edges that might attract fish. And in the process, you should be developing a mental picture of the structure. This is a vital part of the process known as setting a pattern. Patterns are the essence of walleye fishing, or any kind of fishing, and something we'll be discussing at length later in the book. The more you can understand about the makeup of the structure, the sooner you'll be able to pinpoint fish location, and the better equipped you'll be to duplicate a pattern that may evolve. You want to develop a mental picture of the edges and food shelves so precise, that if it were possible to drain the water out of the lake, the actual structure would appear exactly as you envisioned it. If you get the idea from all this that you're becoming a *hunter* of fishes, you're on the right track.

Many of these areas won't be as obvious as an island or point. There are, for example, many edges in and around the weedline. The inside and outside edges of the weedline will be fairly easy to locate. If there's a good lip, cut or point along that edge, you've found a good potential spot for walleyes to be hanging around.

But there are other edges within the weedbed. A gravel run through the weeds or perhaps a pile of rocks within a weed bank can be a real fish magnet.

Changes in weed types or in density of weed growth can attract fish. A thick clump of coontail bordered by cabbage weed, for instance, might well attract active walleyes.

In the last chapter we talked about pH edge, a breakline where a sudden drop in pH levels occurs. While you need a pH Monitor to find these edges, the fish can easily sense them and will relate to them.

Thermal edges also exist within many bodies of water. One example is the thermocline, a stratification of water according to temperature. At times, the fish will actually relate to the thermocline as if it were the bottom of the lake.

Wind and wave action can create other types of thermal edges. Should the wind blow out of the south for several days consecutively, it will stack up the warm surface water on the north side of the lake.

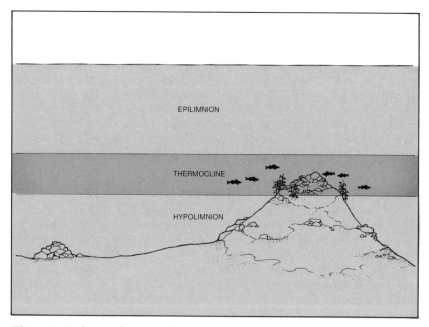

**Figure 8.** Understanding stratification is important to the angler. In some lakes, the only layers that will get any amount of oxygen rejuvenation is the upper level and thermocline, which forces the walleyes to use only these layers.

Water cannot be compressed, thus as the warm surface water is moving to the north, it's being displaced by cooler water on the south side. It's possible that for some time after the wind dies down, you'll have a bubble of warm water on the north end of the lake that will result in all sorts of things happening within the food chain.

Obviously, minnows and baitfish will be attracted to the mass of warm water. Because of the wave action, insects and grubs may be unearthed. Organic and inorganic materials will be stacked up on the windy side of the lake. Algae will have drifted in that direction creating a protective umbrella that blocks out the sun's rays.

Sure, it's calm the morning you arrive to go fishing. But the events of the last three or four days may have had such a dramatic effect on the ecosystem that you won't be able to buy a fish on the south end of the lake, but they'll be feeding on the other end.

How about current edges? You can have current in a natural lake following the events we've just described. When the wind pushes water in one direction for a period of time, something called a seiche is created. The windy side of the lake can be as much as a foot or two higher than the lee side. When the wind stops blowing, all that water that was forced to one side of the lake will now begin to move back as the lake balances out. That can actually create a current that fish may relate to. This is especially true in a neck-down area of the lake where the current is concentrated.

You will also encounter water color edges. If the waves break over a soft-bottomed area for any length of time, water clarity will be reduced, allowing baitfish and gamefish alike access to shallow water that normally would be subject to too much light intensity. If there's a distinct mud line, fish will often relate to it, working the edge between the stained and clear water.

As you can see, there are many different kinds of edges. Some are obvious, some are downright obscure.

## Super-Structure

Now let's take our look at structure one step further and talk about "super-structure." Not all structures are created equally. One island may have the ability to attract fish only under certain conditions while the next seems to host active fish a good percentage of the time.

It could be that the first island is relatively featureless. It's merely a dome with some scattered rock on the top. But the super island has a multitude of features that can attract and hold fish. It not only has rock, but it also has a good weed growth on one side. There are three different points coming off the island at varying depths, one attached to deep water by a rock finger. This island very simply has more features or edges that will attract and hold fish.

Close proximity to other structures is another element of a super-structure. An island, by itself, is good. But an island connected to a point by a saddle, with a pronounced food shelf and a major weed bed on top . . . well, that's dynamite. Look at all the options fish have. They can be relating to the weed bed, the point, the saddle or the island. You can bet that somewhere within that little complex there will be walleyes a good percentage of the time.

A long point that extends out to deep water can, at times, attract a big school of fish. But, if the surrounding shallows are void of any distinguishing features, there's not as much of a chance that fish will ever utilize that point. Now, if the shallows happen to be a huge, tapering flat with dense cabbage and coontail growths, some gravel runs and a few rock beds, both become super-structures worthy of your attention.

Starting to get the picture? Some bodies of water simply don't have many options for the fish to use. On those lakes you may not encounter super-structures. But on many of the larger natural lakes and reservoirs, structure seems to be everywhere. In those lakes, the ability to eliminate water by selecting super-structures can be a real key to finding bigger fish.

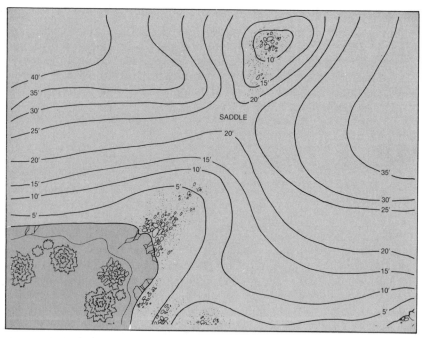

**Figure 9.** A saddle formed by a hump on the end of a point is a perfect place for walleyes. This "super-structure" will often hold fish from the spawn period all the way through fall.

At this point, we should talk a bit more about food shelves. The actual size of the food shelf can be critical. In my experience, the larger the food shelf, the more apt you'll be to find fish on it. That's not always the case, but it holds true more often than not.

The reason, of course, is forage. A very small food shelf simply doesn't have the carrying capacity for large concentrations of forage fish. And if there's only limited forage available, walleyes aren't likely to frequent the area. But with a large food shelf, there's a much better chance that a large school of fish will migrate in that direction at meal time.

A tiny island isn't as likely to hold numbers of fish as a large island. Granted, small islands have been known to attract schools of big fish, schools that because of attrition, are reduced to only a few walleyes. But, generally, I'd select a large island first, working smaller islands as a last resort. A series of small humps all clustered together would be the optimum situation you could encounter. The key here is the number of edges or particular features within the framework of the island or humps. A large food shelf might not hold anything in the way of baitfish or gamefish if it's void of features. And a smaller food shelf could harbor some fish if it contains the proper features to attract and hold baitfish.

That leads us to the next important consideration—mini-structure.

## Mini-Structure

You've found a good food shelf on what you'd consider a super-structure. Let's assume there's a large flat with dense growths of cabbage and coontail with an ample food shelf on the outside edge of the weeds. You've narrowed your search down to a relatively small section of the lake. Next, you want to seek out the "mini-structure," or that *exact spot* along the weedline that is most likely to hold fish.

A mini-structure is nothing more than a particular feature the fish can relate to. Some might call it a "break on a break" or a "structure on a structure." I simply coined the term "mini-structure."

Moving down the outside edge of the weed bed you may encounter a hook or a cut in the weeds. That's a specific feature walleyes will relate to. Maybe there's a rock finger extending down the break with a few larger rocks contacting the edge of the weeds. That's another likely fish-holding spot. It could be something as seemingly insignificant as a gravel bed surrounded by clay bottom. Or a clam bed.

The point is, it's another edge, something more the fish can relate to. Pinpoint such a spot and you'll increase your chances for finding and catching fish by 50 percent.

While you're appraising that sunken island you just found with your sonar, check for "mini-structures." Maybe there's a stairstep ledge that occurs a few feet below the top of the island. That stairstep might not

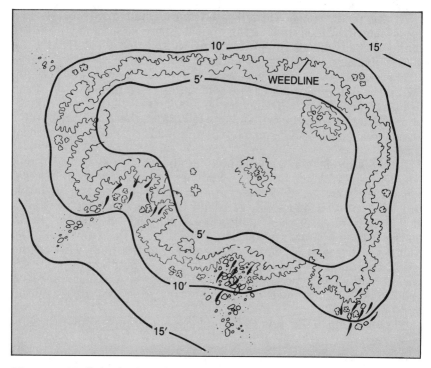

**Figure 10.** *Troll slowly along the weedline looking for a pocket, a weed point or a rock point. These **mini-structures** hold concentrations of fish.*

only hold fish, it may have the ability to attract some big fish. Perhaps one side of the island drops more quickly to super deep water while the other three sides taper more gradually. The quick access to deep water constitutes mini-structure. So does a small but dense patch of weeds on top of the island. Or that rock finger that extends all the way down to 35 feet . . . or a single large boulder on the rock finger.

Again, you're looking for changes. Initially you're looking for big changes, but as the search narrows, you're down to seeking out the minute changes we call mini-structure.

The availability of different types of structures will change from one body of water to the next. For example, the weedlines that produce so many summertime walleyes on some natural lakes, are non-existent in many sections of rivers and reservoirs. The classic structures like rock piles and deep sunken islands are apt to be very rare in your older, eutrophic lakes. So understanding the body of water you're fishing can be quite important.

But don't put too much emphasis on the importance of identifying the various lake types. I have seen too many fishermen waste the first two days of their vacation trying to figure out if they're fishing a late-stage mesotrophic lake or an early stage eutrophic lake. What's the difference? The key is looking at choices.

When you boil it all down, successful fishing involves three basic steps. First, you must analyze the options available to the fish. Where can they be? Where do they *have* to be? Second, you start hunting for the fish. And the third step to successful fishing is setting a pattern. Examine the options available to the fish, hunt for active fish, then use the information at your disposal to set a pattern. It's the same whether you're fishing a lake, a canyon reservoir, a plateau reservoir, an oligotrophic lake or a carp lake. The procedure never changes.

Our good friend, Gary Roach, is generally considered one of the finest walleye fishermen alive. Certainly he's one of the top promotional fishermen in the country. He's also a "seat of the pants" fisherman. It's doubtful Gary can even spell oligotrophic. But he sure as heck can catch fish out of an "oly" lake, or any other body of water. He follows the same procedure we just talked about . . . he *hunts* for fish. He eliminates the possibilities until he encounters active fish. He seeks out different types of structures, works a variety of depths and constantly changes his presentation until the fish tell him where they are and what they want. Gary's a *walleye hunter*.

## Lake Types

There's a tendency to classify natural lakes as young, middle-aged and old. That's misleading. What you are actually concerned about is the fertility level, forage and the basic bottom configuration of the water. These are the factors that will dictate the options available to the walleyes.

The process of aging is called eutrophication. In many cases, I've seen this aging process accelerated. Pollution, agricultural runoff and erosion can result in chronologically young lakes actually dying of old age. Conversely, acid rain is taking some very old lakes and turning them into sterile environments. So, rather than using age as a guideline, I will refer to fertility levels of various lakes.

At one end of the scale lies the oligotrophic lakes. These are extremely infertile bodies of water. The surrounding terrain is basically rock and often contains very little soil that could contribute nutrients to the water.

Oligotrophic lakes have very deep basins with high concentrations of dissolved oxygen even at the greatest depths. They have very low nutrient levels and limited aquatic life in the form of organic or inorganic materials. These lakes do not have the carrying capacity to hold large numbers of fish.

Oligotrophic lakes are best suited for lake trout, although they do have some walleyes, smallmouth bass, pike, and muskies as well. Because there's room for growth within the bio-mass and because of limited fishing pressure, oligotrophic lakes can contain some very large walleyes. Because of the cold water of these systems, the walleyes grow very slowly. But they live substantially longer than walleyes in warm-water environments.

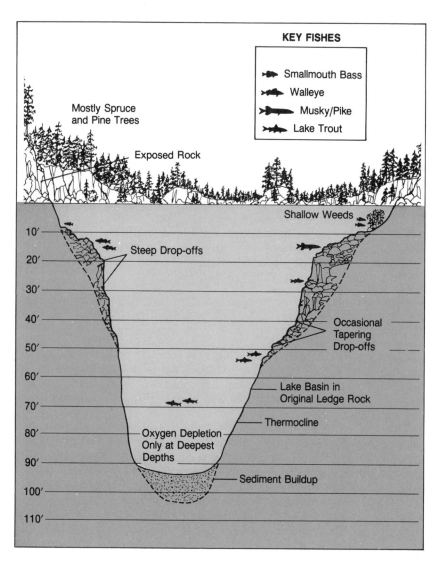

**Figure 11.** *Oligotrophic lakes are characterized by deep basins and infertile water. They are, by nature, best suited for salmonids like lake trout but can also support small populations of walleyes, smallmouth bass and northern pike. The warm-water species like walleyes and smallmouth won't be abundant, but can reach a very large size.*

Oligotrophic lakes tend to be very deep with abrupt drop-offs. Most are located in Canada, but a few exist in the northern reaches of some states as well. The forage base in these deep, clear, oxygenated bodies of water typically includes cisco, tullibee, whitefish, shiners, and the various members of the dace family. However, perch are not uncommon in many oligotrophic lakes.

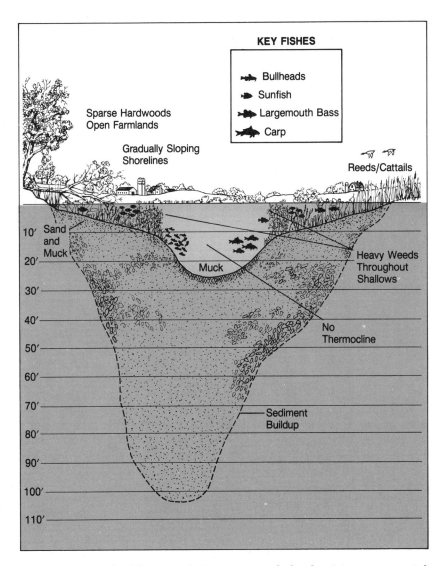

**Figure 12.** *Eutrophic lakes are rich in nutrients and often low in oxygen, especially in the latter stages of eutrophication. These lakes do not support naturally producing populations of walleyes, but many contain good numbers of walleyes because of stocking programs. The water is off-colored and by summer becomes thick with algae growths which limit oxygen levels. Most of the summer walleyes will be relating to the weeds.*

At the other extreme are the eutrophic lakes. These lakes are characterized by very high fertility, considerable weed growth, low oxygen levels and a fairly shallow muck bottom. Water clarity is extremely poor and weeds usually grow only to a level of five to eight feet, depending on how far the aging process has progressed.

Most eutrophic lakes do not contain naturally-producing populations of walleyes. However, excellent walleye populations do exist in some eutrophic lakes, thanks to stocking programs. While not native to these environments, walleyes thrive because of the availability of food. Still, you'll rarely see any giant fish in a eutrophic lake. A walleye in the six or seven pound class is generally considered a biggie. Most of the walleyes in the population tend to be stunted, at least in some lakes.

Eutrophic lakes in the late stages of life can support only carp, bullheads, and other rough fish. In the earlier stages, largemouth bass and sunfish thrive in these systems.

When stocked into these lakes, walleyes have limited options. Oxygen is in short supply during most of the summer, especially in the deep water. Thus the walleyes must relate to their environment much like bass, prowling the weedlines where oxygen and forage are available. I have taken some unreal catches of walleyes from these lakes, tossing spinnerbaits, crankbaits, and yes, even plastic worms, along the edge of the weedline.

Rock piles and hard bottom areas rarely exist in these lakes. But one other option that in some cases might be available to the fish is moving water in the form of an incoming river or stream.

Sedimentation and erosion have left the basins of these lakes quite shallow, in many cases 25 feet or less. Production of blue-green algae threatens to deplete oxygen levels during the hot, summer months and fish kills are frequent. Under the ice, as all the vegetation is decomposing and burning oxygen, fish kills once again pose a serious threat.

Right in the middle of these classifications lie the mesotrophic lakes. Mesotrophic lakes are not nearly as fertile as eutrophic lakes, but are far more fertile than oligotrophic lakes. Meso lakes are generally considered the prime environment for walleyes and smallmouth bass and also may contain good populations of northern pike, muskies and largemouth bass.

Mesotrophic lakes may contain some of the features common to each of the other lake types. They can have deep-rock-capped sunken islands like oligotrophic lakes and at the same time contain shallow, weed-infested bays common to eutrophic lakes. Bottom content consists of rock, sand and gravel along with muck, marl, and clay.

Vegetation is common in these lakes. Unlike the junk weed that grows in eutrophic lakes, meso lakes contain plush growths of cabbage weed and coontail, two weed types that attract walleyes.

Oxygen-wise, meso lakes lie somewhere between the two extremes. They won't be as oxygenated as the oligotrophic lakes, but don't experience oxygen depletion like the eutrophic lakes. Thermal stratification is quite common in meso lakes.

Mesotrophic lakes are considered top producers of walleyes. Walleyes reproduce naturally and have the necessary nutrient levels to attain excellent size and numbers.

Mesotrophic lakes can be very diverse, structurally. They can have sharp, hard-bottomed drop-offs; large, tapering flats with dense weed

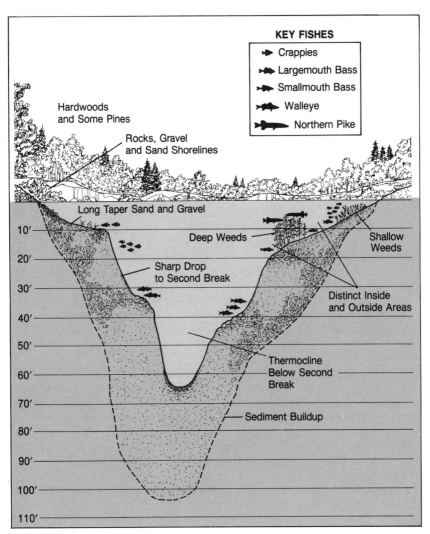

**KEY FISHES**
- Crappies
- Largemouth Bass
- Smallmouth Bass
- Walleye
- Northern Pike

Hardwoods and Some Pines

Rocks, Gravel and Sand Shorelines

Long Taper Sand and Gravel

Deep Weeds

Shallow Weeds

Sharp Drop to Second Break

Distinct Inside and Outside Areas

Thermocline Below Second Break

Sediment Buildup

**Figure 13.** *Right in the middle of the natural lake types is the mesotrophic bodies of water. These lakes have medium fertility and can support a wide range of fish species. They are perhaps best suited for walleyes but also can hold good numbers of smallmouth, largemouth, muskies, pike, crappies and bluegills. Sedimentation has started to fill in the basin of the lake, but the rock-gravel shorelines provide excellent spawning habitat for walleyes. Mesotrophic lakes have ample and varied weed growths.*

growths; muck bays; rock islands; and points . . . just about anything you can think of in the way of structure.

Add to that a diverse forage base and you can see that the walleyes in a "meso" lake have a lot of options. Which is probably a major reason that these types of lakes are best suited for our old friend the walleye.

## Reservoirs and Rivers

Obviously, natural lakes are not the only bodies of water that contain walleyes. Rivers and reservoirs offer some of the finest walleye fishing known to man, especially if you're talking about big walleyes.

In truth, rivers and reservoirs have many similarities functionally. After all, a reservoir is nothing more than a river that's been dammed up, forming a large pool of water on the backside of the obstruction.

Like lakes, rivers and reservoirs can be classified. But rather than devoting a lot of time to putting labels on different bodies of water, you're far better off considering the options available to the fish.

Reservoirs have the capacity to harbor excellent populations of fish and grow some of the biggest walleyes you'll find anywhere. The current world record of 25 pounds came from Old Hickory, in Tennessee. I've caught reservoir walleyes from the Virginias to the mountains, and many of these impoundments have never really been tapped for big walleyes. The Arkansas and Dakota reservoirs have attracted a lot of attention in recent years, but many other states have excellent walleye fishing as well.

In some ways reservoirs have a distinct advantage over other types of waters. Reservoirs flood nutrient-rich topsoil (an exception being canyon-type reservoirs) which contributes to a stong food chain. In some reservoirs, the bio-mass is capable of supporting as much as 250 pounds of fish per acre. Contrast that to a mesotrophic lake, which can carry perhaps 25 to 40 pounds of fish per acre.

Excessive buildups of nutrients and the resulting oxygen depletion are usually not problems in larger reservoirs because of the rate of water exchange. Blue-green algae, for example, never gets the opportunity to develop to any extent because of constant in-flows of fresh water. This is not the case on some of the smaller reservoirs, which tend to function more as eutrophic bodies of water.

Reservoirs are among the most diverse bodies of water in the world. On the lower, deeper ends, some are oligotrophic in nature and capable of supporting chinook salmon, lake trout and other salmonoids. In the middle reaches, they might function more as mesotrophic bodies of water and can have fantastic populations of walleyes. The upper thirds can be shallow and turbid, more of an environment that would be suited for largemouth bass.

Reservoirs exhibit some of the characteristics of lakes and some of the characteristics of rivers. Current is common in reservoir systems, especially in the middle and upper thirds. But there's moving water even in the lower, deeper sections of the lake . . . it's just not as noticeable.

Fluctuating water levels tend to move fish around in reservoirs and rivers. Reservoir fish are, by nature, river fish. And river fish are nomadic. If the water levels in a reservoir drop several feet, the fish usually will begin migrating downstream. An increase in water levels tells the fish to move upstream. Reservoir fish also make seasonal migrations, sometimes 100 miles or more. These migrations are most common in fall and prior to the spring spawn.

Most reservoirs offer peak fishing during the first decade of their existence. Rising water levels inundate surrounding farmland, providing brush and other types of vegetation that results in an explosion in baitfish numbers. All the nutrients and organic materials that are being flooded bring the food chain to life. Fishing success can explode.

As the system matures, vegetation dies and decomposes. The basic nature of the system undergoes a change. In some instances, the topsoil is eroded away by wave action and deposited in the basin of the lake. As the topsoil vanishes, it's replaced by a rock-rubble substrate, the kind that's ideal for walleye reproduction.

The peak fishing that was experienced during the early years of the reservoir's development will be replaced by a more predictable kind of angling. Water levels will stabilize and the fish will settle into particular niches in the system.

Of course, water level fluctuation is always a factor on reservoirs. In the very deep, steep-walled reservoir systems, water levels may fluctuate 20 feet in a single day. On the shallower, flatland systems, water levels can fluctuate 5 to 10 feet in a season. Regardless, the fish will acclimate themselves to particular niches within the system.

If major changes occur in the lake's bottom, some species of fish may almost disappear while other species, better suited to the new environment, take their place.

Stocking efforts—both with gamefish and forage species—can play an important role in determining just which species will wind up dominating the system. It could be that a suitable species will make its way into the main lake through one of the many feeder rivers along the course of the system.

Obviously, our concern here is with those reservoirs that have evolved into walleye fisheries, and there are a bunch of them. From the Flambeau in Wisconsin to Center Hill in Tennessee, to Big Stone in Minnesota, and Lake of the Ozarks in Missouri, to some of the many smaller reservoirs in Nebraska, Kansas, and Iowa . . . all provide exceptional walleye fishing. Some of the best in the world, in fact.

We could devote a lot of time and space to an examination of the different reservoir types, but that really isn't necessary. because reservoirs are extremely easy to "read."

You can get a clear picture of what lies below the surface of any impoundment simply by studying the surrounding shoreline. If the water is lined by 500-foot cliffs on both sides, you can bet you're fishing a very deep, clear reservoir. If the terrain on both sides of the water is flat as a pancake, you're on a shallow, off-colored system. Besides, the Corp of Engineers usually has quite accurate maps available. Normally, these are much more accurate than maps available for natural lakes because they are done prior to flooding. That is not the case with lake maps.

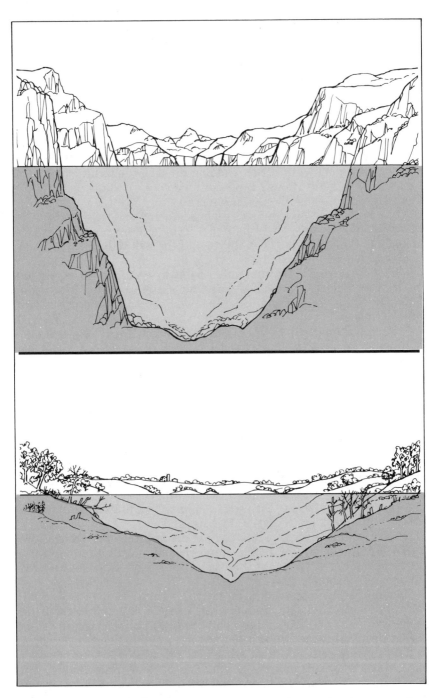

**Figure 14.** You can often "read" the structure in a reservoir by the surrounding terrain. Sharp, steep cliffs indicate the same type of topography under the water. On the other hand, flat, low banks may mean shallow, gentle structure.

You can often determine what options are available to the fish just by watching the shoreline as you move across one of these impoundments. Steep cutbanks usually indicate that the old river channel swings close to shore at that point. Gently rolling hills on the shoreline hint at the possibility of sunken islands below the surface. A slowly tapering shoreline will usually extend out into a large flat.

Remember, too, that reservoirs are likely to contain all sorts of man-made structures, many of which can be superb walleye areas. And these, too, will usually be betrayed by an on-shore feature or landmark. The most common of these would be old roadbeds, railroad grades, and creek or river channels. Under the surface you may encounter a plethora of unique features. You could run across old cemetaries, farm buildings or foundations, bridge abutments, rock piles, drainage ditches, gravel pits, rock rip-rap . . . even car bodies, junk yards and old town sites.

Using a quality flasher and knowing how to use it, can help enormously when fishing a reservoir. You never know what you're going to find under the surface.

The important thing is that you approach a reservoir like you would a natural lake. Study the options available to the fish and be an aggressive hunter.

Pay particular attention to the old river channel and the mouths of creek arms where tributaries enter the system. The river and creek channels serve as highways for walleye migrations. As they move up and down the system, walleyes relate to the deep-water channels. Areas where the channel is adjacent to a major food shelf of one type or another, will collect concentrations of fish stopping to rest and feed up. Long shoreline points, sunken islands or large flats are three good examples of such structures.

The intersection of the main river channel and a feeder creek channel can be a dynamite spot to find walleyes. In most cases, the mouths of these creeks will widen into a large bay with several points that actually extend all the way to the main river channel. You'll want to probe any such area thoroughly, especially if one or more of the existing points is exposed to wind and wave action. And keep in mind that brush and timber may be used in reservoirs like weeds are used in natural lakes.

A final type of water where walleyes are likely to gather is rivers, the natural environment for our glass-eyed friends. In a river, the most important consideration is current.

Fish will not, as a rule, spend a lot of time in direct current. They simply expend too much energy fighting the flow to make it worth their while. However, fish will be relating to the current.

Current washes food to the fish, so they usually won't be far away from the moving water. But they'll position themselves so they can be at rest in slack water and still be within easy striking distance of any meal that might drift past with the current. What you want to look for are current breaks or edges.

Eddies are a good example. Eddies are pockets of slack water directly in the current. The fish can lie in these pockets with fast water swirling all around them, resting the "eye of the hurricane."

Underwater obstructions that break up the current flow serve the same purpose. A rock pile, hole, boulder, sandbar or wing dam will change the course of the current's flow providing hiding places for feeding fish.

It's important to understand that water cannot be compressed. If water strikes an underwater obstruction, it will be forced up and over that obstruction, creating a pocket of dead water on both the upstream and downstream sides. Walleyes usually will hang on the downstream side of these obstructions, unless the obstruction is large enough that a pocket of slack water exists on the front edge as well.

You can locate such underwater obstructions by watching the surface of the water for tell-tale boils. These boils should indicate that something exists under the surface that's disrupting the flow of current.

Large flats with depressions or rocks can definitely attract walleyes. The walleyes will tuck into the depressions or hide behind the rocks, waiting in ambush for a passing meal.

S-curves in the river channel produce slack water areas that attract fish. A sandbar, rock pile, or stairstep that exists along the course of the S-curve will serve as the mini-structure that will hold the majority of the walleyes.

The bigger fish usually hang on the upstream portions of any river structure. That's true whether you're talking about a large food shelf, a pile of boulders, a sandbar, or any typical current-breaking structure. The majority of big fish usually will be on the upstream third of the structure.

River walleyes tend to run smaller than their reservoir counterparts. Because they are fighting the current on their upstream migrations, the river fish seem to be more sleek-bodied . . . leaner and meaner. They're usually stronger than comparable-sized fish from other systems and will out-fight their lake or reservoir cousins.

I have, however, noted exceptions to that rule. The Columbia River is a good example. The Columbia grows some huge walleyes, and those fish spend a major portion of their lives battling current. I suspect that the availability of a high protein forage, lots of current breaks, and an environment that's perfectly suited to walleye growth and development, all combine to produce such big fish.

Another factor is the basic nature of the river itself. Major river systems like the Columbia, the Missouri and the Mississippi have the capacity to grow some real mules. Smaller, older rivers can have good populations of walleyes but rarely produce many monster fish.

Some rivers, like the Mississippi, do not have reservoirs between all dams. In these rivers, walleyes will make long migrations from one dam to the next and, when possible, will actually move through the dams into the next stretch of river.

River walleyes are extremely migratory. Fluctuating water levels and seasonal changes will prompt movements of great distance, sometimes hundreds of miles. For example, tagging studies conducted by the South Dakota Department of Game, Fish and Parks showed some walleyes moving more than a hundred miles the first year after being captured, and as far as 250 miles away the second year.

Movements also can be quite abrupt. One walleye caught in the Grand River in South Dakota was recaptured and released a year later by the North Dakota Game and Fish Department in Beaver Bay, some 75 to 80 miles north of where it was originally captured. Months later, the fish had migrated south to the Gettysburg area, a trip of more than 100 miles.

River fish also display definite homing tendencies. Out of 199 walleyes recaptured in the Cheyenne River in South Dakota one spring, 195 had been tagged in the same place the previous spring.

Regardless of the body of water you're fishing, there are basic rules to observe. First, you must consider the options available to the fish, including forage and habitat. Next, you must actively pursue those fish, becoming a hunter. And finally, you must establish that all-important pattern. By paying attention to the seemingly most trivial details, you will often find the clue that will explain the question "where are the walleyes?"

Once you figure out where the walleyes are hiding, you can move onto the next important step in fishing: presentation.

# Chapter 4
# Presentation

## Ask the Fish

*"Let us, then, be up and doing, with a heart for any rate; still achieving, still pursuing, learn to labor and to wait".*
**—Henry Wadsworth Longfellow**

A late October "norwester" was chasing local ducks to a warmer climate as I drove back to Brainerd after four days of non-stop editing. Shooting our *Good Fishing* television show is fun . . . editing the rough footage into a program is hard work.

Mother Nature's promise on that dreary afternoon was a crust of ice on the sloughs and potholes by the next morning. Winter was on the way. That concerned me, because we still needed a couple segments to fill out our spring schedule. I particularly wanted one more walleye episode, a real blockbuster.

At home I tossed a couple of logs on the fire, poured myself into an easy-chair and wrapped both hands around a mug of hot coffee. I wondered which of the local lakes might be willing to yield a few "movie star" walleyes before ice-up. An unexpected phone call provided the solution to my dilemma.

"Winkelperson," the voice came over the phone. There's only one guy who calls me "Winkelperson." It was Dan Nelson, a longtime hunting and fishing companion from North Dakota. "The big walleyes are committing suicide on Sak," Dan said. "If you want a 10-pounder, better get out here."

"Sak" is North Dakota's Lake Sakakawea, a sprawling prairie reservoir that produces more than its share of trophy walleyes, especially in October and November. I recalled my last Halloween trip to North Dakota several years earlier. An early storm left us stranded in a motel room for three days and we never even wet a line.

But Dan assured me that the weather would cooperate and the fish were on a rampage. I didn't require a lot of encouragement. I made hurried arrangements to fly the television crew out west, stashed my gear, and pulled out early the next day. Along the way I picked up several oxygen bags of jumbo redtail chubs and river shiners.

There was little doubt in my mind that the best thing we could drop into Sakakawea's chilly, off-colored water would be a hot yellow Fuzz-E-Grub jig tipped with the biggest, liveliest redtail money can buy.

My suspicions were confirmed halfway through the first pass when I set the hook on a whopping 9-pounder.

Now, Dan's a bit on the stubborn side. Despite my continuing success, he insisted on trying everything in his tackle box. He fished different-colored jigs, Lindy Rigs, hard baits behind a bottom cruiser, and anything else he figured might put a trophy walleye in the boat.

"We're just practicing now," he said. "When we get down to fishing, I want to know exactly what's going to work best." That's not a bad philosophy. But, I have a philosophy of my own—never look a gift horse in the mouth. In two days of practicing we collected seven walleyes, each over eight pounds. Of those, my Fuzz-E-Grub/redtail combination accounted for six. Dan took the other on a Lindy Rig and big redtail.

At the same time a group of locals, many of them guides, were fishing the same water. These boys are good fishermen, fellows like Wade Williamson from nearby Parshall, who knows Sakakawea like the back of his hand. The second morning we stopped at Wade's Deepwater Bay retreat, a cozy cabin not far from where we were fishing. Just for fun, we all threw some money into the kitty for a mini-tournament.

At weigh-in time that afternoon, I had the biggest fish . . . and the second . . . and the third. My closest competition for the money was Dan, in fourth place.

I'd like to report that my overwhelming skills made the difference; that I simply out-fished those boys. But that would be a misrepresentation of the facts. In truth, they weren't able to get any big bait. Suckers in the three to four-inch range were all that was available to them. Hot yellow Fuzz-E-Grubs were in short supply, as well.

The third day, when we got down to the serious business of filming, Dan made the switch. On the first pass, he caught a 9½ and a 10½-pounder, two of the most beautiful, well conditioned walleyes you'd ever want to see.

That morning Dan had donated a couple Fuzz-E-Grubs and a few of our remaining redtails to local angler Bill Steele. Bill returned to the dock with a 10-pounder, but none of the other boats working the same area had anything even approaching a whopper.

The incident dramatically points out the importance of proper presentation. Sure, you must be able to find the fish. On that particular trip, the big walleyes were tucked into little hooks along a sharp-breaking, rocky shoreline. Finding those hooks and working our jigs into them was a real key to our success. For a lot of anglers, location is the toughest part of fishing. But once you find the fish, presentation becomes all-important.

Very *few* anglers are more conscious of presentation than Bill Binkelman, a legendary walleye fisherman.

*Working out the right presentation helped Babe and Dan Nelson put together this dandy stringer of Lake Sakakawea (N.D.) walleyes.*

Many of us tend to be one-method fishermen. We find something that works ... something we have confidence in ... and that's what we fish. Day-in and day-out, we live and die with that one presentation. Mostly, we die.

There is no one lure that catches fish all the time. The keys to successful fishing are first being versatile enough to experiment with different families of baits and, second, to have confidence that what you're fishing will produce. One without the other is worthless.

There are basically four families of walleye baits–rigs, jigs, crankbaits and spinners. There are dozens of variations on each of those families.

I'm going to walk you through the different families of lures and provide some helpful tips on each. But the rest is up to you. I can tell you the importance of versatility, but only you can develop confidence in a lure. If you don't believe you're going to catch fish on a particular presentation, it's a cinch you won't.

The best way I know to build confidence is from hands-on fishing— and catching—experience. Maybe you're pretty accomplished with a Lindy Rig but haven't experienced much success with a jig. The next time you get into a good bite, cut off that rig and try a jig. After catching a few fish you'll start to get the feel for the jig. You'll learn what it feels like when a walleye picks up a jig. You'll discover when and how to set the hook. You'll build confidence in yourself as a jig fisherman.

The many lures at an angler's disposal are "tools of the trade." The more tools you can master, the better angler you will be.

The more proficient you can become with a variety of different lures, the better over-all fisherman you'll become. My credo has always been, "Ask the fish what they want on a particular day." It doesn't really matter how you want to fish, it's what the fish want that's important.

There are guidelines you can follow from day to day and from one body of water to the next. But, if the fish aren't responding to the presentation they're supposed to hit, try something different.

Lures are only tools. If you took your car to a garage for some major repairs and the chief mechanic had a tiny tool box that held a vice grip, a crescent wrench and a couple of screwdrivers, how much faith would you have in his ability to fix your car? A good mechanic could do wonders with just a handful of tools, but a good mechanic has a tool for every job.

Still, tools are tools. They are not magic. That's the ingredient provided by the angler. Keeping an open mind and paying attention to what's happening on the water can often lead the fisherman to the solution to that day's fishing puzzle.

Take that Sakakawea trip Dan and I made. We knew, and everyone else knew, that the fish were working a 20-foot breakline along the edge of a rocky shoreline. By paying close attention to his flasher, Dan noticed there were a series of hooks, or indentations, along that breakline. These hooks weren't noticeable unless you were really watching the flasher closely and hugging that 20-foot contour. Most boats were drifting right past these hooks. By popping the motor in reverse, as we drifted to the openings in these little pockets, and fishing a vertical presentation, we were able to place our jigs right where the fish were hiding.

On occasion, the fish will actually tell the fisherman what they want. I recall one afternoon we were casting crankbaits to walleyes that were hanging along the edge of a rocky reef. Right in the middle of a fast retrieve, a mosquito crawled into my ear. I stopped my retrieve, momentarily, to remove the little pest, then, in disgust, gave the rod tip a jerk to resume the retrieve. Bang . . . a nice walleye got himself snagged up on my hook.

That fish was trying to tell me something. The message was that a pause followed by a sudden dive by the plug was what those fish were looking for. By duplicating that retrieve, we were able to land a mess of fish from a spot that had been yielding walleyes grudgingly. Can such a minute difference in presentation really make a difference? You better believe it can. And paying attention to the little clues the fish provide can help you zero in on those little presentation refinements that produce.

One final word about presentation before we spin off to look at the individual families of lures. It's been our experience that there will be, within a given group of fish, a few who march to the beat of a different drummer. Triggering those fish can make a real difference in your overall catch.

Setting a presentation pattern includes finding the right lure, color, live bait, speed, action and depth for that particular day. For instance, you may run into a summertime situation where it becomes obvious that the most productive presentation is a 24-inch Lindy Rig tipped with a jumbo leech and dragged very slowly on the outside edge of a bed of cabbage weeds.

It would be safe to assume that most of the fish working that section of water will be susceptible to that presentation. Many fish, within a given body of water, will be loyal to a pattern, assuming weather and light conditions are constant.

The first half dozen passes along that weed edge may produce four good fish. Then the action stops. A natural assumption would be that the fish moved. But that may not necessarily be the case. It could just be that all the fish interested in the particular presentation have been caught.

That's when I'll make some changes and try to milk a couple bonus fish out of the same hole. Maybe I'll hop a jig-and-leech combination over the same spot. Or maybe I'll try a tiny spinner tipped with a crawler. Or a rig and a crawler. Sometimes I'll take a tiny jig, remove the body and thread a crawler nose-first on the hook.

If 50 percent of the fish from that school wanted one presentation, that still leaves the other 50 percent who were susceptible to something different. Of course, some of those fish don't want anything. They're simply not catchable fish. But adding a few of the remaining rebels to your stringer can really add up by the end of the day. Many a tournament has been won because a versatile angler was willing to stick it out on a heavily fished spot using something a little different.

Now let's take a look at some of the different walleye lures that have earned their stripes over the years.

## Live Bait Rigs

The Lindy Rig is generally considered to be a fairly recent innovation in fishing. It wasn't until the 1960s that rigs made their appearance in the marketplace with all the components available in packaged form (see Figure 1).

Actually, the concept of Lindy rigging has been around for a long time. No one knows for sure who was the first to employ a free-flowing line to a bottom rig, but the basic principle has been in use for 50 years or more.

Rigging is a system of fishing that involves a tiny hook, a light monofilament leader and a small weight through which line can be fed without the fish detecting any resistance. It's a highly natural presentation that's likely to appeal to a walleye whose attitude is neutral or even negative. With a conditioned nightcrawler impaled on a No. 8 hook, all the fish sees is the bait. There's no unnecessary hardware or paraphernalia to distract the fish. And sales that pushed over the

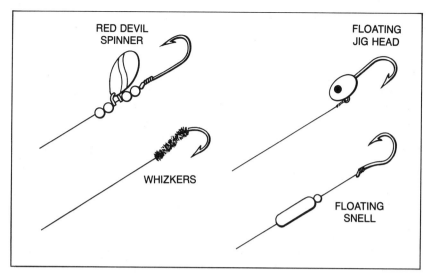

**Figure 1.** *Here are four of the more popular live-bait rigs. Left is the Red Devil spinner, a lure which works well in reservoirs and off-colored natural lakes. Next is the new Whizkers rig, featuring a scent-holding hook. Next is a floating jighead which will float a bait to the desired depth. Right is Lindy's Floating Rig with an adjustable float.*

25 million mark early in the '80s are a tribute to the rig's ability to catch fish.

The standard Lindy Rig has a 30-inch snell with a No. 8 hook for crawlers and leeches and a No. 6 hook for minnows. The walking sinker varies in size from one eighth ounce to three quarters of an ounce. The rule-of-thumb is to select a sinker that's the smallest you can use and still maintain contact with the bottom.

At the other end, a sensitive graphite, boron or kevlar rod is necessary to telegraph the sometimes delicate messages from the bottom. The less sensitivity you have, the more weight you'll be forced to use. A spinning reel spooled with fairly light line is the final piece of equipment in the rigger's arsenal. Oh, don't forget the concentration. That's perhaps the most vital ingredient in rig fishing.

As a rule, a walleye won't strike a rig. Usually he'll gently pick up the bait and slowly swim off. That's where the concentration comes into play. Normally the pickup will feel like a tick. With a crawler, the fish may slowly roll the bait up on its tongue. With small minnows and leeches, it's more likely the fish will swallow the entire bait in one gulp. If the angler isn't paying close attention to what's happening, the fish may swim a short distance and spit the bait without ever being detected.

Early riggers liked to release line to the fish at the first sign of a pickup. The old-school riggers preferred soft, long, fiberglass rods which were more forgiving. In other words, the fish were less likely to feel any resistance from the other end because the buggy-whip served as a shock absorber and compensated for angler error. Most of today's riggers opt for the stiffer-action graphite and boron rods because of their increased sensitivity. After all, the sooner you can feel the fish, the sooner you can react.

Riggers drift or troll very slowly with the bail open and line notched in the top joint of their index finger. When the fish picks up the bait, they drop the rod tip and release their grip on the line with one quick motion. In effect, they are spoon-feeding the bait to the finicky fish.

At this point, the fish can swim off with the bait in its mouth, pulling line through the walking sinker and feeling no unnatural resistance. The angler continues to play out line until the fish has the hook in its mouth. That's the time to set the hook.

And that's where a lot of novice riggers run into trouble. Set the hook too soon, and the fish is missed. Wait too long, and the fish will eventually spit the bait. Either way you reel back a partially eaten crawler . . . but no walleye.

So, how do you know for sure when to set the hook? Experience and the ability to adapt to the conditions are the best ways. Some anglers use the "count" method. They count to five and set the hook. If that doesn't work, they count to 10. They keep experimenting until they find the right count for the day. That method is far from foolproof, however, since not all fish will hit at the same time. While a 10 count might work for one fish, a 25 count might be necessary for the next.

Notch the line in your index finger when fishing a Lindy Rig. At the first sign of a fish, drop the line and allow the fish to swim off while it takes the bait.

Besides, by the time you determine the proper count for the day, the school might have moved off the structure. Or died of old age.

There is a better way. I call it the "feel" method. After the hit, I release line in the same manner as the count method. Instead of counting, I periodically pick up the line and very gently feel what the fish is doing. If I feel a tapping sensation coming up on the line, I'll drop the rod tip again. As soon as I feel a *steady pull*, I close the bail and set the hook. A steady pull, from the business end of your line, is a pretty good indicator that the fish has the bait in its mouth.

Needless to say, this method requires a good sense of feel, a sensitive rod, quick reflexes and lots of concentration. But it's about 90 percent effective.

That brings us to the third technique, now employed by rig fishermen, the "tease." I developed this method and coined the term while fishing with Jim Wrolstad when the two of us were on assignment for *Fishing Facts* magazine back in the early '70s. Instead of dropping line back to the fish, you take it away. At the first sign of pickup, very gently (very, very gently) put pressure on the line by squeezing your index finger, the one with the line notched through it. When teased this way, the fish feels his meal is struggling to escape and is apt to chomp down on the bait. That's the time to set the hook.

Any sudden or unnatural movement of the rod tip will alert the fish and it will spit the bait, pronto. But a steady, easy resistance will often result in success. This is a trick maneuver, at best, and requires a lot of practice. However, under certain conditions it will improve the rigger's hooking ratio tremendously. It's the best way I know to handle those walleyes that are biting the crawler in half, then losing interest.

Which method is best? That depends on the conditions and the attitude of the fish. It will be necessary to experiment from one day to the next. I usually release line to the first couple of fish. If they drop the bait, I'll try teasing.

If neither of those work, I like to change live bait dressing. If the walleyes continue to toy with a crawler, they could be telling you they'd rather have a leech. Usually smaller fish will play with a bait while the larger fish are more aggressive . . . when they decide to feed, that is. If you find it impossible to get a fish on the hook with all of the above methods, chances are you're dealing with a school of immature walleyes.

With practice, anyone can get the hang of catching fish on a rig. It will be possible to catch more fish, however, by using some variations of the standard techniques.

It's important to first establish where the fish are, in relation to the bottom. Are they hugging the bottom? Are they riding a foot or two off the bottom? Are they six feet off the bottom? Or more?

A good flasher or recording graph will show exactly where the fish are in relation to the bottom. Weather conditions also may provide clues. On dark, windy days the fish are likely to be more active. And as they get active, they tend to ride up off the bottom. After the passage

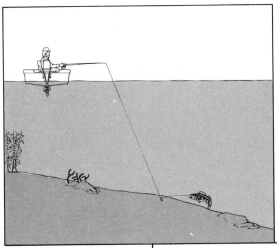

**Figure 2.** Lindy rigging has evolved to the point where it is the "bread and butter" technique of many walleye fishermen. However, knowing how to handle a "rig" properly is imperative if you are going to be succesful.

The whole idea of this concept is to allow the fish to pick up the bait and run with it without feeling anything unnatural. So, when you feel a hit, freely give the fish all the line he wants. The fish will normally peel off several feet of line, then stop, and after a brief moment take off again.

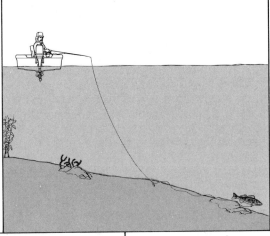

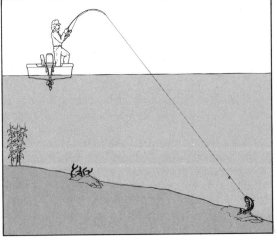

When that happens, close the bail and drill him a good one. You've got to use a long sweep set in order to take up all the slack line the fish peeled off as well as set the hook. So do it with authority.

of a cold front, when the sun's rays are penetrating deep into the water, chances are the walleyes will be lying belly-to-the-bottom.

It's important to adjust your presentation accordingly. For high-riding fish, try inflating a nightcrawler with a shot of air. That air bubble will float the crawler up to where the fish are. Some riggers like to give their crawler a shot of air in the harness, that dark bank around the upper portion of the body. Others like to inject the tail. I prefer the harness because the skin is tougher in that section of the crawler. I also think it gives the crawler a better action.

If you suspect the fish are hugging the bottom, shorten up the snell to 10 or 12 inches and forget about inflating the crawler. Keep that bait right down on the bottom, in the fish zone.

Should the fish be six or eight feet off the bottom, it will be necessary to use a longer snell and a float. Lindy makes a floating snell that will take a bait to the desired elevation. It's nothing more than a tiny, colored float-a-bobber that is adjustable. By moving the float up or down the line, it's possible to control the exact depth at which the bait will suspend.

There also are a wide variety of floating jig heads on the market, like the floating Quiver jig. For super-active fish, you might want to go with a Spin & Glo, a floating attractor with tiny propellors that gives off fish-attracting vibrations.

Color is an important consideration when selecting a floater of any style. The floats not only carry the bait up to the fish zone, but they also work as an attractor. Thus, finding the right color is important.

The type of attractor also is a factor. The plain floater might take some fish, while others will be lured by the movement of a floating jig and still others might prefer the vibrations given off by the spin-float.

We can't over-emphasize the importance of keeping the bait in the fish zone. An active fish will swim up to take the bait. It *rarely* will swim down for a meal. If the fish are three feet off the bottom and the bait is coming through the water six inches off the bottom, you may fish through a whole school of active walleyes without so much as a touch. You want to put that bait right in front of the fish's mouth, and using a floating rig is an excellent way to do that.

Scent has become a recognized aspect of fishing the last few years. More and more, anglers are realizing the importance of scent in triggering a strike from an otherwise disinterested fish. Now it's possible to purchase a Lindy Rig that holds scent. Whizkers rigs have tiny bits of fuzz embossed on the hook. The fuzz absorbs and holds scent, slowly releasing it into the water and laying down a scent track. Get a good product like Chummin' Rub and layer scent on the hook for a long-lasting incentive to lethargic fish.

There's another little trick I've picked up the last couple years that involves scent. For generations, bass fishermen have been tipping jigs and spoons with different varieties of Uncle Josh pork rind. A "jig and pig," for instance, is one of the deadliest bass combinations ever devised. So why wouldn't a pork rind work for walleyes? It does. The

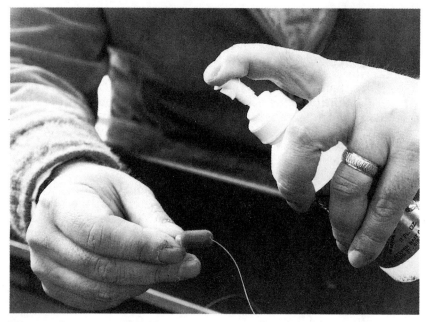

The new floating, scent-holding spinner from Lindy promises to be a walleye killer. Scent is an important aspect of fishing.

Uncle Josh leach or ripple rind have obvious eye appeal, but the pork rind also holds scent well. Pork rinds can be fished behind a Lindy Rig as well as floaters and jigs.

Under most conditions, the standard walking sinker, which is designed something like a shoe, will be most appropriate for your rig fishing. It literally walks over obstructions. When fishing the weeds, I prefer a bullet sinker like the one bass fishermen use on plastic worms. The streamlined design of the bullet sinker enables it to slip through the vegetation without hanging up as often. I also like to use a weedless hook when fishing in heavy vegetation.

One last thought on rigging. If the fish makes a sideways run after picking up the bait, you may have line heading off at a 90-degree angle to the slip sinker. When you set the hook, all you're doing is taking the bow out of the line. You'll miss that fish.

I always try to reel up *all* the slack before sticking the fish. Once the slack is gone, I like to use a strong sweep set. Don't worry about that tiny little hook ripping loose. If the fish has the hook in its mouth, it won't tear out. Those hooks are a lot stronger than they look. They'll hold any walleye that swims.

Occasionally, a really big fish will grab the bait and make a mad dash for deep water. I've seen big walleyes strip 40 or 50 feet of line off the reel before they finally slowed down. Should this happen, it's usually best to chase the fish with the boat. Position the boat over the top of the fish before attempting to set the hook. With 100 feet or more of line between the rod tip and the fish, it will be almost impossible to get a good set. All you'll be doing is taking the slack out of the line.

Babe's trophy tip No. 1—With floating jigs try lip-hooking a lively minnow upside down on the jig. The minnow will struggle to right himself, presenting an appealing offering to a passing walleye.

Babe's trophy tip No. 2—When fishing a plain rig, try putting a single bead above the hook. I prefer pearl or orange to give the presentation a little bit of color. Maybe it looks like the bait has something in its mouth. Or perhaps it resembles an eye. Whatever the case, it works.

Babe's trophy tip No. 3—Walleyes usually strike bigger baits from the side. Most anglers' natural inclination when missing fish is to tie a stinger hook into the tail of the bait. That would work if the fish were hitting the bait from the back. But usually they attack from the side, swim away and slowly turn the bait in their mouth, swallowing the bait head first. Knowing this, you might find it more effective to attach a tiny treble hook into the bait's back, just a few inches behind the main hook.

## Jigs

If I could have just one lure for all of my walleye fishing–perish the thought–it would be a jig. Of course, only a fool would restrict himself to just one lure for all his fishing needs. But if someone hosted a "one-lure" tournament, I'll bet most of the pros would pick a jig.

While jigs are normally thought of as a spring and fall presentation, they'll actually catch fish all year long under just about any condition. You can make a jig do anything to meet any condition you might encounter. The ways to fish a jig are limited only by your imagination. You can swim it just off the bottom . . . hop it over rocks . . . drag it super-slow for lethargic fish . . . jiggle it in front of the walleye's face . . . I mean there's just about nothing you can't do with a jig.

Let's begin with a basic look at jig fishing. First, you should always use the smallest jig possible for the conditions. In calm water when fish are fairly shallow, that could mean an eighth-ounce or even smaller. In current, heavy waves, or when fishing deep, that may mean three-quarters of an ounce. Conditions will dictate the proper size of jig. And by conditions we mean current, wave action, activity levels of the fish, bottom content, and speed, along with the obvious factor of depth.

Tie the jig directly to your monofilament line. No snaps or swivels are necessary. They only make the offering less natural and inhibit the jig's action.

I always use the lightest line possible for the conditions. I generally use 6 and no more than 8-pound line for jig fishing, but under extreme circumstances I might even step down to 4-pound line, or up to 10-pound or more in dirty, snag-infested water.

The plastic-bodied Fuzz-E-Grub is perhaps the most effective and best selling jig on the market.

The ideal jigging rod is lightweight, about 5½ feet in length with lots of backbone and a fast tip. I like a medium- to light-weight spinning rod for heavier jigs and a light spinning rod for light jigging.

I must admit to being partial about jig styles. Over the years, I've not found any jig that produces so consistently as the Fuzz-E-Grub. Fuzz-E-Grubs have a soft plastic body that feels natural to fish and a tiny marabou feather tail that adds a slight swimming motion. That's important, because at certain times of the year, a walleye will just mouth a jig, doing nothing to betray its presence.

Generally, he'll spit a jig without the fisherman ever being aware that he had a bite. With a plastic-bodied jig, the fish will hang on an extra second or two, giving the angler time to react. Fuzz-E-Grubs come in two different head styles, the ball head for most fishing and the standup, which works best for fishing in current.

There are dozens of ways to fish a jig. One of my favorite stories about jig presentation comes from fishing buddies of mine, Gary Roach and Randy Amenrud of Pro-Mos out of Minnesota. Gary and Randy were fishing spring walleyes on a cold,windy, rainy morning. They were casting tiny jigs into the shallows with absolutely no success. As usual, they'd forgotten their rain gear and were soaked to the bone.

After a couple of hours, Randy got chilled and started to shake visibly. Right in mid-shiver, he got a strike and set the hook on a nice walleye. Several casts later he caught another.

Pretty soon Gary was shaking as well. "The cold finally get to you?" Randy asked.

"Nope," replied Gary. "I just saw you catching fish when your rod tip was shaking, so I'm imitating your presentation."

You don't think a little thing like quivering the rod tip could make that much difference to the fish? Think again. The boys filled out in less than an hour just by making a slight variation in their presentation.

A few years ago I was fishing on Pipestone Lake, one of my favorite Canadian Shield lakes, in the spring of the year. We found walleyes holding tight to the spawning areas, just below the first breakline.

We weren't having much luck until I discovered the right presentation. I found that by swimming the jig slowly just inches off the bottom, closely following the contour of the fast-dropping break, I could entice a few strikes.

That may sound simple enough, but it's really a very difficult presentation. The drop-off was quite sharp and the fish were lying just below the break. The jig had to be swum just inches off the bottom as it moved down that drop-off. With a steady retrieve, the jig would swim horizontally off the breakline and would move over the fish much too high. The fish wouldn't move at all to take the bait.

Using the slow-swimming retrieve, I was able to take several monster walleyes over a period of five days. There were boats all around us and no one, not even the other fishermen in my boat, was having any luck. It wasn't until the third day that my brother, Dave, finally got the hang of keeping that jig close to the bottom coming off the breakline, and I consider him exceptional with a jig! When he did, he caught real beauties.

The pickups were very light. The fish would gently scoop the jig up in the corners of their mouths and swim along with it. You couldn't really feel anything. It just seemed as if the jig got heavier, like it had fallen into a cup of molasses. If you didn't set the hook quickly, they'd spit the jig . . . if you set too fast you'd never stick 'em. Timing was split-second critical.

I'm certain some of those other fishermen were getting hits, they just didn't realize it. I guess the best way to describe the hit is that it feels different. It doesn't feel like a hit, it just *feels different.*

At other times you'll have better luck popping that jig off the bottom and letting it settle back down. At still other times, just dragging that jig along the bottom will produce most of the strikes. The only way to know for sure which presentation will appeal to the fish is to experiment with a number of different variations until you find the one that works. The time of year and weather conditions should provide some clues.

For instance, in spring and fall, when the water's cold, it's often best to just drag the jig, giving it an occasional quick hop. In warm water, short hops off the bottom, with the occasional big jump, work best. At other times, just swimming the jig as we described earlier can be deadly.

Most anglers have a tendency to put too much action on a jig, especially in spring and fall. Repeating the same motion over and over

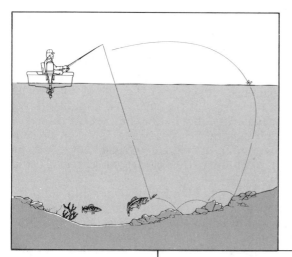

**Figure 3.** The ways to fish a jig are limited only by your imagination. For very active fish, it's often best to work the jig with big sweeping hops.

For inactive walleyes, it's usually best to just drag the jig slowly along the bottom. In spring and fall with very cold water, this is often the only way to entice a walleye.

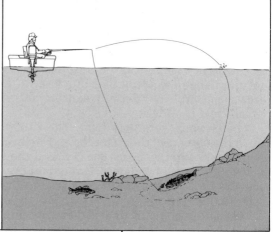

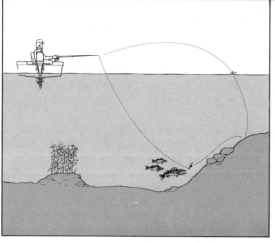

Swimming a jig, as in this drawing, requires a lot of practice and concentration, but it's an excellent way to catch walleyes under certain conditions.

without a break gets too monotonous. The best action is usually more subtle, with a slight variation to get the fish's attention.

Again, paying attention to the little clues provided by the fish can often result in a heavy stringer. Once I was fishing fall walleyes with a good friend. It was late in the season, just before ice-up, and those walleyes should have been very, very slow. To my surprise, dragging a jig along the bottom wasn't producing much action. My friend was one of those nervous types who was constantly reeling in to check his bait. A few times he got a hit as he was lowering his jig back into the water. I noticed this and decided the fish must be riding off the bottom, hitting the jig while it was still falling. I switched presentations, giving the jig big sweeps, pulling it upwards three to six feet and letting it settle back to the bottom. That was the answer.

There's one rule about jig fishing you should understand. If you raise the jig three feet and it falls back two feet, there's a very good chance it landed in a walleye's mouth.

When that happens, reel up the slack and put a little pressure on the fish . . . then set the hook quickly. That's exactly what was happening in this case. By the time my friend took up the slack and felt the fish it was too late. But, by watching my line and realizing what was happening under the surface, I was able to start catching fish.

The most important thing to remember about action is that different kinds of retrieves will work under different conditions. Keep changing until you find one that works. Look for those little clues the fish will provide.

Two of the most critical aspects of jig fishing are when and how to set the hook. As a rule, a walleye will take the entire jig, or at least enough of it, in its mouth on the first bite. The hit may be very light and the tendency is to think the fish is still taking the bait. The angler hesitates for a split second before setting the hook and misses the fish.

As with rig fishing, concentration is essential. Fish with the rod tip pointed towards the water and every muscle in your body poised like a trap about to be sprung. When you feel any resistance from the bottom, put pressure on the fish by raising the rod tip slightly and . . . snap . . . set the hook. And I do mean *snap*. Don't try to jerk the fish three feet through the water. Just set the hook with a quick, but firm snap of the wrists.

If you watch a good jig fisherman in action, he's a study in concentration. He's so involved in what's happening at the other end of his line, that you could probably fire a cannonball six inches past his ear and he wouldn't flinch.

Jigs can be tipped with minnows, leeches, crawlers, salamanders, or just about anything in the way of live bait, plus a host of artificial dressings like Uncle Josh's ripple rind or leeches.

Crawlers should be hooked once through the head and trailed back behind the jig. Under most conditions, that's the best method. However, with active fish, try hooking the crawler in the middle and trailing it behind the jig in a V. When the jig moves up and down, the twin tails give off an exciting action that active fish find hard to resist.

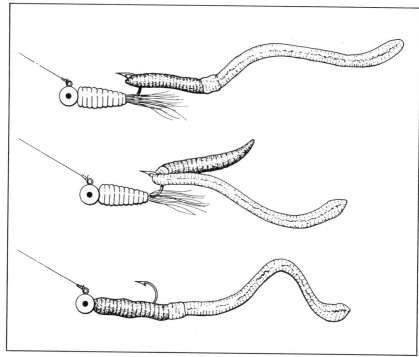

**Figure 4.** This drawing illustrates three ways to attach a nightcrawler to a jig. First, simply trail the crawler straight back. For added attraction with more active fish, try hooking the crawler in the middle and trailing it back in a V. For finicky fish, it's often best to remove the body and thread the crawler all the way up to the jighead.

Color, like lures, can be a critical factor. The only sure way to determine the color most visable under the conditions you're fishing is with Dr. Loren Hill's Color-C-Lector, a device we'll look at a little later. However, I've developed some color guidelines over the past 20 years of fishing jigs that work more often than not.

In cold, clear water, early and late seasons, I'll start with all white. Chartreuse yellow on a white body, with a fluorescent orange or pink head, will be favored in water that is over 55 degrees or in water not ultra-clear.

In stained water, I'll usually start with fluorescent yellow, but keep a second rod rigged with a fluorescent orange/brown combination. For night fishing, I'll start with black, blue or straight brown.

Finally, when fishing extremely deep water, I'll opt for blue or purple to start my search. However, no matter what the condition or time of the year I'm fishing, I always let the walleyes decide what color they like best.

On occasion, when dealing with finicky walleyes, I like to remove the body from a light jig and thread the crawler all the way up to the jig head (see Figure 4). Fished slowly, this can be a real killer. Bill Binkelman's tiny jigs are especially suited to this technique.

A jig-and-minnow combination works best during the spring season. As the water warms to around 60 degrees, leeches and crawlers will take over as preferred bait. August may see days when minnows will again be good, particularly with weed walleyes. Late fall calls for minnows normally, but big ones . . . like four to seven inches big.

During the spring transition period, most walleyes may be hitting minnows. But again, not all fish will be susceptible to the same thing. After you've given a jig-and-minnow combination a thorough dunking, try working a crawler through the same water. This tactic may result in some of those bonus fish.

In fall, I like to go with big baits. And I'm talking about redtails, suckers, or shiners in the four to eight inch range. With baits that large, you will not be able to set the hook immediately. It's best to fish with the bail open and allow the fish to run with the minnow, giving it a chance to get that monster turned around in its mouth.

Reluctant to use such a big bait? Don't be. A biological study conducted on the food preferences of walleyes showed that fish usually like a bait that's 25 to 40 percent of their total weight. In fall, when you're looking for trophies that might run from 28 to 34 inches long, you're dealing with fish that prefer a bait from 7 to 14 inches long. Those fall fish are larding up for the long winter ahead. Their objective is to acquire as much nutrition as possible while expending as little energy as possible. Don't offer those fish an after-dinner mint when they're looking for steak.

For really finicky fish, try using a stinger hook. Attach a small (No. 6, 8 or 10) treble hook to your jig with a piece of light monofilament line and hook it through the back of the minnow. Remember, walleyes usually strike large prey from the side, not the back. And this is especially true of bigger baits. The fish want to stun a big minnow before they try to swallow it.

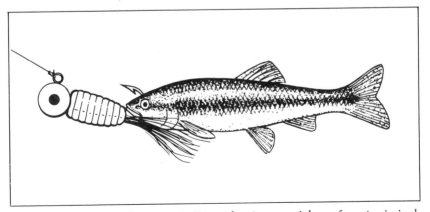

**Figure 5.** Fall is a good time to tip jigs with minnows. A large four- to six-inch chub is a favorite.

A stinger hook has its drawbacks. The bait won't swim as naturally as it would if slightly lip-hooked. And you're more apt to get hung up on the bottom. But, at times, it's the only way to put a finicky fish in the boat. You can tie the line either to the eye of the jig or to the hook itself.

Babe's trophy tip No. 4—Always, always, sharpen the hook on a jig using a file like the one made by Luhr Jensen. Touch up the top of the hook as well as the underside until it has a razor edge. Sharp hooks will improve your hook-setting success by 50 percent or more.

Babe's trophy tip No. 5—For finicky fish, try going with an unpainted leadhead. No body . . . no color. Just a plain old leadhead tipped with live bait.

Babe's trophy tip No. 6—Changing line often will retain limpness which is essential for successful jig fishing.

Babe's trophy tip No. 7—A few aggressive fish will often give away the location of a school. When *looking for* fish, go with a slightly heavier jig than conditions would dictate and fish fast, covering a lot of water. Once you locate the school, switch to a lighter jig.

## Spinners

Spinners have been used by walleye fishermen for generations. The old standbys like Prescott, June Bug and strip-ons were about all some folks ever used for walleyes. With the advent of the live bait systems, spinners went the way of the hula hoop. And in some cases, that was a mistake.

Studies show that walleyes prefer to feed mostly by sight. Of course, they also depend on hearing, taste, scent and their lateral line.

In the typical mesotrophic lakes, with their relatively clear water, a spinner might not be very productive during the daylight hours. But on reservoirs and eutrophic lakes, where the water tends to be off-colored, the added flash of a spinner blade moving through the water will help get a walleye's attention. Not only can the fish see the bait better, but he can also hear and feel it much better.

There are a number of factors at work here. One is definitely water clarity. Another is fish population. Still another is forage type.

The dirtier the water, the more likely the walleye will be to snap up an attractor bait like a spinner. In off-colored water the fish tend to be shallower and more active.

Large populations of fish tend to be more active than smaller populations. If you're working a large school of fish, they will usually be competitive and attracted to a fast-moving, vibrating lure.

The type and abundance of forage also has something to do with the effectiveness of spinners. On many large reservoirs and on some of the small, eutrophic lakes, there's an abundance of forage. When the fish feed, they go on a real binge. They're accustomed to chasing a meal and are aggressive.

I'm not sure which of these factors is most important. Likely it's a combination of all three. But I do know that, at times, spinners can be the most productive lure no matter where you chase walleyes.

Let's begin with the basic hardware. A standard spinner has a 36-inch snell with a No. 3 Indiana blade and a No. 2 or No. 4 hook. When fished slowly, it can be worked behind a plain slip sinker. When fished fast, it will be necessary to use a bottom cruiser weighing anywhere from one to three ounces, depending on the depth and speed you wish to fish.

The size and color of the blade can make a world of difference. For dark waters I've had my best luck with fluorescent reds and oranges. For moderately stained water, I prefer chartreuse, hot yellow and green. For fairly clean water, I like nickel and gold.

Color, of course, is something that's going to change from day to day and even from hour to hour. We'll take a comprehensive look at color preferences of fish in the next section of this chapter.

It's been my experience that big fish prefer big blades most of the time. On some reservoir systems, it's not unusual to use a No. 5 Colorado, or No. 6, or No. 7 Indiana blade (see Figure 6). And most of my biggest summertime fish—8, 9 and 10-pounders—have come on oversized blades.

Speed is perhaps the most critical factor when fishing spinners. I've experimented with trolling speed indicators and learned that the fish show a definite speed preference from one day to the next. I've seen days when 1/6 of a mile an hour difference in speed would spell the difference between success and failure. I've run spinners at two and even three mph and caught fish where a slower presentation was totally worthless.

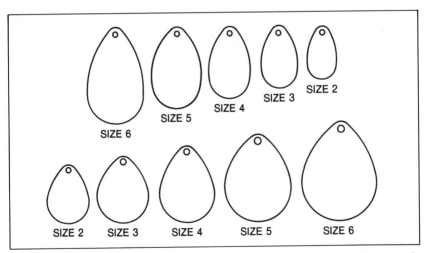

*Figure 6.* Spinner blades come in a variety of sizes and styles and the versatile angler will want to experiment with all of them. The top row are Indiana blades and the bottom row are Colorado blades. Blades from 0 all the way to 6 are likely to work under different conditions.

If you don't have a trolling speed indicator, you can gauge speed one of two ways—by feeling the resistance from your rod tip or by listening to the engine's RPMs. Listening to the engine isn't always reliable because waves or current will affect boat speed. With a sensitive graphite or boron rod, you'll be able to feel the blade spinning on the other end. Once you find a productive speed, make an effort to duplicate that speed on every trolling pass.

The length of snell can also make a difference. On some days I'll shorten the snell to nine or ten inches. At other times, we'll go with snells as long as four feet. As usual, let the fish tell you which they prefer on a given day.

Normally, a shallow, active walleye will hit a spinner so hard it'll about rip the rod right out of your hand. But, that's not always the case. When confronted with short-hitting or lethargic walleyes, there are several possible remedies.

First, try varying speed. Usually by increasing boat speed, you'll eliminate the short hits.

If that doesn't work, try teasing the fish. When you feel a fish riding along with the bait, don't drop line to the fish. Instead, gently take the bait away by pulling the rod tip towards you very slowly. The next thing you feel will be that fish trying to catch up with the meal . . . and that's the time to set the hook.

Finally, try a different live bait dressing. If they're not attacking a leech, try a minnow or nightcrawler.

There's a new product on the market that promises to revolutionize spinner fishing. It's the floating, scent-holding spinners from Lindy/Little Joe. These spinners have a float just above the blade to keep the bait off the bottom. The float is wearing a fur coat that will hold and slowly release scent in the water.

When fishing spinners, it's best to do a lot of experimenting with color, size and speed. Check the snell frequently. At high speeds, a clevis is making hundreds of revolutions on the line and eventually will wear through. Winkelman's Law says this always happens about the same time one of those monster walleyes attaches itself to your hook.

I like to use a medium to medium-heavy baitcasting outfit for most of my spinner fishing. Shimano makes two that really good for this kind of fishing, the medium-weight XL 1602, and the heavy-action XL 1553. For reels, you can't beat the Shimano BGT 2000P. With baitcasting gear, you can use fairly heavy line—which is OK in off-colored water—and still have a light-weight outfit.

Babe's trophy tip No. 8—On occasion, reservoir walleyes will crawl up into three or four feet of water and will be extremely active. Try fishing with a heavy weight right in the motor's prop wash. This will only work on rare occasions, but for shallow fish it's worth a try.

Babe's trophy tip No. 9—With over-sized blades, add a few beads to keep the blade safely away from the hook. This practice will cut down on the number of short hits.

Babe's trophy tip No. 10—Mix and match colors. If you own a Color-C-Lector, you may find that two or three colors are likely to work under a particular situation. Use a primary color—say chartreuse—on the spinner blade. Use secondary colors—maybe yellow or green—on your beads or float.

Babe's trophy tip No. 11—Put a small spinner and six beads in front of a jig. This trick will sometimes trigger a strike from a reluctant fish. It might also result in a big fish from a school that's been producing smaller walleyes on jigs.

## Crankbaits

Pappy used to fish with River Runts and Lazy Ikes. He caught some walleyes that way, too.

But plugs fell from favor with walleye enthusiasts who decided that slow and natural was the only way to fish. You might say crankbaits became victims of the live bait revolution.

Perhaps, Pappy wasn't too consistent with his plugs. But we have to consider that he didn't have a depth-finder. He fished heavy braided line. And he thought structure was the new building going up on the corner of Fifth and Main.

There have been a lot of changes in plugs over the last decade, most of them prompted by bass fishermen. We don't call them plugs anymore; now they're crankbaits. They come in all sorts of sizes, shapes, actions and colors.

But today's crankbaits catch walleyes . . . lots of 'em . . . and big walleyes.

*Crankbaits catch walleyes . . . lots of walleyes and big walleyes.*

111

For purposes of this discussion, we're going to lump all plugs under the headings of crankbaits and minnow baits. Actually, there are a number of different families of crankbaits or hardbaits. And all are designed to accomplish something different.

Let's begin with minnow baits. These are slender-bodied plugs like the Lindy Baitfish, Rebel's Minnow, and the floating Rapalas. Basically a shallow-running lure, these minnow-initating plugs perform best when fished slowly, whether right near the surface or deep behind a bottom cruiser.

Several ideal situations come to mind when talking about minnow baits. One is night fishing over the tops of weedbeds. The bait can be cast out and twitched back over the tops of the weeds or trolled with long-lining techniques. On clear-water lakes that receive a lot of boating traffic, this type of fishing is one of the best ways to turn a big fish forced to spend the daylight hours holed up on the bottom of the lake or tucked into the dense weeds.

On a lot of natural lakes, especially the older ones, night fishing can be most productive during the spring transition period when lunker walleyes move onto the mud flats or shallow rock piles at dark to feed on insects.

These minnow-like crankbaits are also extremely effective at night on lakes that are otherwise hard to fish. On very clear lakes, walleyes frequently adopt a "night-only" feeding policy. You can't buy a walleye when the sun is up. Those fish move to the shallows in the evening to feed, and walleyes of trophy proportions might be found in just a few feet of water. Live bait will catch them, but no method is as efficient for finding and catching these fish as trolling something like a Rapala or a Baitfish because that way you cover more water in a short time. These are aggressive fish that will hit a pretty big lure. Other crankbaits will work too, but the longer minnow-shaped lures are the proven producers.

In many of the country's reservoir systems, spawning activity occurs on rock rip-rap areas along highway and railroad bridges or bank stabilization areas. During the height of spawning activity, anglers troll Raps or Baitfish in just a few feet of water from dusk until dawn. Most of the action is on males, but a lot of those males run pretty good size. And the occasional female shows up as well.

Then there's the winter fishing on some of the open-water impoundments up north. Water from these impoundments is used to cool the turbines that generate electricity. Baitfish are drawn to the warm water, and the big walleyes usually aren't far behind.

In certain years, the power plant at Big Stone Lake, on the South Dakota/Minnesota border, produces walleyes of unreal proportions. We're talking about 10, 12 and 14-pound fish caught in open water when temperatures outside hover well below freezing.

The tactic? Cast a shallow-running minnow bait and retrieve it just under the surface. Those big walleyes will come up and explode that bait in the middle of the night.

*Many anglers think that only "cigar" walleyes use the weeds. Not true! This hefty stringer was taken by trolling a minnowbait over weeds at night.*

The most recent development in crankbaits is also the most productive, as far as walleye fishing is concerned. I'm talking about the long-bodied, deep-diving models like Lindy's Shadling, or Rebel's Deep Shad. These baits were designed primarily to catch bassmen who fish waters where shad is the number one forage. Bass? Well, walleyes take a real shine to them as well.

On some rivers and reservoirs, the shad-like cranks could well be producers of big walleyes. They also have proven very effective on certain of the shallow, eutrophic-type lakes. And they've even done some damage on a few of the larger, medium-fertility lakes.

From Sturgeon Bay to the Missouri River, to the Winnipeg River to the Columbia, crankbaits have demonstrated an uncanny ability to fool walleyes.

On two successive trips to the Columbia River, Dan Nelson, Gary Roach and their parties caught more than 20 walleyes over ten pounds, most of those coming on Lindy's Shadling.

Later, they took the same techniques employed on the Columbia to other systems like the Winnipeg and the Missouri and duplicated those successes, although the fish ran somewhat smaller.

As recently as a few years ago, the experts would have insisted that any effective river presentation meant moving with the current. Since a walleye usually lies facing the current, that was the most natural presentation. Moving against the current meant bringing the bait at the fish from the rear. But that rule isn't always true. Trolling plugs like the Shadling against the flow of water is a deadly way to catch walleyes...big walleyes.

When walleyes move onto a flat to feed, they find something that provides a hiding place from the current. From these protected areas— a rock, boulder or depression—they can swim out and ambush a passing meal. Trolling against the current enables the angler to run the bait at just the right depth, bouncing it off rocks or running it down into the depressions. When the bait hits slack water, it will free-float for a second before the current catches it once more. That's when the walleye will make its move.

On many of the older, weed-choked lakes, walleyes opt to spend their summers in the dense vegetation. These shallow, fertile bodies of water leave the fish no choice. Most of the available food moves into the weeds, and the predators must follow.

Some fish will be caught by speed-trolling a spinner or crankbait on the outside edge of the weedline. In fact, this was always thought to be the most effective presentation for summertime walleyes on this type of lake. But some of the fish—and a percentage of big fish—will be taken by casting crankbaits right up into the slop, hitting tiny pockets or holes in the weeds. You'll catch something on every cast. Usually it will be green and have leaves . . . sometimes it will have teeth.

It's very similar to bass fishing. And when you think of it, the walleyes in these systems have no choice but to act like bass. They'd probably rather feed in deep water on rocky humps. But, since their

Deep diving crankbaits do take big walleyes, such as this trophy Dan Nelson caught in a reservoir system.

Dan Nelson (left) and Gary Roach boated this beautiful stringer of Columbia River walleyes trolling Lindy Shadlings on shallow food shelves.

watery world has no deep rock humps, they'd rather feed in shallow weeds like bass than die of starvation.

Whereas spinners, jigs and live bait rigs might fail to produce walleyes during the "dog days" of late July and August, crankbaits can often do the trick. And I'm talking about big fish.

At first, this doesn't make sense. For the most part, walleye anglers have learned to go to small, natural-looking live bait presentations when things are tough. But these warm water walleyes are feeling good and feeding often. The only reason they're hard to catch is because there's so much natural food available to them. They can just about open their mouths, roll over and pick up a meal.

Crankbaits work at these times because they evoke a strike reflex. When that hard-swimming plug races by, the walleye strikes on impulse. This fish isn't really hungry, just mean enough to smash something that zips by while putting out vibrations of a distressed baitfish. Much of the year, you tease a hungry but inactive walleye into eating. At times in summer, you slap him in the face with a crankbait and count on his predatory instincts to result in a strike that will jolt your wrists.

Immediately after the spawn on many natural lakes a certain number of walleyes move onto shallow rock piles. These areas won't necessarily attract the greatest numbers of fish, but the ones moving in will be good-sized and hungry. They often become active in the middle of the afternoon, and there's no better way to catch them than with a hard-swimming crankbait.

Another type of crankbait, popular with bass and pike fishermen, is the short-bodied, deep-diver. Examples include Lindy's Snipe, Bomber's Model A, Rebel's Deep Wee-R, the Fat Rap and others. These lures look more like a bluegill than a shad or minnow, and bluegills are not primary forage for walleyes. That doesn't mean these baits won't catch walleyes, but they aren't as consistent as the other crankbait types mentioned.

I can, however, think of a situation where they excel. On some reservoir systems walleyes are forced into deep water late in summer when mountain runoff leads to clear water. These fish, though they are in water from 25 to 50 feet deep, are aggressive feeders. They want a fast-moving bait. You can get them by combining a deep-diving crankbait with a bottom cruiser type of sinker and trolling quickly.

Too many anglers think of all crankbaits as being more or less the same. The opposite is true. Little differences in body shape, balance, weight and the action-giving front lip will cause noticeable differences in behavior and vibration. Anglers don't notice the differences, but walleyes do. The Lindy Shadling and the Shad Rap have very similar shapes and actions. Yet on a given day, one of those lures might outproduce the other by a factor of ten to one.

The "banana plugs" like the Lazy Ike, Flatfish and Canadian Wiggler offer another example. The superficial resemblances break down when you look at them closely. The Flatfish must be trolled extremely slowly, slower than just about any crankbait made. When fish are negative or inactive (perhaps because they're in cold water) the Flatfish will sometimes produce stringers of fish when other banana lures are worthless because they have to be trolled too quickly to have any action.

At my seminars, fishermen often ask me what are the best finishes for crankbaits. It is ironic that crankbaits became so much more popular when manufacturers put the natural finishes on them. Some of those natural baits looked so much like real perch, shad or bluegills that you had to get close to them to tell if they were alive or plastic.

But serious anglers learned that natural finishes are hardly the answer to a fisherman's problems. The natural finishes are not nearly so popular today, and manufacturers are bringing back many of the old proven straight colors. I'm not saying natural finishes won't catch walleyes, especially in very clear water, but I think of other factors when picking lure color, factors we'll be looking at in-depth soon. Such things as action, speed and depth are more important than little details of finish.

What fishermen don't ask me about enough at seminars is tuning crankbaits. Even with the best manufacturing techniques, many brand new crankbaits don't run properly. An out-of-tune crankbait will run to one side or the other or maybe it won't dive deeply enough.

It's best to tune baits while standing on a dock or at a swimming pool. Cast out a short distance, then pull the bait toward you rapidly. If it runs to one side or the other, bend the eye of the plug with pliers to move that eye *the opposite way* from the direction the plug is running. If it runs off to the right, bend the eye slightly left. You might need to do this two or three times before the bait runs true, but it is

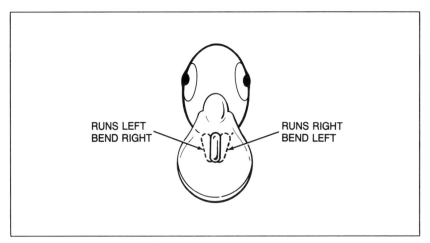

**Figure 7.** Tuning a crankbait is critical. Cast the plug out and retrieve it back towards you. It should run in a straight line. If the plug runs off to the right, bend the eye back to the left. If the plug runs left, bend the eye to the right. Only a slight adjustment will be necessary.

far better to do it on land than to try doing it while fish are hitting and you're in high waves.

Most crankbaits work best if you tie your line directly to a split ring in the nose. High quality baits often come with a split ring; if they don't, it's easy enough to add a light split ring. Otherwise, use a light-weight snap (not a big snap-swivel) that has a round bend (not an off-center, safety-pin shape). Or, tie to the lure with a loop knot, such as the King Sling. If you tie your line directly and firmly to the eye of the lure, the line inhibits lure action.

For the same reason, it's best to use light lines when fishing crankbaits. Light lines don't interfere with lure action. They also let lures dive down deeper, and that's almost always a plus. I prefer eight or ten-pound line, but will go to something like 12-pound for night fishing or fishing in real snaggy water.

Crankbaits work well as fish finders. If you troll a crankbait quickly along a stretch of rocky shoreline you can pinpoint the locations of schools. Then go back and work that area more carefully with a jig, spinner or live bait rig.

Babe's trophy tip No. 12—If you can't get a crankbait deep enough, add a Rubbercore sinker (it goes on and off quickly without hurting the line) about two feet above the plug. Use a sinker as heavy as needed to get that bait down where the walleyes are, which is usually right near bottom.

Babe's trophy tip No. 13—When trolling a crankbait, periodically rip it through the water by sweeping your rod tip forward as if you were trying to clear the plug of weeds. Then drop the bait back slowly, keeping some tension on the lure. This sudden, erratic speed change will often trigger a strike.

Babe's trophy tip No. 14—Vary your speed when trolling. Start slow, but don't be afraid to open up the throttle until you're clipping along at four or five miles an hour. Walleyes, especially if they aren't in terribly cold water, are capable of amazing bursts of speed if they see something that looks good and it's getting away from them.

## And Don't Forget . . .

While the lure families discussed earlier will probably cover three-fourths of your fishing needs, they aren't the whole story. Here are some other lure systems a well-prepared angler will want to carry.

One is the weight-forward spinner, such as Tom's Walleye Lure. This type of lure and Lake Erie are almost always mentioned together. For one thing, Lake Erie is almost a "one-lure" lake, as weight-forward spinners have proven themselves the top choice on this fabulous fishery. For another thing, very few weight-forward spinners are used anywhere else.

Does that make sense? Not really. If weight-forward spinners are the best lure on such an important lake, you can bet your best graphite rod that they'll take fish elsewhere. And they do.

*Weight-forward spinners like Tom's Walleye Lure catch walleyes, not only on Lake Erie but on some of the popular reservoirs as well.*

First, what is a weight-forward spinner? This lure has a piece of wire at the front, followed by a keel-shaped lead head, then a spinner and, finally, a hook that often carries some hackle. The lure pivots in the middle where the wire connects to the lead head. The lure casts well, does not tangle and sinks at a rapid and predictable rate.

This simple lure is known as the "only" way to fish on Lake Erie. Actually, other systems work, but none can beat the weight-forward spinner at its special game. Erie has large schools of walleyes suspended somewhere near the surface. The Erie fishing system is to cast the spinner out, count it down to a certain depth, then retrieve it. The system requires a lure that casts and retrieves without trouble, and which will get down to where the fish are holding. Almost any kind of live bait can be attached to the hook or hooks, but the time-tested winner on Erie is a big, juicy nightcrawler gobbed on the hook (with the hook going through the crawler several times).

In my fishing on Erie, I've found that the boat will spook the shallow suspended fish, sending them to the sides of the boat. The best cast, then, is out to the side. At some point in the retrieve, the drifting of the boat will cause the lure to suddenly turn toward the boat. This sharp turn, called "saving," is when most strikes occur.

You say you don't fish Lake Erie? Well, weight-forward spinners will produce fish (and not just walleyes) in almost any body of water. I've used them effectively under a variety of circumstances on reservoirs, eutrophic lakes and mesotrophic lakes.

120

*Slip bobbers, weight-forward spinners and Musky Shads. Off-the-wall walleye lures? Nope. This trio of lures can put a lot of walleyes in the boat ... and a lot of big walleyes at that.*

Let's say you have located a school of walleyes that hit your trolled spinner rigs, but that school moves up into water too shallow to troll over them. What to do? Easy—crack out the weight-forward spinners and cast in to the school. A regular spinner/bottom cruiser rig is a miserable thing to cast.

For that matter, at times you'll catch more walleyes by trolling a weight-forward spinner than on a spinner/bottom cruiser rig. Dan Nelson reports he's had this experience on the Missouri River system in both Dakotas several times, with the weight-forward spinner sometimes being ten times better than the classic spinner.

I've experienced it, too. Last summer, I went fishing with Bud Riser, president of the American Walleye Association, to check out rumors we'd heard of a walleye comeback in Lake Huron's Saginaw Bay. This kind of research takes time and money, but Bud and I feel somebody has to make the necessary sacrifices in the interest of science.

We found the walleyes, all right, oodles of fish and many of them good-sized. But finding was easier than catching.

The locals said the only way to catch them was trolling crankbaits. We caught a bunch with Shadlings early in the day, but then they shut off. We switched to white and silver Tom's walleye lures and absolutely had a field day on a spot where the locals said they wouldn't work and at a time of day when the locals said you couldn't buy a walleye. That's just one case. I could name more, but you get the point.

The trick lies in the presentation. Yes, the weight-forward spinners can be trolled with some success. Matter of fact, some days they will out-produce other trolling baits. But the weight-forward spinner's, forte lies in its ability as a casting lure.

Each type and size of lure will drop at a certain rate (you have to count them down) and then they will track at that same depth when slowly retrieved. The strike is usually triggered when the bait changes direction, speed, depth or all of the above. That's normally the case with suspended, chasing fish. You have to do something different to trigger them. The easiest way to trigger a strike with the weight-forward spinner is by using the drift of the boat to make the bait change directions. This will result in a change of speed, and usually a strike when you're into the fish.

The best dressing I've found is to simply gob a bunch of nightcrawlers on the back, leaving a two inch or so tail trail behind. I realize that goes against the *Nightcrawlers Secrets* approach of a streamlined bait, but it works . . . and quite well, I might add.

Even though these baits are used primarily for suspended walleyes, on occasion they produce well when fished on the bottom like a jig. That's especially true when working a sharp drop-off or dealing with walleyes hanging a few feet above a sunken rock pile.

One last thing. If a steady retrieve and swing isn't producing, try a semi-stop and go retrieve. Sometimes it'll take a dropping lure to trigger those suspended fish.

Another often overlooked system for walleyes is the slip bobber rig. These lures gained popularity on Mille Lacs in central Minnesota for catching the walleyes suspended above the mud flats during the summer months. It's common for the fish to suspend 5 to 20 feet above the bottom on this lake, obviously making Lindy rigging a bit difficult.

As slip bobbers grew in popularity, anglers found they were ideal for presenting a bait to walleyes working shallow, boulder-strewn reefs and points as well. Many locations were too shallow to troll without spooking the fish and too snag-infested to work with a jig. The simple solution was to hang the bait from the top down, between the rocks. The answer . . . the slip bobber rig.

Actually, the system is very simple. The bobbers are shaped in a teardrop design, with a shaft sticking completely through them, protruding an inch or so from each end. A tiny hook and a couple of split shot are put on the business end, then a bobber stop made of thread or rubber band is used above the bobber, tying it directly over the line. The bobber stop can be adjusted to any depth you desire. The bobber stop can then be reeled right onto the spool, so the bobber comes right up to the tip top for casting, even if you're fishing 20 feet down.

The best dressing is a jumbo leech, hooked once through the sucker end. Place the split shot about ten inches above the leech so he has plenty of room to work. Walleyes, even when in a negative mood, find this rig hard to resist.

Then too, consider the shore caster. Now he can fish at any depth and still be able to cast with ease. These are tools you have to consider to be totally equipped.

I would rather fish with a jig or almost anything else rather than a bobber for walleyes. That's just my style. But I always keep a bunch of slip bobbers in my rigging box for the right situation. With some suspended fish, or fish in ultra-clear water or on shallow rocky shoals, slip bobbers really can't be beat.

There's another way to get at shallow-running fish, and that's with side boards and a minnow-bait. Side boards, or planer boards, are generally used by salmon fishermen to take any fish that may be working close to the surface, away from the rest.

But they're ideal for getting a minnow bait like a Lindy Baitfish right up next to shore or along the edge of a sharp-breaking rip-rap area without having your boat get close enough to spook the fish.

Side boards are a little bit of a hassle until you get used to working with them, but they'll put fish in the boat under conditions where nothing else will work.

Looking for really big fish? I've found a couple of lures intended for fish of other species that will take huge walleyes.

One is Lindy's Giant Shad, a musky bait. Anglers in certain areas of the country have been trolling the Giant Shad for suspended walleyes over very deep water.

You can make a Giant Shad run down 20 to 30 feet with no problem. Because of its size, the Giant Shad throws off vibrations that will attract fish from a long distance. Some walleyes will actually streak 35 feet vertically to smash these monster baits. I prefer the jointed version and have personally caught some huge fish deep-trolling with these musky lures and others.

For anyone who thinks a bait this size is too big for a walleye, remember what we've been saying about a walleye preferring something between 25 and 40 percent of its total length. An active, warm-water fish will think nothing of hitting a Giant Shad. Another big bait, called a Grandma Lure, comes in sizes up to 13 inches in length. And they definitely produce their share of big walleyes.

And talk about off-the-wall . . . are you ready for this one? Anglers chasing salmon with Lindy's new Pop-Tail were suprised to find that walleyes love 'em. And why not? The big shiny body and tinsel tail ought to attract anything that swims.

We know of several 10-pound walleyes that were taken on Pop-Tails by salmon fishermen who got a little close to a shoreline-connected structure. Again, a bait this size isn't too much for a walleye, it's just about the right size.

How about spoons? Bass fishermen know how effective a Johnson Silver Minnow can be, especailly when fished in the slop. Well, I know some walleye fishermen who use spoons when trolling reservoirs and they catch a lot of nice fish. When jerked up and fluttered down, a spoon looks like an injured baitfish falling from the school. Any walleye is likely to jump all over it.

Obviously, just about anything in your tackle box has the capability of catching a walleye. We're certainly not saying you should spend your entire fishing year pulling Pop-Tails and Giant Shads through the water. But, under certain conditions, unusual methods pay off.

The important thing is that you keep an open mind and be ready to experiment with different baits and presentations. If you use them as tools to give you the greatest advantage under the conditions you're facing, they will not let you down. On the other hand, if you're looking for a magic lure that will fill stringer no matter how bad you present it, you'll be looking for a while. A *long* while.


## Color

I've heard a lot of crazy, unexplainable color theories. I never understood the mysteries of color until I got to know Dr. Loren Hill, inventor of the pH Monitor and the Color-C-Lector. Dr. Hill's research really opened my eyes to a lot of things about color.

I recall a trip to Pipestone Lake in Canada with my brother Dave. It was spring and the walleyes should have been hitting hot yellow or white. And for the most part, we were taking all our fish on hot yellow Fuzz-E-Grubs. That didn't surprise me one bit.

But, one day they went crazy for brown-orange, a color I call root beer. The day before they wanted yellow and the day after they wanted yellow. But on this particular day, root beer out-produced everything else, five to one. I didn't understand it at the time . . . my philosophy was always to keep experimenting with colors and shades until the fish told me what they wanted. Now, thanks to Dr. Hill, I have a better grip on the whole question of color preference.

I guess I could list two hundred examples of how color was one of the key ingredients—in some cases the most vital ingredient—in setting a pattern. I have always believed strongly in the importance of finding the right color for every situation.

Same with Dan Nelson, the North Dakota boy who's helping me write this book. When we sat down to develop an outline almost a year before the actual work on the book was to begin, we both decided to do an in-depth section on the importance of color.

But at that time, we didn't really have much information. Enter Dr. Hill. Dan came down to Minnesota to meet Loren with the idea of learning more about pH. When he learned about Hill's forthcoming Color-C-Lector, well, that's about all those two talked about for two days.

They set a date to fish Lake Sakakawea out in North Dakota, Dan's home base, to put the Color-C-Lector to the test. If Dan was excited about the new product before the trip, he was absolutely wild about it after the trip. Dan was one of the first anglers in the country to

Dr. Loren Hill is the man who invented the pH Monitor and the Color-C-Lector.

witness the Color-C-Lector in action. In fact, the unit was still in the prototype stages during his test.

Because he spent so much time picking Hill's brain and has, at the time of this writing, some on-the-water experience with the unit, I decided to let Dan write this section of the book. Color has been an unexplored aspect of fishing, and I think this section is perhaps the most comprehensive look at the subject ever written.

## Color-C-Lector

I first started recognizing the importance of color many years ago while fishing walleyes on Lake Oahe in South Dakota. Prior to that time I believed–as did many Missouri River fishermen–that chartreuse was the only color that consistently produced walleyes. But as I traveled around the Dakotas, I discovered an interesting fact about color. In one community everyone seemed to prefer chartreuse. But, just down the road the favorite color of most fishermen was red. At the next stop, everyone was wild about orange. And so it went.

Obviously, these anglers were all enjoying some success or they wouldn't be so loyal to a particular color. I figured maybe the guys fishing chartreuse were catching fish on Monday, but the guys who preferred green did better on Tuesday and the nickel boys kicked tail on Wednesday. It stood to reason that anyone who was willing to be versatile in his approach to color selection could catch fish every day of the week.

I started to experiment and very quickly learned that there was hardly a color in the rainbow that wouldn't produce under certain conditions. And while some colors, like chartreuse, were pretty consistent, no single color produced day-in and day-out. Further, I learned that as light conditions and water clarity changed, color preference shown by fish actually changed from hour to hour, not just from day to day.

As the years went by, the importance of color became more and more obvious. I learned that versatility in color selection was the only way to be assured that you were going to be fishing what the walleyes wanted on that particular day.

I recall one dreary July day when I was fishing a tournament in the New Town area of Lake Sakakawea. It was so overcast at mid-day that it seemed like dusk. Now, the standard rule-of-thumb is "light colors on bright days and dark colors on dark days." Right?

Well, my partner and I had tried just about every color spinner blade in the spectrum. About the only thing we hadn't tried was white. And white should have been our last choice for those conditions. As a last resort, we switched to white and quickly caught four fish. When the sun finally burned off the clouds, you couldn't buy a fish on white.

Babe and I discussed this phenomena at length and determined three basic facts about color: 1) color does make a difference; 2) as light conditions change from day to day, or even from hour to hour, color preferences will change, and 3) fish have the ability to distinguish not only different colors, but different shades of the same color.

Now you could get into an argument with a lot of fishermen on the first of those three points. The second will raise a lot of eyebrows and the third could get you laughed out of a lot of bait shops. Still, we were convinced, based on our personal observations, that we were right.

It wasn't until we got the chance to visit with Loren Hill that we began to understand all the ramifications of color preference. Dr. Hill came to Brainerd to appear on Babe's *Good Fishing* television show to talk about pH. But he arrived with a briefcase full of scientific data on color. This guy could write a book on the subject. He devoted nine years of research to determining the importance of color.

Studies by other biologists show that walleyes have two sets of cones in their eyes—single cones and twin cones. The twin cones are most sensitive to orange, but also very sensitive to red and green. Formerly, fishermen felt red was a poor choice for deep, murky water. Red was thought to be the first color to fade as it went through the water. And it is...for human eyes. But, unless you're trying to catch a human, you want to use something that's visible to fish.

The product of Hill's research was the Color-C-Lector, a light-sensitive probe that can be lowered through the water and will indicate, on a color bank, which shade will be most visible at that depth under existing light conditions.

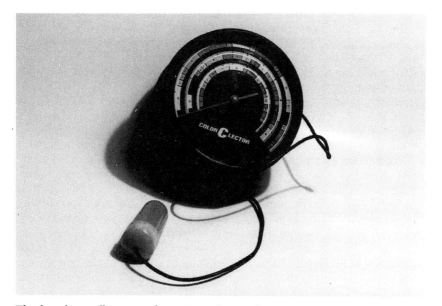

*The fact that walleyes can determine colors and are attracted by different colors at various times will often determine the heft of your stringer at the end of the day. The Color-C-Lector is a valuable tool that will help you choose the "right" color lures for varying conditions.*

We were drifting the deep edge of a wind-swept shoreline break in 34 feet. It was October, and experience told me that hot yellow would be the best choice of jigs for the conditions. Loren lowered the probe and announced that brown and fluorescent orange would be the best colors to fish under these conditions.

I about swallowed my chaw, Brown and orange? In the fall? I could have believed pink-and-white...or white...or even chartreuse. But brown-orange? I tied on a hot yellow Fuzz-E-Grub and tipped it with a six-inch sucker minnow. I gave Loren a brown-orange jig with the same live bait.

We knew we were over fish because my flasher indicated several large schools of smelt stacked against the edge of the drop-off, all schooled up in a mushroom cloud. Any time smelt are mushroomed like that, they're being herded by walleyes or sauger. So this would be a good test for the Color-C-Lector. I had the run of the rainbow. I could fish any color I wanted. Loren worked only with the primary colors indicated by the color band.

Loren played out line until his jig hit the bottom, and about that quickly, he was wrestling with a chunky six-pound walleye. Before we completed the drift he hooked another nice walleye and two sauger in the three to four-pound class. I was still waiting for my first bump.

I switched to brown-orange for the second pass and promptly set the hook on a fish that felt more like the bottom than a walleye. I couldn't move that pig. I wound up losing the fish, but I gained a lot or respect for Loren Hill and his Color-C- Lector.

The Color-C-Lector came through again the following day. Loren studied the light transmittancy levels and predicted chartreuse would be most visible to the fish. Sure enough, chartreuse out-fished everything else we tried.

If the sun went under a cloud, Loren would dutifully check light intensities and change colors. If we moved out from 24 feet to 35 feet, Loren would announce that another color would work best for that depth.

Unfortunately, I only had three days to work with the Color-C-Lector. And since we were fishing right in the middle of the turnover, the action was anything but fast and furious. But I made three basic observations on that trip: 1) the fish definitely did show a color preference, and that preference changed as light conditions changed; 2) the Color-C-Lector demonstrated amazing accuracy in predicting which color would be most visible to the fish under different conditions, and 3) bigger fish seemed more impressed by the "proper" color than small fish. There are several times when I would pull in a small walleye or sauger using the color I'd selected, while at the same time Loren would be struggling with a big fish caught on the color indicated by the Color-C-Lector.

I came away from that experience more convinced than ever that color is a key element in fishing and completely sold on Hill's new invention.

It isn't necessary here to present all of the research that led to the creation of the Color-C-Lector, but a quick review might help. The work began in the early 1970s, on largemouth bass. Hill's first experiments established the fact that bass could distinguish between different colors. For example, bass quickly learned that striking a blue disk brought them a reward, while striking a green disk did not.

The next experiment showed bass could distinguish between similar colors and shades of the same color. Bass trained to hit a blue disk would not hit a blue-green disk. They could tell a dark blue from a light blue, as well.

Another experiment demonstrated that bass have color preferences. Green was a highly attractive color to the fish, whereas yellow seemed to put them off.

Then came a key series of experiments to learn how well bass see particular colors in a variety of circumstances. It turns out that the key circumstances are: 1) how clear the water is, and 2) how much light reaches the colored panels. The amount of light striking the panels was affected by two things: the brightness of the sky (early morning light is less intense than mid-day light) and water depth (less light reaches into deep water). Hill broke water clarity into three categories: clear, stained and muddy.

This set of experiments showed that under certain conditions, some colors were just about invisible to fish. Those same colors often became highly visible when light levels changed. For example, in early and mid-morning in stained water, bass can barely see grey. At mid-day they see it quite well. There were many surprises here.

Finally, Hill spent years feeding painted crayfish to bass to learn which color of food bass preferred to feed on under the various conditions of water clarity and light level. The key finding: *bass preferred to feed on the same color of food that they find easy to distinguish.* In other words, a grey crayfish offered to a bass in stained water early in the morning would be ignored, while that same crayfish would be snapped up by a bass at mid-day in the same water.

Let's sum up: at a given time and place, there are tremendous differences between which colors (both fluorescent and non-fluorescent) a fish sees well and which colors it cannot see well. Your guess and mine are just about worthless when it comes to predicting which color fish will find easy to see. (Would you guess that fish have trouble seeing yellow at noon in clear water? They do!) But if you know what colors a fish sees well, you know what color bait will be most visible.

The Color-C-Lector does three things: 1) determines water clarity, 2) measures light transmittance at the depth you'll be fishing, and 3) indicates which fluorescent or non-fluorescent colors will be most visible to fish. It is simple to use.

You'll still have to try different lures and use your head. If the meter suggests using yellow-orange, you might have different shades of yellow orange or maybe a yellow-orange spinner with silver stripes. You'll have to fish to see what specific color or combination works. That will be a whole lot easier if you have the Color-C-Lector pointing you in the right direction.

I'm also convinced that not all the fish in a school are susceptible to the same color. Always use the top producer until it has worn out its welcome. Then switch to something different and you'll often be able to milk another fish or two from the school. Consider switching from a hot color if light conditions change. Hill's experiments show that differences in light levels really change what colors fish will hit.

If you don't own a Color-C-Lector, constant experimentation is needed to identify the best color. It helps to fish with friends so you can all try something different.

I can offer a few general guidelines. The old "light colors on bright days, dark colors on dark days" axiom is useful. Keep in mind, though, that fishing deep is just like turning the lights down because less light gets down there.

In spring, I've had my best luck with lighter colors. White, pink-and-white and hot yellow have all been good. A little later in the spring, chartreuse green will take a lot of fish. There's also a time in spring when walleyes come up on the mud flats to feed on insect hatches. Brown-orange jigs work well then.

When fishing very muddy water, I've had my best fishing on red, fluorescent red and orange. Any time I am working a mud line or fishing a wind-swept shoreline where the water is riled up, one of those three colors will be my top choice.

It's a good idea to experiment with fluorescent colors. Take some time in winter to paint up jig heads and spinner blades in real fluorescent paints. Hill's research shows that fish preferences for fluorescent colors are different from their preferences for non-fluorescent colors, so the fluorescents are like a whole separate world of colors.

Purple, for some reason or other, seems to be a dynamite fall color.

We are going to see a tremendous increase in interest in color—among fishermen and from lure manufacturers—in the next years. Loren Hill's research makes it clear that color is far more important than most of us guessed.


## Scent

If fishermen are just about to wake up to the importance of color, they already have begun sniffing out the importance of scent. Catfish and carp anglers have long known how critical scent was in their fishing. But the last years have seen a revolution in the awareness of walleye, bass, trout and pike anglers about how scent can help (or hurt) them.

You see evidence of this on the shelves of your favorite bait shop. Products that didn't exist a few years ago are now very much in evidence, and products like Chummin' Rub, as well as the many spray-on scents, are helping people catch fish.

I've long been a believer in the importance of scent. Even before all these products appeared, I used to put anise oil in my tackle boxes, letting that licorice fragrance permeate the lures throughout the season. And I have for a long time washed my hands in Lindy's No-Scent Soap to remove foreign odors like gasoline, after-shave, sun lotion or insect repellent.

A wealth of research has been conducted on the sensitivity of fish to scent. We'll just look at some highlights.

Fish vary, by species, in terms of their sensitivity to scent. This seems related to differences in their bodies, namely the number of folds in the olfactory organ, the smelling organ of fish. It stands to reason that fish living in dark or turbid environments will have more highly developed senses of smell. Catfish, for example, have large olfactory glands with lots of folds, 142 in the case of the channel cat.

But what about walleyes, the fish we're most interested in? Walleyes, though they are called "sight feeders," fall about in the middle of the spectrum when judged against all other fish. Again, that makes sense. Walleyes spend most of their time in the semi-gloom of deeper water. And if walleyes weren't so sensitive to smell you wouldn't see them preferring live bait over artificials as often as they do.

Looking at it another way, a fish only has so many senses. It seems foolish to totally ignore one of them. You may not pay attention to scent, but the fish do.

Few anglers know that the number and size of folds in the olfactory organ also increase *with age*. That means the old fish—those big fish we'd all rather catch—are more sensitive to scent than the little "cigars" we see so much of. We all know fish aren't dumb (or they wouldn't get to be big fish!), but now we know they are physically more sensitive to their surroundings than little fish. If you fish without considering the scent factor, it's the same thing as intentionally fishing for little fish.

All mammals, humans included, exude an amino acid called L-serine. This amino acid has often been demonstrated as highly repulsive to fish. Different people have different amounts of L-serine, which is one possible explanation for those crazy days when two guys fishing side by side have entirely different "luck." One of them might have stinkier hands, from the fishes' point of view.

There are two substances to be concerned about, starting with amino acids. Amino acids are the building blocks of protein, and some (like L-serine) are highly repulsive to fish. The introduction of a tiny drop of L-serine in a salmon stream caused a major upstream spawning migration to stop in its tracks. Salmon can detect L-serine in dilutions as small as one part in 80 billion.

Fish are also highly sensitive to pheromones. Pheromones are the chemical messengers that help fish communicate with each other. Pheromones, for example, are important in courtship behavior.

Pheromones also alert fish to danger. For example, an injured minnow pumps fear pheromones into the water through the cut in its skin, causing all nearby minnows to panic. Would that mean you will panic walleyes if you drop down a minnow with a hook through its skin?

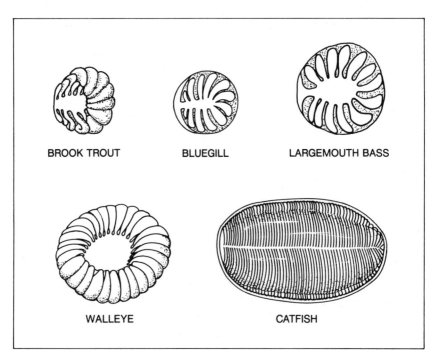

**Figure 8.** *This drawing depicts the olfactory glands of several popular fish. Notice the large olfactory of the catfish, a species that lives in very dark water and relies heavily on scent to feed. Scientists tell us that the size and number of folds in a fish's olfactory glands increase with age.*

No, of course! Fear pheromones are "species specific." One species will not pick up the messages in the water put out by other species.

I'm willing to bet a walleye can smell a northern pike 50 feet away in the water. Goodness, I can smell one at the other end of the boat, and I don't have the nose of a fish!

What you have with scent, then, is two types of substance that are putting out various messages to fish. Some messages will be positive, telling fish that this bait tastes good. Some messages will be extremely negative, telling fish to keep away. And most fishermen don't even know this is happening, and they sure don't have any control over it.

That's where the new fish-attracting scents come in. Most of them can mask the negative effect of the L-serine we all have in our skins. And a good fish scent can add attraction to our baits, especially the artificial baits.

Some baits hold scent better than others. Hard-bodied crankbaits will let scent wash off faster than other types. Soft plastic-bodied lures, like plastic grubs or twistertails, hold scent well. Lindy's now makes a variety of jigs and rigs that carry a flocked "whizkers" substance to hold scent better. Scent will wash off a bare hook far faster than from a hook with a whizker fuzz.

132

A product that I've worked with extensively, and that shows great promise in avoiding many of the pitfalls of early scent products, is Chummin' Rub. It comes in a sort of "Chap Stick" applicator, and you can just "goo" it on your hooks, whizkers material, soft baits, and even hard crankbaits. It really stays on well, and I've seen it really make a difference in my catch.

Now some days, as you might guess, no scent product is going to make a difference. And some days, the difference might be so subtle as to be nearly undetectable. But you better believe it makes a big difference on other days!

If I'm catching fish as fast as I want, I'll probably not bother to use a scent attractor. If I'm not catching that many fish, though, I'll sure reach for that "something extra" that could tip things my way.

That's like much of my fishing. I tie extra-good knots, change colors frequently, and do a lot of other things that bring me a fish here, a fish there. Don't expect the fish to dive in your livewell the moment you make some little adjustment in your presentation. But, if you pay attention to the little things and keep experimenting, you'll consistently do better than lazier fishermen.

Scent fits into that overall approach. The little things count. And, some days, little details aren't little at all. They're very big, indeed.

Take a day this last fall on a lake near my home in Brainerd. Six anglers were out, fishing in three boats. I consider three of the other

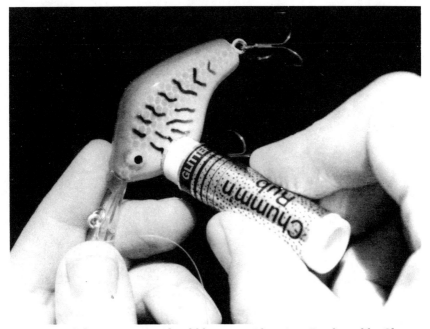

*For serious fishermen, scent should be a consideration. Products like Chummin' Rub, a waxy "Chap Stik-like" scent, will stay on even hard baits. Some days, it can make a big difference.*

These two nice walleyes came on a jig that was "spiced up" with a scent product. Does scent always make a difference? Probably not. But on this day, I really believe it did.

guys true experts with a jig. I was the only one using a scent product. At day's end, I had caught seven walleyes from six to ten pounds. The other five anglers caught, all together, two small walleyes.

Now, maybe the scent factor wasn't important that day. On the other hand, maybe it was the only reason I did so much better than those good fishermen who weren't using a scent attractor.

It's always hard to prove that one factor is the one that really works . . . but nobody has to prove to me that I should be aware of the scent factor. I've seen enough to know I want to carry fish-attracting scent with me at all times.


## Boat Control

Racing a late-afternoon storm back to the boat ramp, my attention was drawn to a group of wide "blips" on the flasher in the 30 to 45-foot depth range.

Curiosity got the better of me and I swung the boat around and turned on the graph recorder to take a better look. There, suspended over 50 feet of water, was a school of big fish I suspected might be walleyes.

I combed the area in ever-increasing circles looking for the nearest structure those fish might be relating to. Not far away I found a tiny rock finger, no bigger than my boat, lying in 32 feet of water at the tip of a sunken flat.

It was late October, prime time to catch big walleyes. I knew this particular central-Minnesota lake held some real pigs, and judging from the hooks on the graph paper, a lot of them were right under my boat.

Even though I wasn't dressed for the occasion and despite a strong wind coming up out of the northwest, I couldn't resist the temptation to wait and see if those fish would eventually move in the direction of that rock finger. If they did, I knew I stood a good chance of sticking some trophy-sized walleyes.

As dark, snow-filled clouds drifted over the lake, the fish started a horizontal movement towards the point. I tied on hot yellow Fuzz-E-Grubs tipped with big redtails and positioned the boat over the structure. That lasted all of a few seconds before three-foot waves blew me off the spot.

This was a tricky situation. I wanted to stay over the top of the rock finger, but it was too small to back-troll or drift. The wind was too strong for the electric motor. And I didn't want to take a chance on dropping the anchor and bouncing it off a fish's nose.

I picked out two sets of coordinates on shore and got rifle sightings on each. Watching the flasher, I backed the boat over the top of the finger and held it in position using the motor, which was in reverse.

In doing so, I was able to hover over the spot, vertically fishing with only quarter-ounce jigs. This may sound easy, but believe me, not. With each gust of wind it was necessary to increase engine speed to maintain position. In a lull, I'd have to back off or even pop the motor into neutral. And when the bow drifted slightly, the boat began to slide off the spot sideways. Holding my position required constant attention to the engine, the graph recorder and my shoreline markings. At times like these, it would be nice to have three sets of hands and four eyes.

But it paid off handsomely. In the 25 minutes those fish were up, I hit nine walleyes running from 5 to 12 pounds. And I missed at least that many because my sense of feel was reduced greatly by the depth I was fishing and the velocity of the wind—to say nothing of half-frozen fingers.

I believe this story illustrates vividly the importance of boat control. I usually tell people that boat control is at least 25 percent of successful walleye presentation. But under certain conditions, like the one I just described, it's probably more like 90 percent.

Boat control is best described as "using your boat to maximum advantage to present the bait in the most effective way." That may sound easy enough, and it is under ideal conditions. But things get a little complicated if you're bucking four-foot waves or fighting strong current.

Every fisherman's goal should be absolute boat control. That means using your boat to move the bait at the exact depth, speed and direction necessary to catch fish. You can be doing everything else right, but if your boat is moving too fast or too slow, or if you're a foot or two off the contour, you simply won't catch many walleyes.

## Step No. 1 to Absolute Boat Control

Before you can achieve maximum boat control, you must first know where you want to be. When you hook a fish, there are two things you should try to do instinctively. First, check your sonar to determine the exact depth at which the fish was caught. Second, look to shore for marking that will lead you back to that exact same spot. Line up a distictive tree with a big rock . . . a dock with the front window of a cabin . . . whatever's available. You should get rifle-sightings on at least two sets of landmarks no less than 45 degrees apart. Armed with that information, you'll have a pretty good idea of where the fish was hooked and be able to return to that exact spot.

Of course, it's easier to toss out a marker buoy, and that's just what I do under many circumstances. But if you're fishing in a crowd, markers are not the answer because they tend to attract a lot of boats. In heavily fished areas, I prefer to use landmarks.

On ensuing passes over the area, learn everything you can about the water. At what depth does the breakline occur? Is there a ministructure? Where are the fish in relation to the structure? The more information you can feed into your computer the better your chances of capitalizing on the situation.

If you're not sure where you want to fish, you can use boat control to "check and clean" an area. Start deep and systematically eliminate water, moving up a few feet on each ensuing pass until you've worked the structure thoroughly. Again, precise boat control is necessary to accomplish this goal.

## The Equipment

Like any job, boat control requires a complete set of tools. The first and most obvious of these tools is the boat itself. You'll achieve the best control with a low-profile boat that's less subject to wind drift. A big, heavy boat with high sides will be tough to control under any circumstances. It's like the difference between driving in heavy freeway traffic in an 18-wheeler as opposed to a sports car.

I like the Ranger 1600 V-II, because it's the sports car of walleye boats. Its low profile, and excellent tracking ability allow me to follow the tightest contours, even under tough conditions. And wait until you take your first ride in the newest Ranger line, the **Fisherman.** I helped design this boat, and believe me, it can take big water, and it really performs.

A lot of the boat control work will fall on your outboard motor. In the past, most serious walleye fishermen used smallish engines in the 6- to 15-horsepower range. In fact, I can remember when a 15-horse was considered a big engine. But the introduction (or popularization) of walleyes in many of the big waters around the country has necessitated going with bigger boats and bigger engines.

Thankfully, we have some viable options that weren't available a few years ago. Mariner has a 45 horse with power to burn, yet thanks to four tiny cylinders it still trolls down like the 15 horse of pappy's day. I run a 45 Mariner with a tiller handle, because of its trolling capabilities. If you're serious about walleye fishing, you'll want a tiller motor rather than a steering console. You can react more quickly to those sharp inside and outside turns in the contour with a tiller than a console.

If attaining ultra-slow speeds is necessary—and that's often the case in fishing situations—you'll want to have an electric trolling motor. A strong case, in fact, can be built for having two electrics in your boat, one on the transom and the other on the bow. I have a MinnKota 95 on the transom, and a 395 on the bow. These high-powered electrics produce 35 pounds of thrust that can handle rough water and strong current.

The back-trolling rig offers complete boat control. A 50-horse engine, an electric motor and splash guards are all integral parts of the perfect fishing machine.

Obviously, you can't follow a contour you can't see. For that reason, a good flasher at both ends of the boat is a must. Two flashers are preferable for one simple reason: If you're working a sharp-breaking contour, the depth at one end of the boat won't be the same as that on the other end. If you're running the bow-mounted electric motor, but reading the depth given by the transom-mounted flasher, you really won't have a good idea of what the actual depth is where you are fishing. You could even be following the wrong contour.

Splash guards, nothing more than mud flaps you mount on the transom of your boat, provide protection from incoming waves when you are backtrolling in even a moderate wind.

If total boat control is your goal (this all depends on how deeply you want to get involved with your fishing), you'll also want to have a set of sea anchors, two regular anchors with at least 75 feet of rope each, and a trolling speed indicator.

A trolling speed indicator is an essential piece of equipment when fishing crankbaits or spinners. Often, a difference of just 1/6 mile per hour can cut your success in half, or double it.

## The Basic Concept

During the course of your fishing experience you may find it necessary to improvise many different boat control tactics. I can't possibly cover every condition you're likely to encounter.

The idea is that you develop a method to meet every new situation. Each day will be different and will require a different boat control approach. Current, wind direction and velocity and the contour to be followed will dictate what sort of improvisations you'll have to come up with.

If you have all the tools we've discussed, you should be able to make your boat do just about anything you desire. You can hold over a tiny area in four-foot waves without using an anchor, crawl along at jigging speed in a strong current or follow a tight contour at very slow speeds with a 40 mph wind hitting that contour at a 45-degree angle.

Some jobs will require just one of the pieces of equipment you have installed on your boat. Some jobs will dictate using both electric motors and a Boat Brake.

The methods of controlling a boat are limited only by your imagination. When faced with a tricky boat control problem, size up the situation carefully, taking into consideration the direction of the wind, the speed you wish to move and the contour to be followed.

Now let's take a look at the basic boat control tactics, along with a few tricks that can help save the day when conditions prove difficult.

## Front-Trolling

Front-trolling is perhaps the most basic and widely used method of boat control (see Figure 9). You simply engage the engine and start trolling forward. As recently as ten years ago, front-trolling probably accounted for 90 percent of the fishing that occurred on walleye waters.

Front-trolling is preferable under certain conditions. The major consideration is speed. When fishing a crankbait or a spinner at three or four mph, it may be impossible to maintain the proper speed unless you're forward trolling.

When we talk about boat control, two of the most vital aspects are speed control and depth control. If following an exact depth along an irregular contour is the most important consideration, front-trolling isn't the answer. But if maintaining the proper speed is essential, and if that speed is something over two mph, you may have no choice but to front-troll.

Front-trolling has drawbacks. When moving forward, you are pushing the boat with the outboard motor. Since the transducer for your flasher is usually mounted towards the rear of the boat, you won't see a change in the contour until the boat has already passed over the spot.

Say you're headed due north following a 17-foot break. Suddenly the contour takes a 45-degree turn to the left. By the time that change is indicated on your flasher, your boat has already moved well off the spot. You swing the motor to the left, but it takes you several yards to recover and get back on the contour.

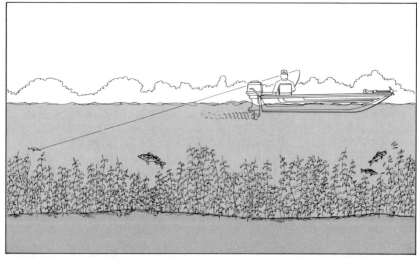

**Figure 9.** *When working a crankbait over the top of a weedbed, front-trolling is best. In this situation following a contour is a secondary consideration to maintaining the right speed.*

If the fish happened to be tucked into the bend in the contour, your lure won't ever get close to the school.

Another problem with front-trolling is wind drift. In a strong wind, the bow of the boat is most likely to be blown off course. When a gust of wind catches the bow and moves it in one direction or another, you have to compensate by chasing the bow with the motor. Again, you'll find yourself too deep or too shallow as you maneuver to get back on the breakline.

Still, there are instances when front-trolling is preferable. Obviously, if you're fishing downriggers for deep walleyes front-trolling is the only way. With suspended fish, following a tight contour is a secondary consideration.

When trolling minnow baits over the tops of weedbeds or across a shallow flat, depth control becomes secondary to covering water quickly and locating active fish. Again, front-trolling is the answer.

When running lures behind planer boards next to shore or looking for suspended walleyes, front-trolling is the ultimate answer.

Sometimes you'll locate fish scattered over the top of a large flat where the depth is more or less constant. Here, speed control becomes the primary consideration and front-trolling is appropriate.

## Back-Trolling

Unless you're brand new to walleye fishing, you're probably familiar with back-trolling.

Most anglers, when they first discover back-trolling, think it's a great concept. They understand that by putting the motor in reverse, they'll be able to move at a slower rate of speed (see Figure 10). And reducing speed is one of the reasons for back-trolling. But there's more to it than that.

When back-trolling, the engine becomes the pivot point for any change in direction, allowing you to precisely follow the tightest contour. The engine is pulling the boat rather than pushing it, and thus you are less subject to wind drift.

Remember that 45-degree turn on the contour we encountered when front-trolling? If we'd hit that turn while back-trolling, the flasher would have indicated the change and with a quick left turn on the tiller we could have swung the boat around and hugged the 17-foot break, dragging our lure right past those fishes' noses.

And with the motor pulling the boat, wind has less effect on the bow. The wind may still swing the bow from time to time, but we can compensate quickly and easily without passing over any prime water.

The basic back-trolling movement is accomplished by running the motor in reverse and backing squarely into the wind. By adjusting the speed to match the force of the wind against the transom, you can run your boat at a variety of speeds. That's assuming you have a 50 horse

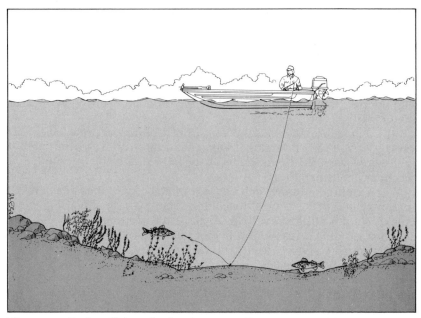

**Figure 10.** *Back-trolling is by far the most efficient means of boat control for walleye fishing.*

or smaller engine. With a 60, 75 or larger outboard, you'll need a small gas engine, sea anchors or a powerful electric to slow down to the necessary speeds.

In some cases it may be necessary to shift the engine in and out of gear to maintain slow speeds. If the water's calm and you're having difficulty holding down your speed, I'd suggest using the electric.

Back-trolling sounds simple enough, but adverse weather conditions can make it tough. If three-foot waves are crashing into the contour at a 45-degree angle, following the breakline requires a lot of concentration and hard work. Especially if the contour has slight irregularities. Remember, the goal of boat control is to remain on an exact contour 100 percent of the time—not 50 or 75 percent of the time.

If you carefully size up each situation, the wind may actually become your ally. While you're back-trolling, pop the motor into neutral once in a while and let the wind push you along. You may even have to put the motor in forward to hold your course. This tactic is known as sliding and is illustrated in an accompanying diagram (see Figure 11).

Another back-trolling tactic is called hovering. We described hovering in our opening comments. Turning the transom against the wind, you simply hold the boat in position by increasing or decreasing speed according to the velocity of the wind. This allows you to dangle a bait in front of a walleye's nose without dropping an anchor into the middle of the school. It requires a lot of concentration but it can be effective.

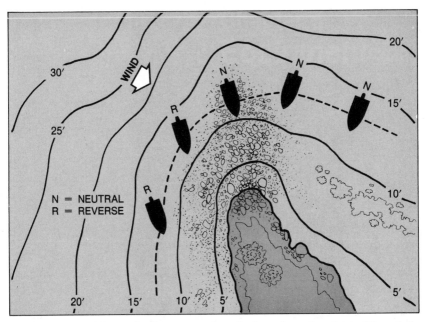

**Figure 11.** *Sliding is another boat control tactic that takes advantage of the wind. The boat back-trolls out to the tip of the point following an exact contour. Then the motor is placed in neutral and the boat "slides" along the contour with the wind.*

In some situations, you may want to rock in place. Here, again, the wind becomes an ally. You back-troll through and past the school of fish moving against the wind. Then you shift the motor into neutral and let the boat drift back over the school. If the wind is too strong for a slow drift, use the electric motor to slow you down during the drift.

### Slipping

Slipping is a terrific boat control tactic when fishing current. It's also fairly difficult to master.

Let's say you want to present a jig very slowly along a 25-foot contour in heavy current. Obviously, the current will move the boat along faster than you wish to move. Still, you want to drift with the current because that's the most natural presentation as far as the fish are concerned.

The solution? Slipping. Here's how it works. Point the boat into the current and leave the engine idling. The boat will still move downstream. The engine merely allows the speed of your drift (see Figure 12).

143

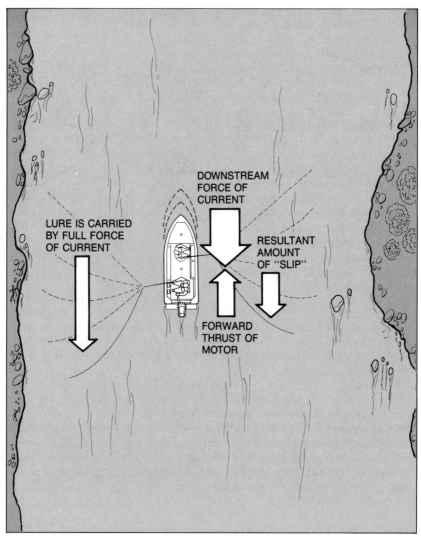

**Figure 12.** Slipping a river is tricky but effective. The boat is pointed into the current with the motor in forward. But the boat moves downstream with the current. The motor is used to control the speed of the drift.

By motoring weakly against the current, you can slow the boat down to meet the speed the lure is moving through the water. A 3/8 ounce jig has less resistance to the water and won't move nearly as fast as a boat, with all that hull surface contacting the water. If you just drift, your boat will be racing down the river leaving the jig behind. By slipping, you can slow the drift rate of the boat to roughly the same speed as that of the jig, or even slightly slower.

It's imperative when slipping to keep the bow pointed directly into the current. If the bow turns at even a slight angle to the current, the water will catch the bow and swing it sideways. It's a lot of work and takes some time and experience to master. But slipping is deadly on river walleyes.

## Drifting

Drifting is extremely popular with walleye fishermen. Drifting is easy; just shut down the motor and let the wind do all the work. The problem with drifting is that the wind won't always be moving you at the speed or in the direction you wish to go.

The waves may propel your boat too fast for an effective presentation. And very, very rarely will the wind push the boat along the desired contour.

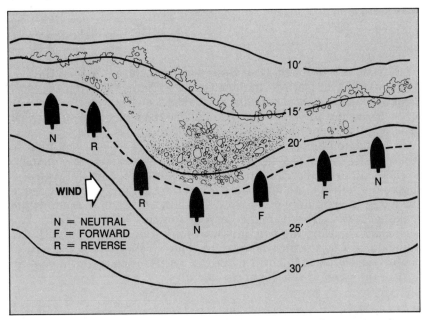

**Figure 13.** Drifting is an excellent way to follow a contour "if" you remember to use the motor to maintain the proper course. That's what is known as a "controlled drift." By putting the motor in forward, neutral and reverse it's possible to hug the contour while letting the wind do most of the work.

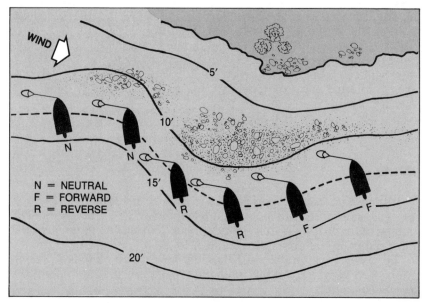

**Figure 14.** *Boat Brakes help slow even large boats to a crawl in big waves. Using Boat Brakes and the outboard this boat is moving along the contour at a very slow speed even though the wind is extremely strong.*

If speed is a problem, Boat Brakes (manufactured by Blue Harbor, Hopkins, MN 55343) are the answer (see Figure 14). Attach a Boat Brake, which is a parachute-like device that catches water, to the bow eye with a short piece of rope. By adjusting the outlet hole on the Boat Brake, you can control the speed of the drift.

But direction remains a problem. That's where we get into the *controlled* drift. That means using your outboard to adjust to any changes in the contour. If the contour breaks in, put the motor in reverse. If it goes out, put the motor in forward. If the contour is straight, leave the motor in neutral. In other words, you drift much of the time while making occasional adjustments in your course.

Sometimes using the bow-mount electric in conjunction with the outboard will be the answer. Several times I've used the outboard to control the course of the drift while my partner used the front electric against the wind to slow the boat down.

### Anchoring

Under most conditions, I do not prefer to anchor. I want to be free to cover a lot of water until I locate fish.

But there will be times when anchoring and fishing just one area will be highly effective. One example is in the spring when the walleyes are super slow. Maybe you have a school of fish working a rocky point where they've gathered to spawn. You want to cast jigs up into the shallows and work them back slowly through the school. Here, you'll want to anchor and cast.

During the post-spawn period you may encounter a concentration of lethargic fish. You may want to dangle a jig or a floating jig right in front of their noses for long periods of time, daring them to pick it up. Again, anchoring is the answer.

And there will be days when wind is so strong that anchoring is your only viable option. Trolling is out of the question because of the size of the waves.

There's another neat trick I picked up a few years ago that involves anchoring in current. Say you want to fish the lip of a deep hole in the river. Anchor on the upstream side of the hole and let out just enough anchor rope to position the boat right over the lip.

Shut the motor off and let the current slide you from side to side. If you turn the motor, the skeg will move the boat like a pendulum back and forth, allowing you to work the entire lip without casting (see Figure 15). In effect, you're trolling the lip without starting a motor.

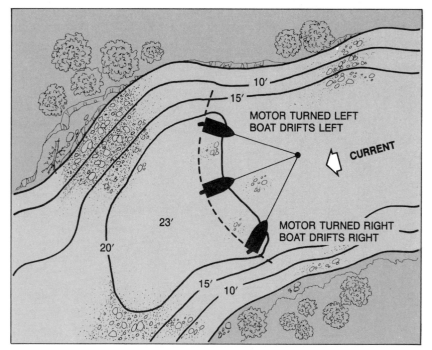

**Figure 15.** When anchoring in current you can silently move from one side to the other just by turning the motor and letting the current drift the boat like a pendulum. This is a great way to work the edge of a hole in a river.

## Electric Motors

I've already mentioned several instances where an electric motor can save the day. Whenever possible, I prefer to use my electric rather than the gas outboard because it's quieter and less likely to spook fish. You have better control with an electric and can attain much slower speeds, not to mention the noise factor.

For casting to the shallows, you can use the bow-mount electric to slip in and out of pockets in the weeds without spooking any fish.

Electrics also allow you to change directions quickly, a tactic I've found to be highly effective for walleyes. Maybe I'm trolling a jig over the top of a rocky point that's holding fish. I'll work that jig up and over the point, then quickly reverse directions and go back over them. You'd be amazed at how many strikes this sudden change in direction will produce.

I could list boat control methods that would fill volumes. But the point is that you must develop a system that works for the conditions you face on a particular outing.

That could mean tying off to a tree stump on a reservoir, using both electrics at the same time, back-trolling with a sea anchor, or any of a thousand combinations.

Every situation will be different and will require a different approach. But if you have all the tools and keep an open mind, you can come up with the solution to just about any boat control problem. Once you do that, and realize where to put your boat, you're on your way to walleye heaven.

# Chapter 5
# Equipment

## A Man and His Toys

*"The one with the most toys when he dies . . . wins."*

**—Anonymous**

It was such a dirty trick that even now, several years later, I'm almost ashamed to talk about it. Still, it was kinda fun!

It was a beautiful September afternoon and I was sitting at my typewriter half-heartedly working on a magazine article. My mind wasn't on the job. I was really looking for an excuse to go fishing.

When the office door flew open, I didn't really know who to expect. Much to my surprise it was my old buddy, Dan Nelson, from North Dakota. Dan explained that he was passing through on business, and since it was such a lovely fall afternoon, he figured we should go catch some walleyes.

"It's our Christian duty," he reasoned.

Since he put it that way, I really had no choice. I grabbed a few extra rods and reels for Dan, loaded the boat, and we were off in a matter of minutes.

We hadn't been on the water long when I stuck my first fish. Then another, and another. All the while, Dan didn't have so much as a bite.

Now the kid from North Dakota didn't fall off the turnip truck that morning. He knew there was a reason he was getting out-fished. First, he switched from his Lindy Rig to the same white Fuzz-E-Grub I was using. Then he started to fish out of my side of the boat, suspecting he was the victim of a meat hog conspiracy. Can you imagine that? He even went so far as to walk back and practically sit on my lap so he could see the depth-finder.

But all to no avail. I wound up with a limit of walleyes and Dan never set the hook. He just couldn't figure it out. I didn't catch any monsters, but I did have a couple of fish in the four to five-pound range.

That evening, Dan insisted on a rematch. He still wasn't sure what had happened, but he was bound and determined to figure it out.

Just before we retired that night, Dan disappeared for a few minutes. I peeked out the window and saw him snooping around in the back of my fishing truck. I cringed, because I knew he was getting close to finding the answer.

Next morning he disappeared again, and when he finally came out the back door, he was wearing a big smile.

On the lake, I caught the first fish. Then Dan caught one. And another. Then I caught a couple. If the fish Dan was catching didn't tell me he was onto my game, the cup of coffee he poured for me did. When I went to take a sip, there was a fathead minnow swimming around in my java.

Dan had put two and two together and come up with 12—12-pound line, that is. You see, I had six-pound line spooled on the reels I was using. But the reels I gave Dan were spooled with 12-pound line. I was surprised he hadn't noticed when he rigged up the day before. I guess he was too excited about going fishing to check for details.

That night he inspected our equipment. And next morning he grabbed two ultra-light rods and spooled on some fresh 4-pound line. And if you don't think the difference between light line and heavy line can affect your overall catch in fall fishing, you'd better guess again.

## Line/Knots

My rule of thumb is to use the heaviest line I can get away with for the conditions I'm fishing. If, as was the case on our September walleye trip, the water is clear and the fish are finicky, you'll probably have to use six or even four-pound line. On the other hand, if the water is stained and you're trucking along with a spinner, you might be able to get away with heavy line.

I'll never forget the 1980 North Dakota Governor's Cup on Lake Sakakawea. Nelson and I were teamed up, but because of scheduling difficulties, I couldn't get to Garrison until the night before the tournament. Dan knows "Sak" pretty well and had done a good job of scouting. He had located several areas that were holding good concentrations of fish.

When I arrived, Dan told me to spool 14-pound line on my baitcasters. I said there was no way I'd fish walleyes with 14-pound line, a baitcaster and a spinner. As hard as he tried, he couldn't convince me.

Our number one spot was an island with lots of jagged rocks and— get this—an old car body. That island was a line-eating monster. Now, when you get a fray in 14-pound line, you still have eight or ten-pound line in the water. But if you get a fray in six-pound line, like I was using, there isn't much left. That line will break under the slightest pressure.

We got frays. You couldn't make one pass over the rocks and car body without nicking your line. In two days of tournament fishing we broke off more pounds of fish than we caught. We wound up with close to 50 pounds of walleye, good for a 10th place finish. We could easily have been close to the top, we maybe even could have won it, had I been using heavier line.

Later, I visited with the winners, Mort Bank and Dave Jensen of Bismarck, and learned they'd been using 20-pound line. In Sakakawea's off-colored water, line size just doesn't seem to make much difference in overall success, at least not during the summer period.

Obviously, light line is not *always* the correct choice for walleyes. Lesson number two.

Line is the most vital link in your fishing tackle system. You can read books about fishing, attend seminars and invest a fortune in equipment. Yet, the moment you set the hook on a big fish, the only thing between you and the fish is your line. And if that line fails, you've lost the fish.

If line is the most vital link in your tackle system, it's also the most overlooked. Guys will spend $8,000 on a boat motor and trailer, equip it with all the latest electronic gadgetry and fill several tackle boxes with expensive baits. They own the most sensitive graphite or boron rods and super-smooth, high-tech reels. But, when it comes to spending a few bucks for fresh line, they balk.

I like to ask seminar audiences this question: "Which would you rather have, a ten-pound walleye or $20?" Invariably, every hand in the place goes up for the ten-pound walleye. And why not? A ten-pounder is a once-in-a-lifetime catch for most fishermen. If you don't get excited about a ten-pound walleye, you should quit fishing and take up golf.

Yet, when you ask those same people how often they change their line, most will have to admit it's once a year, maybe less often.

I'd be willing to wager that 75 percent of the trophy walleyes that are hooked each year are lost because of line failure. And 75 percent could be a conservative estimate. If those fishermen would take the $20 we talked about and invest it in a bulk spool of line, like clear or blue Stren, a lot of those big fish that wind up dying of old age might end up on someone's wall.

Speaking of money, you really begin to understand the importance of using fresh line in a tournament situation. In your everyday fishing, the "one that got away" is something to talk about over a beer that evening. In a tournament, the big one that broke your line means lost cash. I haven't seen the tournament yet where an eight or ten-pound fish wouldn't have put hundreds—maybe thousands—of dollars in my pocket.

I change line a lot—at least once a week when I've fished heavily and *every day* during a tournament. I always buy the best line available. The average weekend fisherman should change line several times

*Line is the most important link in your tackle system. A premium monfilament line like Stren will help put more fish in the boat.*

a season. And if you buy your line in 3,000-yard bulk spools, it doesn't have to be a budget-straining experience.

But, just changing line is no guarantee that line failure won't occur. There are some other precautions that must be taken to avoid having a big fish swim away with a hook and piece of string attached to his lip.

First, cut off a few feet of line several times during each fishing trip. That portion of line down at the business end is being exposed to the bottom and is going to become frayed. Cutting off the bottom few feet of line several times each day will assure that when Mr. Big comes to call, the entire length of your line will be at full strength.

Second, check rod guides and the roller guide in your reel for breaks or scratches. When snagging up or fighting a big fish, the tip guide of your rod is under a lot of pressure. Sometimes the line will wear a notch in the guide and that notch will literally eat up line as it passes through the guide. Same with the roller guide in your spinning reel. Sometimes those rollers will freeze up and become worn.

If either of these things is a problem, you'll see your line breaking within a few feet of the rod when it's under pressure. You can check your guides by running a cotton swab, like a Q-Tip, around the inside edges. If any cotton sticks to the guide, you've got a problem.

You should also store rods and reels and spare line in a cool, dark place. Monofilament line can be stored indefinitely under these conditions. But extreme heat and sunlight destroy fishing line in a hurry. If you store rods and reels in the trunk of your car all week when it's 101° in the shade, by Saturday that line will have aged ten years.

It goes without saying that your line is only as strong as its weakest link. And that's usually the knot.

Let's say you start with ten-pound line. If you tie a knot that breaks at 50 percent of the line's strength, you're actually fishing with five-pound line. If you tie an 80 percent knot, you're fishing with eight-pound line. But if you tie a 100 percent knot, you can be confident that the line will break before the knot gives out.

Over the years I've had fun testing fishermen's knots. I take a piece of fresh line, have the angler tie it to a stirrup and place the line on a special machine that checks line strength.

You simply wouldn't believe how many knots check out at less than 50 percent. One season I used 12-pound line in the tests. Less than five percent of the fishermen tied a knot over 90 percent efficiency the first time. Most fell into the 50 to 75 percent range. And perhaps 20 percent of the knots tested came apart between two and five pounds of pressure.

"But, I've never lost a big fish," they say, staring at the results. To that, I say one of three things: a) you're lying, b) you don't do much fishing, or c) you've never hooked a big fish.

The most reliable knot I've ever run across is the Palomar. The Palomar is a relatively simple knot to tie and checks out consistently in the 95 to 100 percent range.

The Improved Clinch is a good knot except for one thing. There's a right way and a wrong way to tie it. If you tie it right, it should check out at nearly 100 percent. Tie it wrong, as many anglers are prone to do, and you'll see it come apart at 50 to 75 percent. The best advice I can give you about the Improved Clinch, or any other knot for that matter, is practice, practice, practice. Take a few minutes in the evening to tie and re-tie the knot until you've got it down pat.

The World's Fair Knot is another good knot. I've seen this knot check out between 80 and 90 percent. Again, the ultimate strength of the knot is determined by the way it's tied.

There are a few other knots you may want to learn for special situations. The Blood Knot is used for connecting two pieces of line together. The Snell Knot works best when rigging up spinners or Lindy Rigs on snell hooks. And the King Sling is an excellent knot to use on crankbaits. Study the diagrams of these knots and experiment with them.

## Palomar Knot

This knot is equally as good as the Improved Clinch for terminal tackle connections and is easier to tie, except when using large plugs. It, too, is used by most of the pros.

1. Double about 4 inches of line and pass loop through eye.

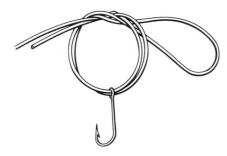

2. Let hook hang loose and tie overhand knot in doubled line. Avoid twisting the lines and don't tighten.

3. Pull loop of line far enough to pass it over hook, swivel or lure. Make sure loop passes completely over this attachment.

4. Pull both tag end and standing line to tighten. Clip tag end.

## Improved Clinch Knot

This is a good knot for making terminal-tackle connections and is best used for lines up to 20-pound test. It is a preferred knot by professional fishermen and angling authorities.

1. Pass line through eye of hook, swivel, or lure. Double back and make five turns around the standing line. Hold coils in place; thread end of line around first loop above the eye, then through big loop as shown.

2. Hold tag end and standing line while coils are pulled up. Take care that coils are in spiral, not lapping over each other. Slide tight against eye. Clip tag end.

## World's Fair Knot

Created by Gary L. Martin of Lafayette, IN, this terminal tackle knot was selected by a panel of outdoor writers as the best new, easy-to-tie, all-purpose fishing knot from 498 entries in the DuPont Great Knot Search. Martin named it the World's Fair Knot because it was first publicly demonstrated by him at the Knoxville '82 World's Fair.

1. Double a 6-inch length of line and pass the loop through the eye.

2. Bring the loop back next to the doubled line and grasp the doubled line through the loop.

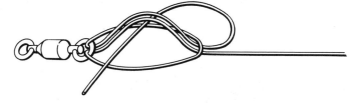

3. Put the tag end through the new loop formed by the double line.

4. Bring the tag end back through the new loop created by step 3.

5. Pull the tag end snug and slide knot up tight. Clip tag end.

## Simplified Blood Knot

This is used for tying monofilament line to leader or one length of leader to another. It works best with lines of equal or nearly equal diameter.

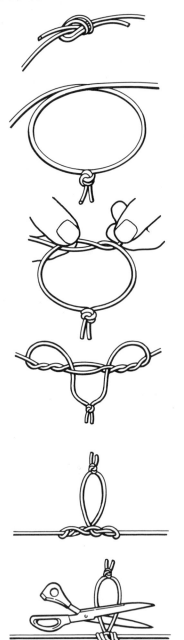

1. Take the two lines' ends and tie a simple overhand knot (which will be clipped off later). Then tighten to combine the two lines into one.

2. Form a loop where the two lines meet, with the overhand knot in the loop.

3. Pull one side of the loop down and begin taking turns with it around the standing line. Keep point where turns are made open so turns gather equally on each side.

4. After eight or ten turns, reach through center opening and pull remaining loop (and overhand knot) through. Keep finger in this loop so it will not spring back.

5. Hold loop with teeth and pull both ends of line, making turns gather on either side of loop.

6. Set knot by pulling lines tightly as possible. Tightening coils will make loop stand out perpendicular to line. Then clip off the loop and overhand knot close to the newly-formed knot.

**Snelling a Hook**

This is a common snell, hook and leader combination. It can be made up to suit the length and strength needed for various types of bait fishing.

1. Insert one end of leader material through eye of hook just past turn and barb. Pass other end through eye in opposite direction, leaving large loop hanging down.

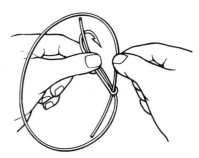

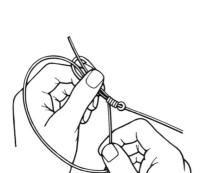

2. Hold both lines along shank. Use line hanging from eye to wind tight coils around shank and both lines from eye toward hook. Take 5 to 10 turns.

3. Move fingers to hold coils tightly in place. Pull leader extending from eye until entire loop has passed under coils.

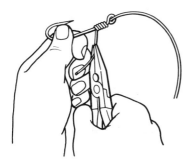

4. With coils snugged up neatly, use pliers to pull tag end, clinching up snell. Clip off tag end and tie loop knot in end of leader.

## King Sling

This knot is used for putting a loop in line that is attached directly to lures.

1. Insert end of line through lure eye and double back about 10 inches.

2. Bring the doubled line around to form a loop and spiral the bait four times around the doubled line above the loop.

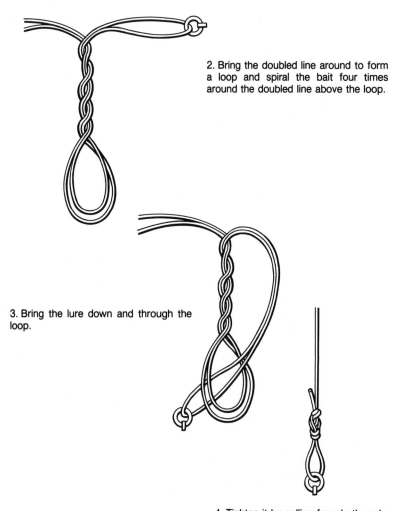

3. Bring the lure down and through the loop.

4. Tighten it by pulling from both ends.

With any knot there are a few things to keep in mind. First, always wet the line before setting the knot. If you set the knot dry, line-burning friction will occur, weakening the line just above the knot. You may see a wave in the line at this point. Heat rearranges the molecules of the nylon. You've seen what happens when you touch a cigarette to your line. When you set a dry knot, much the same thing happens. The friction won't create enough heat to actually break the line, but it will weaken the line considerably.

Second, if you don't like the way the knot looks or feels when you set it, cut off and try again. Sometimes even the best fisherman ties a knot that just doesn't set the way it's supposed to. When in doubt, try again. It takes only seconds and it's a good guarantee that your knot won't break at a critical moment.

That brings us back to the question of which line size is best for your particular fishing needs. And the best answer to that question is to let the conditions dictate the line you select.

As a basic guideline, I use six or eight-pound line for most of my jig fishing; six, eight, or ten-pound test for rigging; six, eight or ten for crankbaits and anywhere from eight to 17-pound for fishing spinners. I'll beef line size up a bit if I'm fishing snag infested waters.

The most important consideration when selecting line is water clarity. The cleaner the water, the lighter you'll want to go. In ultra-clear water I've been known to step down to four and even two-pound test. In really turbid water, 17-pound line may be adequate. If you're planning on releasing any fish, a practice we strongly endorse, you should stay away from ultra-light line. It simply takes too long to get the fish into the boat and the fish's chances for survival are almost nill.

The diameter of the line affects the drop rate of the lure. The heavier the line, the more resistance it has to the water and the slower it will drop. Heavy line is also more visible to the fish and affects the natural look of your presentation.

With six-pound line, a crankbait will run with the maximum side-to-side action. Step down to ten-pound line with that same crankbait and you not only will be unable to fish the lure as deep, but also will note a slow-up in the lure's action.

However, there are cases where the slower action may be desireable. I've used Lindy Shadlings with 14-pound line and caught some nice fish, because the walleyes seemed to prefer the more lethargic action that resulted from the heavier line.

If you want a Shadling to run down to 18 feet, you'll have to use six-pound line. If you're fishing ten feet, the Shadling can pull 14-pound line to the bottom with no trouble. Trial and error is the best instructor here.

At this point, you're faced with one of the really confusing issues of choosing a fishing line. The consumer really has no idea what he's buying when he walks into a store for a spool of line.

I may get into trouble with some line manufacturers for this, but most companies underrate their line. The label on the box really is not an accurate reflection of what's on the spool.

For instance, if you purchase a spool of ten-pound line, that mono may actually break under 16 pounds of pressure. The angler says, "Boy, is this line tough. I can pull up trees with it."

Sure it's tough. It's not really ten-pound line at all. It's actually 16-pound line that's been mislabeled. Why do the manufacturer's do this? I assume it's because fishermen are so impressed with the strength of a product.

But if it's your intention to use six-pound line on a jig, that's what you want to spool on your reel—six-pound line. Not 8, 10 or 12. You want the fast drop rate, natural-looking action and low visibility of six-pound line.

Were there regulations governing the advertising of fishing products, all lines would be labeled according to their actual break strength. That way, the fisherman would know exactly what he was purchasing.

A lot of anglers have discovered this basic fact of fishing the hard way. They buy what they believe is ten-pound line. On their next trip they hook a monster fish of one species or another. A check of the record books shows their catch is bigger than the existing world line class record in the ten-pound category. Oh boy, a world record.

They fill out all the applications and have the catch verified by the proper authorities. They submit their catch along with the required sample of the line they were using. A few weeks later their application is returned with "rejected" stamped across the front. The reason? The line broke at 15-pounds of pressure and didn't make the minimum for the ten-pound category.

I never go fishing expecting to make a world record catch. But I do want to know what line I'm fishing with.

Fortunately, you can buy lines that are properly labeled. The one I use is Stren's Class Line, a product that's designed for fishermen who are chasing a world record. Class Line checks out at the rated strength and is the line I recommend you should be fishing, whether you're seeking records or just out to put lunch in the boat.

Line color is also an important factor. In those instances when you want to be a line-watcher, I'd suggest fluorescent blue Stren, or Stren Class Line. The fluorescent blue is more visible and is a real plus for jig fishing. If line visibility is spooking the fish, I'll go with clear Stren.

Big fish didn't get that way by being dumb. And anyone who wants to catch a trophy (and who doesn't) will improve his chances greatly by using the right line, tying a strong knot and making sure every inch of that line is at full strength. One slip could cost you the trophy of a lifetime. Can you afford to take that chance?

## Electronics/Rods and Reels

Some 225 boats were milling around the bay, awaiting the storm-delayed start of a major walleye tournament.

At times like this, it's easy to pick out the veterans. Their boats casually move through the maze as they exchange greetings and barbs with other tournament regulars.

You can spot the novices, too. They're nervously tinkering with equipment and going over their maps, trying to decide which spot to hit first.

"Look around, what do you see?" asked my partner, Dan Nelson.

"A couple hundred boats and a bunch of nasty looking clouds," I replied, pulling on my rain gear.

"No, I mean look inside the boats. Three years ago in this same tournament not ten percent of the guys even owned a flashlight. Today, I'll bet at least half are running graph recorders.

He was right. Most of the boats were decked out with all the latest electronic gadgetry.

Dan noticed a boat that had slipped off to the side of the traffic jam. Inside, two fellows appeared to be mounting a graph. They were carefully studying the instruction booklet as they hooked up the power cord and transducer. Everything in place, they sat back and turned on the unit. You could see their eyes light up when the stylus started spinning, scratching out a picture at the bottom.

"Looks like they bought it last night so they could win some money in the tournament," I said.

"Watch this," Dan smiled with a twinkle in his eye. Sliding closer to their boat, Dan hit the switch on his graph creating a wave of interference on the other guys' graph paper.

One grabbed the instruction manual while the other adjusted the knobs and re-checked all the hookups. Nothing would make the interference go away.

Finally, one of them slapped the new unit on the side, as if to calm a hysterical person. At the same time, Dan shut off his unit and it was as if the new toy said, "Thanks, I needed that." The interference was gone and so was the look of terror on those guys' faces.

Just when they thought everything was OK and they were starting to graph some carp (which they thought were walleyes) on the bottom, Dan would turn his unit back on. This went on for several minutes until those poor boys were on the verge of a nervous breakdown.

When the electrical storm had passed and the shotgun blast finally signalled the start of the tournament, I looked back to see those two fellows still sitting there, tinkering with their new gadget.

There's no question that today's sophisticated electronic instruments give the modern fisherman a decided advantage over anglers of past generations. Even the more advanced fishermen of 30 years ago were restricted to dragging weighted lines, or to letting plastic jugs drift across the lake until the cords hung up on an underwater obstruction.

But when Carl Lowrance introduced the first sonar devices for public consumption over a quarter of a century ago, he gave us a very special gift. He gave us eyes; electronic eyes that enable us to see under the water.

Unfortunately, too many fishermen—like those fellows in that tournament—don't fully understand how all the expensive, space-age equipment works. They pay no attention to the flasher until they catch a fish. Then they tell their friends, "Yup, we caught 'em in 25 feet today." The owners of such graph recorders have been known to spend a whole weekend following a school of suspended carp. Worse yet, they pull onto a point teeming with walleyes and immediately leave

*Each year I use my graph-recorder more and more. The Eagle Mach 1 is one of the most reliable graphs money can buy.*

because nothing shows up on the graph, which they failed to properly "tune."

There is no magic involved in using sonar. The angler must understand what he's looking for and be able to make accurate interpretations of what he's seeing. Just because fish are showing up on the graph paper doesn't mean they're the species of fish desired for that particular outing. A graph cannot differentiate between walleye, bass, carp, northern, or any other species of fish. However, with practice and with an understanding of how fish relate to structure, the skilled angler can make a highly educated guess as to just what's swimming around under his boat.

The sonar equipment most of us use, whether it be flashers, or graphs, or both, are nothing more than tools. Our rods and reels are tools, each of the many lures we employ are tools, boats and motors are tools. The number of fish we ultimately catch will be determined by how wisely we utilize the tools at our disposal.

My good friend, Dave "Hot Tip" Jenson, is a tune-up specialist who uses a very expensive computer to pinpoint engine problems. It's a high-tech tool. That same piece of equipment in the hands of a novice, such as myself, would be about as helpful as a toy crystal ball. Only someone with the knowledge of how that equipment works and an understanding of automobile engines could benefit from such a sophisticated engine analysis machine.

In this portion of our chapter on equipment, we'll be looking at sonar and how it works. We'll study some of the different signals and how to interpret them. In the final analysis, the only way anyone can become proficient with sonar is through time and experience on the water. Fact is, there are still some signals I encounter that I'm unable to interpret with any amount of confidence. So, don't be discouraged if confusion sets in from time to time.

When purchasing a sonar unit, there are several things you'll want to consider. The most important considerations, in my opinion, are power, durability, scales, cone angle, and price. I listed price last because, in reality, it's the least important consideration. It may seem important at the time of purchase, but that $50 or $75 you save by buying an inferior unit will come back to haunt you.

Let's talk first about power. Different companies rate power output in different ways, making the question of power a confusing issue. I'm no technician and don't pretend to know the difference between peak-to-peak and RMS. I am a fisherman, and I know performance when I see it. I personally use the Eagle Silent Sixty 2, a flasher that's rated at 250 watts of power (peak-to-peak). Another excellent unit is the Lowrance 2330, which is rated at 300 watts. In graph recorders, the Eagle Mach I and II and the Lowrance X-15's and X-16's are rated at 1,600 watts of power.

How important is the power output of a particular unit? Perhaps we can best explain by relating it to your car radio (see Figure 2). You leave home listening to a 10,000 watt radio station. As you get further and further from the transmitter tower, the signal begins to fade (usually right in the middle of your favorite song). You are forced to turn up the volume. You're not increasing the power output of the station—that remains a constant 10,000 watts. You're merely increasing receiver sensitivity. As a result, you begin to receive a lot of unwanted signals, like interference from spark plugs, electrical wires and static electricity in the air. You're just amplifying unwanted noise.

Finally the signal fades altogether, and you punch up a 100,000 watt station. You are able to turn down the volume and eliminate the unwanted signals, receiving a clear, sharp signal once again.

It's the same with sonar. I've seen flashers that were so weak they couldn't read a 20-foot soft bottom at 30 miles an hour. I've seen units so lacking in power that to read a 50-foot bottom at trolling speeds required turning the volume to the max, resulting in all sorts of unwanted interference.

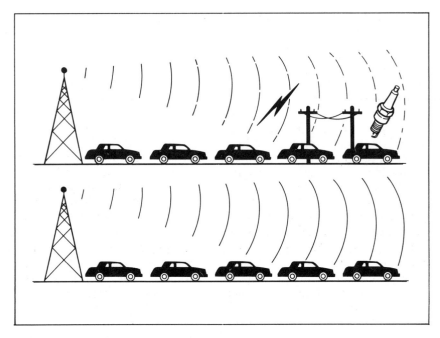

**Figure 2.** Like your car radio, the sensitivity of your locator is determined by the power of the signal it receives.

Some manufacturers include all sorts of whistles and bells on their units as a sales gimmick. Don't be misled by the options you may be offered. You're looking for a powerful unit with the power to penetrate the water and show you what's down there, with the durability to last and the resolution to pick out even those fish that are hugging the bottom.

In terms of durability, I don't think you can beat the units offered by Eagle and Lowrance. I fish upwards of 200 days a year, in all sorts of weather, and I've yet to experience any down time with either brand. That's not to say they never break down. Everything breaks once in a while. But it's tough to beat the reliability of the two brand names I just mentioned. Maybe I'm a bit biased, but 20 years of solid performance is reason to be.

Resolution is another important aspect when selecting a sonar device. Some units cannot pick out a fish 12 inches or even 24 inches off the bottom. The fish just blend in with the bottom.

Lowrance and Eagle flashers have six-inch resolution, which means a fish six inches off the bottom will be displayed as an individual fish as opposed to part of the bottom. And the graph recorders from Eagle and Lowrance, with their 1,600 watts of power, have one-inch resolution. The best in the industry.

Which scale you select will depend on the waters you fish. I use two flashers on my boat. The Silent Sixty 2 from Eagle is a dual scale unit with 0 to 60 feet on the first scale and 0 to 120 on the second in the back. I also use a Eagle Silent Thirty 2 on the front. My next choice would be the triple-range 2330 from Lowrance, which has 0 to 30, 0 to 60 and 0 to 300 feet.

Model numbers are likely to change over the years, but performance should be constant. Check out the specs on any unit thoroughly before you make your final decision. Look at warranties, power output, resolution and availability of scales.

The graph I use on my walleye boat is the Mach I from Eagle. It has range options that include 0 to 10, 20, 40, 60, 80, 100, 140, 200, 300, 400, 600 and 1000. As an added feature, you can split the screen, seeing only the bottom half of the range. For instance, if you're on the 0 to 60 scale and just want to see the bottom, you can punch up 30 and 60 and eliminate the top 30 feet of water.

Lowrance's X-15 series has the ability to enlarge any section of water in ten-foot increments. You can see 0 to 10 feet, 60 to 70 or any other conbination of depth ranges.

Should you buy a permanent mount or a portable unit? I guess that depends on the situations you're likely to encounter. If you spend a lot of time fishing Canada, ice fishing or renting boats, the portable would be the best way to go. If all your fishing is done out of your own boat, I'd suggest a permanent mount. If in doubt, buy a permanent mount—you can always get a portable power pack if you want to travel.

Cone angle is another tricky subject. You can purchase cones that send sound waves to the bottom in a very tight eight-degree cone, a wider 20-degree cone, or a very wide 45-degree cone (see Figure 3).

The eight-degree cone is preferable if you want to look into a very small area and get the clearest possible picture of what's directly under the boat. The 20-degree cone gives you a wider search pattern and will display more of the bottom. The 45-degree cone is preferable for fishing with downriggers because it enables you to graph the cannon-ball and know exactly what depth you're fishing.

If you're really into fishing, you might want to consider having two transducers and a switch box. You can use the 20-degree cone when looking for fish and structure, and switch to the narrower eight-degree cone when you zero in on the area to be fished.

Lowrance just introduced a new product, the X-16 graph. The X-16 has the capability to run a 20-degree cone and a 45-degree cone, giving the angler a dual-purpose unit. The X-16 would be a good investment for anyone who splits his time between walleyes and salmon.

Whatever unit you choose, it's important that you understand its functions. Only through a basic understanding of how sonar works can you get the most out of your unit. I'll offer a basic look at sonar in this segment of the book. For an in-depth look at sonar, you might want to pick up my new cassette-book package, *Babe Winkelman's Comprehensive Guide to Fish Locators,* for the rest of the story.

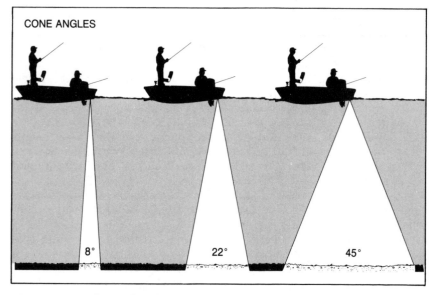

**Figure 1.** Transducers that shoot a 20-degree cone angle are generally preferred by walleye experts. But there are situations where an 8-degree or even a 45-degree cone angle is useful.

I'll begin this look at sonar with a discussion of the basics. Sonar stands for Sound Navigation Ranging.

A sonar device is a three component product: the power source, the head unit, and the transducer. The head unit serves both as a transmitter and a receiver, and is sometimes called a transceiver.

The power source provides electrical current which the head unit converts into an electrical impulse. The impulse travels along a coaxial cable striking the crystal transducer, causing it to ring like a tuning fork. The shock waves travel through the water, reflecting off any objects along the way and returning to the transducer.

Inside the flasher is a spinning wheel or disk which has mounted on its face a tiny bulb. Each time another shock wave is fired the bulb lights up at zero. When the sound wave returns, it lights up the bulb again. The second burst of light represents the distance the wheel has traveled since the initial shock wave was fired.

Because sound travels at a constant rate of 4,800 feet per second (fps) through water, it's possible to calibrate the spinning wheel to accurately display the exact distance the sound wave has traveled. In the case of a graph recorder, a stylus spins on a belt, scorching a piece of paper instead of illuminating a bulb.

The shock waves leave the transducer in an ever-increasing circle or cone. The size of the cone varies from unit to unit. Some cones are as small as eight degrees while others are as large as 45 degrees. The primary application for wider cone angles is deep-water fishing, where it's important to be able to track your downrigger weight through the water. For most walleye fishing, smaller cones are preferable.

In most cases, the ideal cone for walleye fishing has a 20 or 22-degree angle. In 15 feet of water, a 20-degree cone will cover 28 square feet of the bottom. A 9-degree cone sees only three square feet at the same depth. Obviously, the wider search pattern of the 20-degree cone affords the fisherman a greater view of the bottom and enhances his chances of detecting fish, drop-offs or whatever else lies beneath the boat.

However, there are practical applications for the smaller cone. For instance, when jigging over a shelf that contains numerous giant boulders, the angler might want to access the spaces between each boulder, a likely place for the fish to be hiding. Using a wide cone angle, the boulders will blend together. With a narrow cone, it becomes possible to pick out individual fish among the boulders.

For this reason, some crafty fishermen mount two transducers on a boat, using a factory switch box to change from one to the other as conditions dictate. In 90 percent of the walleye fishing I encounter, the 20-degree cone is preferable to the 9-degree cone. But there are times when the narrow cone performs better. In most cases, the wide-angle cone provides far more useful information; for instance, when determining bottom content.

The sound waves traveling down the center of the cone are strongest while those on the outer edge are much weaker. A hard bottom, such as gravel or rock, is an extremely reflective surface for those sound waves. Even weaker sound waves, on the outer portion of the cone, will be reflected back to the transducer. The result is a wide, bright line. If the dial of the flasher is lit up from 20 to 23 feet, the actual depth beneath the boat is 20 feet. The bright signal on the dial indicates that some of those sound waves traveled a greater distance—21, 22 and 23 feet. Just a glance at a properly tuned flasher will tell the fisherman he's working a hard bottom.

Should the boat move over a muck bottom, the signal's intensity will fade. Only a narrow line at 20 feet will appear. That's because sound waves on the outer part of the cone are being absorbed into the bottom. They are too weak to bounce back to the transducer.

This type of information will not be provided using a narrow cone. The sound waves on the outer part of the cone aren't traveling much farther than those going directly down the middle. Thus, a narrow line results at every depth and with every type of bottom.

There's another way to determine bottom content, and that's by the presence of a second echo. Over an extremely hard bottom, some of the shock waves traveling through the water will strike the boat and make a second trip to the bottom, coming back and hitting the transducer again. The result is a double reading on the dial of the flasher. In 20 feet, over a very hard bottom, there'll be one flash at 20 feet (the bottom) and another in the vicinity of 40 feet (roughly, twice the bottom depth). The second echo indicates a very hard bottom.

The second echo is the best way to distinguish bottom content when using a narrow cone angle.

Under certain conditions, unwanted signals will appear with just about any unit. To erase them, most manufacturers have installed another control, the suppressor.

Each impulse kicked out by the transducer is of a predetermined wave length. The shorter the sound wave, the greater the resolution. With extremely short sound waves, it will be possible to distinguish individual fish only inches apart.

If turbulence from under the hull is creating interference, it can be eliminated by merely turning up the suppression. The suppressor stretches the sound waves enabling them to pass through the turbulence. At the same time, it reduces the unit's resolution.

Let's say, just for the sake of discussion, that your unit sends out sound waves six inches in length. With such a unit it should be possible to detect an individual fish only six inches off the bottom, or two suspended fish six inches apart.

If you turn up the suppression adjustment, the pulse width (length of each sound wave) increases to two, three or even four feet. Now that fish six inches off the bottom blends in with the bottom and the two suspended fish look like a small submarine. With maximum suppression, a fish suspended four feet above the bottom becomes part of the bottom.

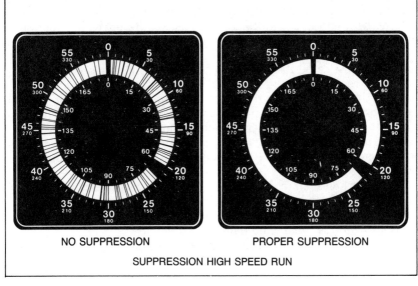

**NO SUPPRESSION**  **PROPER SUPPRESSION**

**SUPPRESSION HIGH SPEED RUN**

***Figure 3.*** *The suppression control is used to filter out unwanted signals that clutter the dial.*

Under most conditions, it will be necessary to use suppression only when running. Unless there is electrical interference from within the boat or unless the transducer is improperly mounted, suppression will not be necessary at slower speeds. Suppression should be used *only* when necessary.

Some units, usually the least expensive models in a particular line, feature built-in suppression. Manufacturers considered this feature a desireable advantage—one less adjustment to worry about. In truth, such units have very limited resolution and certainly don't have the capacity to discriminate between individual targets.

A quality, high-powered unit, properly installed, will be subject to very little interference, even on high-speed runs. However, the transducer must also be properly installed. And that's where many sonar owners run into problems.

Basically, there are only two ways a transducer can be mounted: on the transom, or on the floor of the boat for a through-the-hull reading. The fact that you cannot shoot a signal through aluminum (according to our authorities at Lowrance), simplifies your choice of mounts. However, some manufacturers argue that it is possible to get an accurate reading shooting through aluminum.

Make your own decision. I personally do not believe a signal can pass through aluminum without at least a 25 percent and as much as a 40 percent loss in resolution. The density differences between aluminum and water are simply too great. Sure, with a high-powered unit, it will be possible to read the bottom. But as we're going to see, today's sophisticated flashers and graphs can provide more than a simple depth reading.

Many boat owners are reluctant to mount the transducer permanently on the transom because they are concerned about weakening the boat structurally. Nonsense. Before mounting the transducer, locate the area along the hull which has the smoothest water flow during high-speed operation. This is where you'll want to mount the transducer.

Drill four holes, attach the transducer bracket with four sheet metal screws and add a dab of silicone sealant before tightening. You'll never get so much as a drop of water coming through the holes and the transom won't be weakened one bit.

Boat owners may also fear potential damage to the transducer when running over rocks or pulling on gravel shorelines. Think about it. The motor's lower unit hangs nearly a foot below the boat and the transducer is just a fraction of an inch under the hull. If you run so shallow as to damage the transducer, you'll likely also be replacing a lot of rivets and probably a whole lower unit.

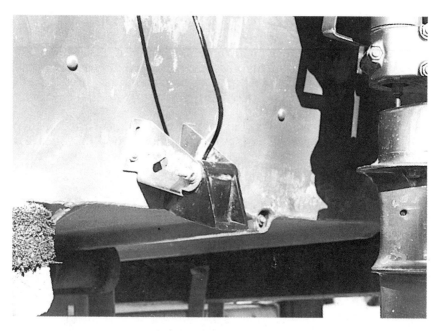

*Even though a transducer can shoot sound waves through a fiberglass hull successfully, an aluminum hull will cut your sensitivity in half. Make sure you mount transducers on the stern of aluminum boats to get a clean, accurate signal.*

Avoid mounting the transducer behind any keels or rivets or anything else that might create turbulence. Remember, no unit can shoot a signal through air, and that includes air pockets and air bubbles. For this reason, it's always best to position the transducer a good distance from the outboard.

Check other, similar boats, to see where and how the transducer is mounted. You'll find that every aluminum hull is slightly different, even in the same model and brand of boat, so it will be necessary to do a bit of experimenting.

For final installation, follow the manufacturer's instructions to the letter. In some cases, you'll want to mount the transducer flush with the hull, while with other models the transducer should be located slightly below the hull line. Tilting the transducer forward one to three degrees will facilitate high-speed readings. If the transducer slips backward a degree or two, the boat will actually be running away from returning signals.

Fiberglass hulls are another story. Fiberglass is roughly the same density as water and thus it is often possible to mount the transducer inside the boat and shoot a signal through the hull. However, this is not always possible. This mounting method is dependent upon the process by which the fiberglass was laid and the location of the transducer.

Some types of fiberglass have very tiny air bubbles created during a roven-woven process. On such boats, which are very structurally sound, the fiberglass is hand-laid. And while these tiny air bubbles won't block out the signal, they will affect overall resolution.

Some boats have false floors with air pockets. Other boats sandwich floatation between layers of glass. In either case, a transducer will not be able to shoot a sound wave through the air pocket.

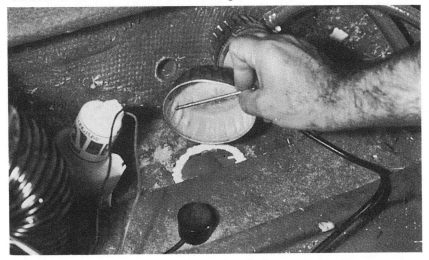

Photo 1 – To install a transducer in a fiberglass boat, first, form a tinkers dam out of caulking compound to trap the epoxy in a pool. Mix equal parts of two-part epoxy and pour into the dam.

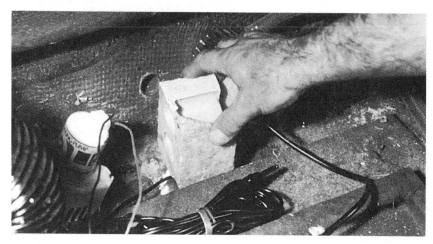

Photo 2 – Press the transducer down into the epoxy and move it around to force out any trapped air. It is recommended to place a half brick on the transducer to hold it still while the epoxy is curing so it won't tilt and allow some air to be pocketed under it.

Photo 3 – The transducer after the epoxy has hardened. The brick is removed, and wire is ready to be attached to the locator unit.

With any boat, it's best to consult your marine dealer before final installation of the transducer. Transducer location and installation is the most vital link in the entire system, and improper installation can reduce efficiency from 25 to 75 percent. In my course on electronics, A Comprehensive Guide to Fish Locators, I covered nearly every kind of transducer mount possible. I strongly suggest you pick up a copy. It will solve any problems you may encounter with transducers.

Now let's get down to the actual operation of the unit, beginning with the flasher.

Before actually going fishing, it's a good idea to take a ride on a familiar lake and observe the different signals the unit will provide. Head into a soft-bottomed bay and notice the signal. Find a weedbed and see how vegetation is displayed on the dial. Seek out a rocky point and study that signal. Find big rocks, small rocks and drop-offs. Study all the various readings the unit is capable of making. In a fishing situation, final interpretation of these signals is the responsibility of the angler, and there's no substitute for hands-on experience.

The most important step of operation is tuning the receiver. When you first turn on the unit, a flash will appear at zero. Every time the transducer fires another shock wave into the water, the bulb will light at the zero position. As you continue to increase sensitivity, another flash will occur at the depth of, say 15 feet. Continue to increase sensitivity and another reading will appear, this one at roughly twice the actual depth, or 30 feet. Earlier, I mentioned second echoes and how to determine hard bottom from soft bottom.

I like to back off on the sensitivity until that second echo is just barely visible. Now the unit is fine-tuned and capable of alerting me to even the slightest change in bottom content. If the boat passes from mud to hard clay, the bottom reading will brighten and the second echo will intensify. Move from gravel to sugar sand, and the second echo may completely disappear. Even the most minute change will be visible.

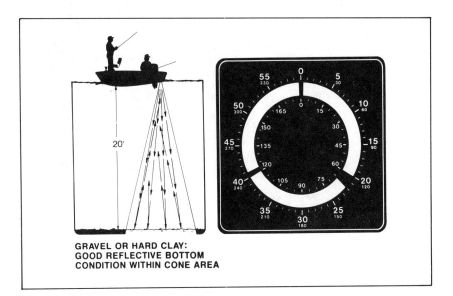

GRAVEL OR HARD CLAY:
GOOD REFLECTIVE BOTTOM
CONDITION WITHIN CONE AREA

*Figure 4.* To "tune" your unit properly, turn up the sensitivity until you get a second echo. Now your unit will clearly display bottom structure, and, of course, fish.

Obviously, it will be necessary to continually fine-tune the unit. As the boat moves from one bottom type to another, or up and down in depth, constant adjustments will be called for. However, if the unit is right in front of your nose—like it should be—that's really not a problem.

A soft-bottom tends to absorb shock waves, giving off a weak, thin line and will require maximum sensitivity to receive a second echo.

A hard-bottom is a far more reflective surface for shock waves and most will rebound back to the transducer. The result will be a wide, bright line and a strong second echo.

Next you'll want to be able to interpret rock. Rock is by far the most reflective surface for sound waves and is also the most irregular. Sound waves will ricochet off rock like bullets, producing a signal that seems to dance on the dial, a "nervous" signal.

It's also important to know when the boat is over the edge of a drop-off. Here again, the importance of a wide-angle cone is demonstrated.

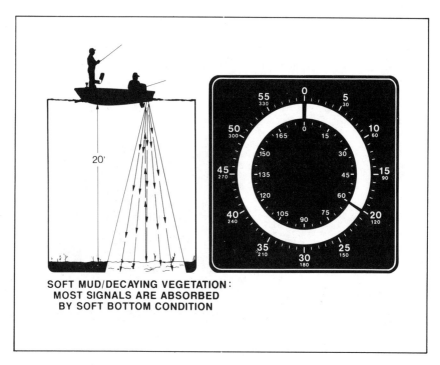

SOFT MUD/DECAYING VEGETATION:
MOST SIGNALS ARE ABSORBED
BY SOFT BOTTOM CONDITION

**Figure 5.** Soft bottoms absorb the sound waves and return a weak signal, resulting in a thin, weak signal.

With a wide cone, some of the sound waves will be striking above the drop-off, say in ten feet. Sound waves at the other side of the cone may be hitting the bottom in 18 feet. The result will be a fairly solid line all the way from 10 to 18 feet. Any time you see a reading like that, the boat is hanging on the edge of a drop-off. Frequently, when working a sharp drop-off, it will seem as though a lot of fish appear on the flasher. That's because sound waves on the outside of the cone are weaker, and only a portion of them are being reflected back to the transducer. These broken signals are often mistaken for fish.

Many of us refer to sonar devices as "fish finders" or "fish locators." Make no mistake, sonar devices detect fish. And the good ones will locate baitfish as well. But I'd caution you not to depend too heavily on sonar to actually find fish. The main purpose of a flasher is to identify those areas that might be holding fish and help you develop a pattern. I like to call my sonar unit a structure finder.

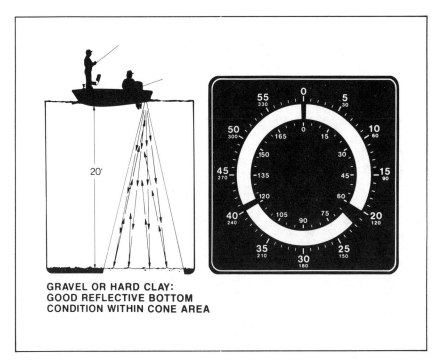

GRAVEL OR HARD CLAY:
GOOD REFLECTIVE BOTTOM
CONDITION WITHIN CONE AREA

*Figure 6.* Hard gravel, clay, or sand bottoms will reflect most of the sound waves, returning a strong, bright signal.

When it comes to actually pinpointing fish, I rely on my graph recorder. Graphs work on the same principle as flashers and they provide a printed readout of everything between the transducer and the bottom. Instead of a bulb flashing on a spinning wheel, a stylus rotates on a belt, printing a mark on a piece of moving paper.

In the last few years, I've relied more and more on my graph recorder, especially when fishing walleyes. Graphs are extremely sensitive and powerful. They are capable of displaying fish, baitfish, rocks, trees and weeds and even the thermocline.

Again, I would caution anyone from relying too heavily on a graph. I've seen fishermen spend an entire day hovering over a school of carp because they believed that what they were seeing was walleye. And I've seen other boats move away from an area that was literally teeming with walleyes simply because no fish were showing on the graph . . . or so they thought.

That's certainly not to say you should ignore the information provided by the graph. These highly sophisticated instruments will display everything that exists between the transducer and the bottom. The tricky part of the whole experience is making an accurate interpretation of what you're actually viewing.

Let's begin our look at graph recorders with a review of the different adjustments. Sensitivity and suppression are about equal to those of the flasher. You should use only as much suppression as is necessary to block out unwanted interference which, under most fishing conditions, will be none. Sensitivity should be turned up until you're

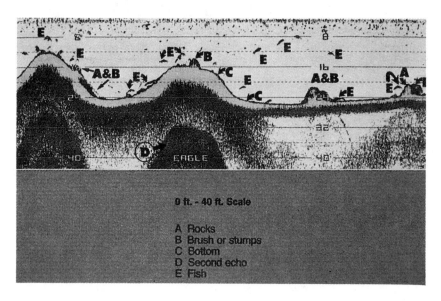

*Electronic fish locators have evolved into highly technological computerized units that can change scale, print out depths, and even print out fish as close as six inches apart.*

receiving the clearest possible picture, in full detail, of the bottom. Too much sensitivity will result in a garbled picture.

A graph recorder is equipped with a chart speed setting that does not exist on flashers. The chart speed determines how rapidly paper moves through the machine. And this is where a lot of anglers get into trouble. Graph paper is a fairly expensive item, but the tendency is to conserve paper by using the slowest possible chart speed, but this is a big mistake.

As a general rule, the chart speed should be positioned approximately at the ¾ setting. The deeper the water, the more slowly you must advance the paper because the expanding cone will be much larger at greater depths and the fish will spend more time inside the cone.

I do not advocate using a graph at speeds greater than five to eight miles an hour. A graph will provide a printout of the bottom even at 70 mph, but for high-speed running, it's best to rely on the flasher.

Fish will be displayed in a variety of ways, depending on chart speed, boat speed, and where fish pass through the cone. When you're trolling, fish will first be picked up at the outside of the cone. The stylus will note the presence of the fish and strike the paper, making a single mark. Remember, sound waves on the outer part of the cone travel further than those closer to the center. Thus, each time the stylus strikes the paper, the fish will be slightly closer to the boat. As the boat moves away from the fish, the distance increases, resulting in an arch across the paper.

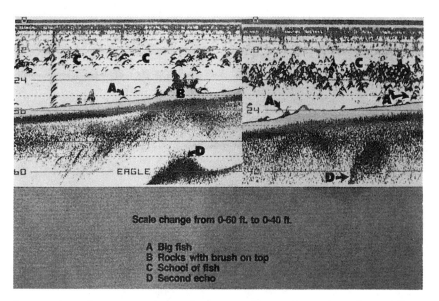

Scale change from 0-60 ft. to 0-40 ft.

A  Big fish
B  Rocks with brush on top
C  School of fish
D  Second echo

*Some units today are so advanced you can change the scale to "zero in" on fish and structure. Notice the change here from 0-60 to 0-40 feet.*

We have a tendency to think that every fish that appears on the paper swam directly under the boat. This, of course, is not the case. Some fish never get any closer than the extreme outside edge of the cone. Those fish will appear as gently rounded arches, like the letter "u" turned upside down.

A fish that passes directly under the boat will appear as a more sharply pointed signal, like the letter "v" turned upside down. The higher the peak of the arch, the more directly the fish passed through the cone. The rounder the peak, the further the fish was from the center of the cone.

You can determine the size of the fish by observing the peak, or that which appears to be the back of the fish. Usually, the thicker the peak, the bigger the fish. This can vary with boat speed, paper speed, depth of the fish and proximity to the center of the cone.

If the chart speed is set too slow, a fish will appear as a vertical line, like a piece of wood floating in the water. If the boat and fish are both motionless, the fish will be recorded as a horizontal line on the graph paper.

Many of today's better units have a grayline feature. The grayline can provide a wealth of important information. The grayline separates the bottom, making it easier to distinguish rocks, brush and fish. There

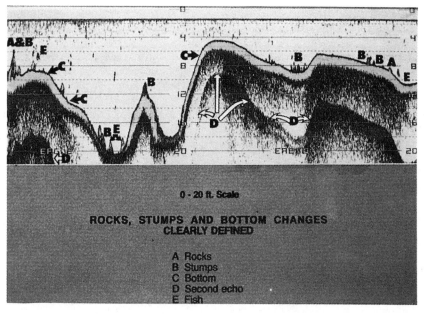

0 - 20 ft. Scale

ROCKS, STUMPS AND BOTTOM CHANGES
CLEARLY DEFINED

A Rocks
B Stumps
C Bottom
D Second echo
E Fish

*Rocks, stumps and brush are clearly visible on this section of graph paper. The second echo shows the unit is properly tuned and receiving a strong signal on a 20 foot scale.*

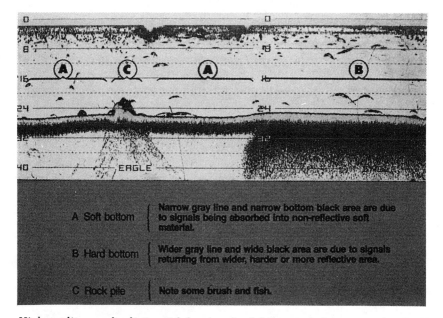

High quality graphs distinguish hard and soft bottoms. Soft bottoms absorb the sound waves and return a weak signal. Hard bottoms are highly reflective and return a strong signal.

will be a black line that represents the bottom, and an area of gray below that. The harder the bottom, the wider the grayline. As the boat moves over a softer bottom, the grayline will become smaller, in some cases disappearing completely.

Still, the operator is likely to have difficulty determining everything that's being displayed, especially with objects extremely close to the bottom. Some of the more sophisticated units, like Eagle's Mach I and Lowrance's X-15B, have one-inch resolution and can actually detect a fish that's only an inch off the bottom. If you see an arch on the bottom that's not completely connected–if there's just a slight break–chances are you're looking at a fish.

Lowrance and Eagle now make units specially designed for deep-water fishing and shallow-water fishing. Eagle's Mach 2 and Lowrance's X-155B are low-frequency, deep-water units which work well for off-shore or salmon fishing. These units have 45-degree cones that enable the fishermen to observe a great deal of real estate.

These units are not recommended for walleye fishermen. At depths of less than 50 feet the wider cone angle will pick up so much information that the angler really has no way of knowing what's under the boat. Fish that are being printed out may actually be 20 or 30 feet from the boat.

Walleye fishermen would be better off with the high-frequency, shallow-water units like the Mach 1 and X-15B. Each of these products boasts an incredible 1,600 watts of power. I've used both and believe them to be vastly superior to anything else in the marketplace.

As with the flasher, the final interpretation of a recording is up to the angler. With experience and lots of practice, you eventually will be able to determine a great deal about fish movements with the help of a graph.

For instance, if you see a group of loosely schooled fish, suspended a good distance from structure, chances are those fish are not active. But keep a close eye on that school. As it begins to bunch up and move toward structure, it will become active. And if you graph a large group of fish stacked on the tip of a point, you can expect some fast action.

Fish hugging the bottom are generally less active than those further off the bottom. If you're graphing fish three, four and five feet off the bottom, it's a good bet those fellows are on a feeding binge.

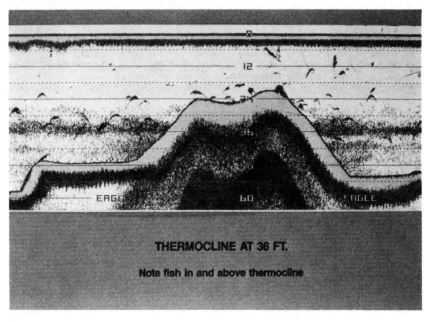

**THERMOCLINE AT 36 FT.**

Note fish in and above thermocline

*A thermocline by definition is a change in temperature of the water at a rate of two degrees per foot. That is a density change too, so the more dense water can send an echo back which will look like pepper specks in a uniform pattern and constant depth. Notice that the fish are prevalent in and above the thermocline.*

Much the same holds true for baitfish. If the graph shows a school of baitfish stretched out horizontally, those fish are probably at rest. And baitfish don't rest when walleyes are in the neighborhood. But if you encounter those same forage fish later in the day and they're mushroomed, they're probably being worked by predators.

I'll never forget the time Dan Nelson and I were fishing North Dakota's Lake Sakakawea. We'd been pounding a wind-swept island for nearly an hour without so much as a pickup. The fish should have been there, but apparently they were not.

We decided to pull out, but a quarter mile up the lake our flasher lit up like a Christmas tree. Using the graph for clarification, we noted several schools of smelt, the walleye's prime forage in Sakakawea, stretching from just under the surface all the way to the bottom in 60 feet of water. Those huge umbrella-like readings told us the smelt were being worked by walleyes. We returned to the island and waited for the walleyes to move. Within half an hour we started catching fish and within an hour we had a limit of nice walleyes.

Finding schools of suspended baitfish, whether it be smelt, cisco, or tullibee, can point the way to walleyes. Wherever there is food, there are predators close by.

Flashers and graphs are highly sophisticated pieces of equipment requiring certain care and maintenance. I strongly recommend that you not trailer your sonar devices on a boat. Boat trailers do not have reliable suspension systems and your equipment can take a real beating as you bounce down a gravel road. The circuitry in a graph, for instance, is nearly as complicated as that of a color television set. And I can't imagine anyone tossing a color TV into a boat and hauling it a couple hundred miles.

Over the years I've used Eagle and Lowrance products exclusively, and can honestly say I've never experienced a breakdown on the water. Dependability is an important criterion when considering which sonar device to purchase. But, I've always taken good care of my units, too. If subjected to undue punishment, even the most reliable unit will eventually fail.

I'd suggest you not trailer your boat with sonar devices on board. Get yourself a Johnny Ray swivel mount and store the unit in the back of your vehicle. If your unit gets wet, dry it out with a hair dryer or use the heater in your car. With Eagle's waterproof unit, that won't be a problem. With some units, it is a problem.

Take care of your sonar device and it will take care of you. It will last a long time, provide hours of dependable service and will help you locate structure and fish. Very simply put, I don't go on the water without my "electronic eyes."

## Rods and Reels

As part of a big promotion, I was fishing with two distributor sales-men, intending to demonstrate different products.

We were into a good "bite," taking four, five and six-pound walleyes about as fast as we could get our jigs to the bottom. Well, two of us were catching them that fast. The third fellow brought along two of his old fiberglass rods and had yet to put his first fish in the boat.

I could tell he was getting hits by the frequent retrieves to change bait. He said "weeds," but we both knew that weeds don't have teeth, and his minnows were practically ripped in half.

Now, I'm not exaggerating when I say two of us had caught and released between 40 and 50 nice walleyes while the other guy was waiting for his first catch. I tried to tell him he wasn't feeling the fish, but he insisted it was just luck.

After considerable prodding, I finally convinced him to try one of my graphite jigging sticks. Within minutes, he was wrestling with a nice walleye. Not only did that salesman have a good time, he also became one of the most enthusiastic promoters of graphite rods in the company.

The issue of fiberglass vs. graphite, vs. boron, vs. kevilar and all the other rod materials is likely to leave the fisherman somewhat bewil-dered. I'm not going to tell you what to purchase in the way of fishing equipment, wouldn't want to try. But, I would like to offer some guide-lines that might help you make a more intelligent decision when it comes time to pick up a new rod and reel.

First, there is no single rod-and-reel combination that will meet all your fishing needs. The rod that handles light line and small jigs will not be properly suited for deep-running crankbaits, spinners or Lindy Rigs. There are different tools for every job. I have nearly two dozen different outfits for walleye fishing alone. But, then I'm known as a bit of an equipment fanatic.

If Mr. Goodwrench set out to overhaul your $15,000 automobile with just a vice grips and a screwdriver, you wouldn't have much faith in his ability to get the job done satisfactorily. It's the same with fishing. One tool performs one function, and you'll need different actions and lengths of rods for different jobs.

Second, always purchase the best equipment you can afford. As we mentioned earlier in this book, faulty equipment probably accounts for more lost fish—and particularly big fish—than any other factor. I don't know about you, but I hate to lose big fish. For that reason, I always go with the best equipment available.

Third, when looking at rods, I'd strongly consider graphite. Graphite is far more sensitive, has a faster reaction time, more backbone and less weight than fiberglass. It will not only make each outing more enjoyable, it truly can put more fish in the boat. But don't think you can purchase a *quality* graphite rod for $19.95. I know they're on the market, but for that price, you're probably buying one or two strands of inferior graphite that may not even run the entire length of the blank. You get what you pay for.

*Babe with four dandy walleyes caught in cold water. A sensitive graphite rod made all the difference in putting this catch in the boat.*

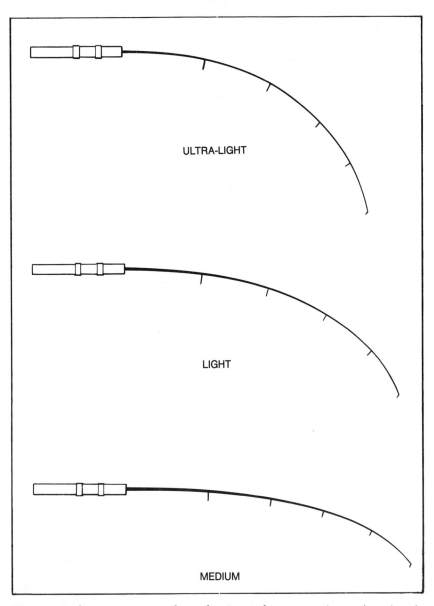

**Figure 7.** It always pays to match a rod action to the presentation you're using. A rod with an ultra-light action is preferred for casting small jigs. On the other hand, a light-medium action is better for larger jigs, and a medium-heavy action rod is best for trolling crankbaits.

Boron is a bit more sensitive and has a slightly faster reaction time than graphite. Personally, I own numerous boron rods. I'd say that if your budget allows it, go ahead and try boron. If you're on a tight budget, graphite will perform admirably and involves less expense.

Finally, always go with a brand name rod-and-reel. Today's angler has a wider selection of rods and reels from which to choose than at any other time in history. There are many excellent products out there in the marketplace. Unfortunately, there are also some products that simply will not stand up to consistent use. Some others I consider downright junk. That's why I stress purchasing the best equipment you can afford. You certainly don't want that once-in-a-lifetime trophy getting away because of a faulty tip guide or a reel with a poor-quality drag system.

If you're on a tight budget, but fish a lot, you can probably get by with four rod-and-reel combinations. I'd suggest spinning rods in ultra-light, light and medium action, and a baitcasting outfit with a medium action (see Figure 7). Obviously, you'd be better off with two outfits from each of these categories, but only your budget can determine how much you own in the way of equipment.

Ultra-light outfits are preferable for, basically, three situations—fishing a tiny jig for shallow walleyes, working a tiny jig for deep walleyes in ultra-clear water and sport fishing. Playing a big walleye on two, four or six-pound line is a real thrill. However, if you're into catch-and-release fishing—which I strongly encourage—you might want to stay away from ultra-lights. Playing fish on very light line usually results in dead fish, because of the necessity of tiring them.

For heavier jig fishing, casting weight-forward spinners and light crankbaits, I prefer a light-action rod with lots of backbone and a fast tip. For most of my rig fishing I'll go to a longer medium-action rod. The longer rods have more forgiveness when you're working a finicky walleye.

For trolling heavier crankbaits or spinners behind a bottom cruiser, I'll go with a baitcasting outfit that's fairly short (5¼ to 5½ feet) with a medium action and a super-fast taper. That soft tip allows you to feel the vibrations from the crankbait as it swims through the water.

Always be sure you have a balanced outfit. A spinning reel big enough to hold 200 yards of 20-pound test line and weighing 22 ounces would not work on an ultra-light rod. Try to match your gear to the type of fishing you're planning to do.

The most important thing to remember is to purchase balanced, quality equipment. The few dollars you might save on a bargain-basement rod or reel will eventually cost you money in repair or replacement, and more importantly, could possibly cost you a trophy fish.

## Boats and Motors

Take one of the more productive walleye lakes in the country, add 25 of Minnesota's best fishermen, stir in a wind strong enough to whip up 8-foot rollers, and you have the makings for what's become known as the "kamikaze tournament."

Officially called the Minnesota Invitational Walleye Championship, the event was sponsored by the St. Paul Pioneer Press. The site was Mille Lacs, a 130,000-acre walleye factory, located just east of Brainerd and about an hour and a half north of the Twin Cities. A good share of the entrants were members of Lindy-Little Joe's now-famous Black Hat Society. The Black Hatters were a group of promotional fishermen and/or guides who comprised the most elite collection of fishing talent in the history of the sport.

There was more than money at stake as 25 one-man boats headed out of Izaty's Resort on the south end of Mille Lacs that morning. It was a question of prestige, ego, status. Our pride got us into trouble, temporarily blocking the flow of blood to our brains.

The wind was out of the south, so it wasn't unusually rough at the start. But by the end of the ten-mile run to a series of reefs that had been producing fish during practice, we were bucking seven and eight-foot waves with two-foot whitecaps. It was rough—damn rough!

On the way out, Rod Romine, one of the original Black Hatters, watched his trolling motor rip loose and disappear into the lake. Not long after, Rod hit another bone-cruncher and broke the motor mounts on his 35-horse Johnson. Rod grabbed the motor with his left hand, pulled it back into the boat and shut it down by hitting the kill switch. In the process, he tore every muscle in the left side of his body.

In pain, but not to be denied, Rod kept going, his left hand holding the outboard and his right hand on the tiller. When he arrived at a reef, he dropped anchor, stashed the motor inside the boat and started casting. His first two casts resulted in two nice fish, but the force of the waves was so great that his anchor rope was cut on the rocks.

With no motor, no anchor and no trolling motor—to say nothing of some painfully torn muscles—Rod had no choice but to call it a day.

One of the first waves that hit my boat spilled a container of jumbo leeches. I arrived at the reef, dropped anchor and started to cast. I caught one quick fish before the boat started to fill with water, from the waves crashing over the bow. I switched on the bilge pump, but it was plugged with leeches.

My only option was to pull the drain plug and run the water out of the boat. As I was to learn, this was easier said than done. My anchor was wedged in the rocks and I was forced to cut the rope. That was only the beginning of my troubles.

I decided to head for the protection of Hennepin Island, where I'd overhaul the clogged bilge pump. There was so much water in the back of the boat that every time I'd climb a wave, the boat would sit on end, threatening to tip over backwards. Each time that happened, I would run the length of the boat, throwing my body on the bow to keep the boat in the water. It was a long, frightening, five-mile trip to Hennepin Island.

It wasn't until 1:30 that afternoon that I reached the island and was able to repair the bilge pump. Needless to say, I was happy to return to the weigh-in alive, let alone with a stringer of fish.

The second day was almost as rough as the first, but I managed to get to the reef without incident and caught three fish, each weighing about seven pounds. That left me in second place behind Denny Schuett of the Twin Cities. Denny and I caught our fish in the same spot.

Several boats filled with water during the two-day ordeal. Outdoor writer, Sybil Smith, pulled her brand new boat on a reef and watched the waves literally destroy her rig.

Randy Amenrud, another Lindy staffer, had one of the top stringers the first day, but was disqualified because a big wave flooded his engine and he couldn't get back in time for the weigh-in.

There were all kinds of special walleye boats in that tournament, from 20-footers down to 14-footers, and nearly every one of them had problems. Under normal conditions, most of the boats could have handled the lake. But these were abnormal conditions and we shouldn't have been on the water in anything smaller than a freighter.

That tournament illustrates one of the biggest problems faced by boat-buyers. The first consideration when purchasing a boat for walleye fishing is boat control, or maneuverability. But, at the same time, you'll want something large enough to safely handle the kind of water Mille Lacs was dishing out that day.

Let's face it, choosing a boat can be one of the most agonizing decisions a fisherman will ever have to make. There are so many considerations, so many options.

I'm going to attempt to make the decision a little easier by narrowing down some of the possibilities. When you look at the situation realistically, there are three factors you should consider when shopping for a fishing boat: 1) safety (comfort), 2) fishability (boat control) and 3) price (economy).

Forget about finding the *perfect* boat. If you want an outfit that will double as a family pleasure boat and will pull three water skiiers, you may as well opt for a pleasure boat and forget about fishing. Sure, you can fish out of any boat. But only a boat specially designed and equipped for fishing will be totally functional. The perfect boat simply does not exist.

The rig that will tame Lake Erie will not be adequate when it comes to back-trolling a tight contour on a small, protected lake. And the boat that's perfect for slipping the Mississippi River will swamp when the wind's whipping across a large reservoir.

Thus, the first question you must address is, "Where do I do most of my fishing?" Your objective should be to tailor your fishing rig to the type of water you're most likely to encounter. If you spend 80 percent of your time on smaller, protected waters, you should select a boat that's suited to that kind of fishing. If you devote 75 percent of your time on big, wind-swept lakes or reservoirs, you should purchase a suitable rig.

If your time is evenly split between big water and small water, you'll have to get as much boat as you can afford to serve a dual purpose. Or, if you can afford it, purchase a small boat, like a cartopper, to supplement your big boat.

The important thing is to give up the idea of finding one boat that will meet all your needs. If you seek the one perfect boat, you'll probably wind up with a boat that will be inadequate in just about every situation.

The next consideration should be hull material. The majority of walleye fishermen over the years have opted for aluminum hulls because of their durability. Many anglers would prefer fiberglass for its obvious benefits—it's quiet, smooth, and attractive. But they're afraid fiberglass wouldn't stand up to the kind of punishment serious fishermen can dish out.

My personal feeling is that the merits of fiberglass have been grossly underrated. Fiberglass can take more of a pounding than anyone might have expected. In some instances, fiberglass takes punishment better than aluminum.

The real advantage of fiberglass is hull design. Aluminum can be bent only so many ways. The configuration of a fiberglass hull is restricted only by the engineer's imagination. Fiberglass can be poured to fit, literally, any mold. As a result, the makers of fiberglass boats can develop hulls that are far more seaworthy than comparably sized aluminum boats. Glass, as a rule, is quieter than aluminum and, in most cases, the price differential is not all that great.

I'm not recommending that you eliminate an aluminum boat from your plans. There are some high-quality, durable, well-designed aluminum boats in the marketplace. I am only trying to point out that fiberglass should not be eliminated from consideration because of what someone may erroneously perceive as structural weakness.

Rounding out the performance team is the outboard engine you'll be hanging on the back of your new boat. And that's where things can become even more complicated.

If you're looking for the ultimate in boat control, you must consider tiller handle operation. But you can't legally go beyond 50 horses and still have a tiller.

In the old days, it was believed that nothing much larger than 10 or 15 engines would troll down slowly enough for a walleye fisherman. But thanks to modern technology, today's 50s troll amazingly slow.

It was only during the last few years that fishermen discovered the four-cylinder 50s from Mercury and Mariner. The old 50 Merc was a commercial offering that had never made its way into the fishing world. Anglers quickly discovered that the engine trolled as slowly, smoothly and quietly as 20, 25 and 35 horse engines. In some cases, more slowly and smoothly. They found it had all the conveniences of a smaller outboard with enough power to cover large expanses of water.

At one time everyone ran a 14-foot aluminum boat with a small engine, but now fishermen could step up to 16 and even 18-foot boats with a 50-horse. That fact, combined with the use of electric trolling motors and Boat Brakes, gives today's boat-buyer a lot more flexibility than he's had in the past.

Ideally, it would be nice to be able to hang a 75 or a 90 horse on the back of a 20 or 22-foot boat and still have the boat control capabilities of yesterday's cartopper. But I don't envision that happening in the foreseeable future. On the other hand, when I was a kid, I never dreamed man would ever walk on the moon.

By now you're probably thoroughly confused and wondering when I'm going to get to the bottom line. You're looking for some specific recommendations. Well, I can't tell you what purchase to make. But, I can talk about some specific boat-motor combinations that have satisfied my particular needs.

A number of years ago, I helped design the Ranger 1600-V. Through the years, that boat has undergone several changes. Today's 1600-V2 is the ultimate fishing rig for fishermen who spend most of their time on small or medium-sized lakes. The 1600-V2 handles well, tracks well, has good stability and superb floatation. It can safely handle reasonably rough water. I've run eight to ten-footers in my Ranger, but only out of desperation.

*The hull design and little "extras" make the Ranger Fisherman the nearest thing to a perfect, all-around fishing rig on the market today.*

Teamed with a 50-horse Mariner featuring tiller-handle operation, the Ranger is just about perfect for most of the natural lakes. With its low profile and modified V-hull, the 1600-V2 is less susceptible to wind drift and offers maximum boat control. It has a comfortable, roomy interior laid out with the fisherman in mind.

The Ranger 1600-V2 is not a good big-water boat. I have, on many occasions, made it home safely in six, seven and eight-foot waves. But the boat simply wasn't designed for that kind of water. And if waves of those proportions are common to the lakes you fish, perhaps you should consider another choice.

If you fish exclusively on big water the size of Lake Erie or Mille Lacs, I can't think of a better choice than the Ranger 380 Chief. The Chief will handle any big water you might encounter and get you back safely and comfortably.

Yet, like other large boats, what you gain in rough-water capability, you sacrifice in boat control. There simply isn't a boat that will do everything.

If you go with something like a Chief, you can strap up to 175 horses on the back, allowing you to cover a lot of water in a short time. Big engines don't have to drain your pocketbook at the gas pump, either. At ⅔ throttle, you'll be able to cruise at 50 miles an hour with gas consumption surprisingly low.

If you select a boat the size of a 380 Chief, you'll have to equip it with a high-thrust electric trolling motor, like Minnkota's 24-volt model 99 or 399. A pair of Boat Brakes (sea anchors) will help slow you down on those windy days. And I'd seriously look at two 70 horsepower outboards as opposed to a single 150 horsepower.

Even with all the options, you still won't have the turn-on-a-dime boat control capabilities of the 1600-V2, but that's one of the sacrifices you'll be forced to make.

*For "big water" like some of the major reservoirs across the country, you can't beat the spacious Ranger Chief 380.*

If you're fishing moderately large waters (not including the Great Lakes), there's another outfit you may find to your liking. Yar-Craft makes a fiberglass V-hull that's deeper and wider than the 1600-V, but small enough to be powered by a 50-horse. It's smooth, dry and quiet and offers excellent boat control, although it is subject to a bit more wind drift than the 1600-V2 because of a somewhat higher profile. Dan Nelson uses a Yar-Craft for fishing the Missouri River system and says it can handle anything you might encounter in a wind-swept reservoir.

Local prices vary, but the boats I've discussed will run anywhere from $5,000 to $8,000 for the 1600-V or Yar-Craft, and all the way from $10,000 to $15,000 for the Chief. The final price tag will depend on accessories.

Keep in mind that fishing is my business and I only buy what I consider to be the finest quality rig available. Cost is secondary to me. However, that may not be the case with you, so shop accordingly.

If your budget doesn't allow an expenditure of that magnitude, you'll be forced to look at something smaller. It's possible to purchase a 14 or 16-foot aluminum boat that will perform well under most conditions and, when teamed with a 25-horse Mariner, will be a bit more economical, but still fairly quick.

I've found that preferences in aluminum boats differ from region to region. A few of the more popular ones include Lund's Pro Angler, AlumaCraft's Backtroller and MirroCraft's Pro Angler.

If you get an aluminum boat in the 14-foot range, there are some 25-horse engines that are suprisingly powerful, giving you nearly as much speed as a bigger boat with a 50-horse.

Understand that aluminum boats, as a rule, will not be as quiet, smooth or dry as some of the glass boats. Your budget will have to dictate the choice you make. All of the major boat manufacturers have done a creditable job of developing boats designed specifically for the fishermen.

What about outboards? We've already discussed the Mariner 50. It's no secret that the Mariner and Mercury 50 are identical engines with slightly different cosmetics, the main difference being that Mariners usually sell for a few hundred dollars less than the Mercury. The 50s, with their four tiny cylinders, have exceptional trolling capabilities. My Mariner will troll as quietly, as smoothly and yes, as slowly, as just about any 25-horse that was ever manufactured. And with the boats we've been discussing, it's possible to attain speeds up to 30 miles per hour or greater.

The Merc and Mariner 50s are not without their drawbacks, however. One disadvantage is lack of torque. The four tiny cylinders do not have the torque to get on plane with an excessive load. The solution is to step down to an 11 propellor, which results in a slight loss of top-end speed. Some anglers have gone so far as to have specially cupped props built to solve the thrust problem.

Another handicap is the limited turning radius. The reason for going with a tiller-handle engine is maximum boat control. The limited turning radius of the Mercs and Mariners places some restrictions on what you can accomplish, especially in a wind. It's possible to add 10 to 15 degrees in either direction by drilling out the stops on the motor mounts. However, I can't endorse this practice because if drilled too far, the mounts could be weakened. Also, drilling could result in a voiding of the warranty. Insurance claims might also be voided.

The folks at OMC are also making some progress in the 50-horse category. Johnson has two large cylinders and, therefore, will not troll down as slowly as the Mariner. However, they do have a much wider turning radius and more torque coming out of the hole.

Dan Nelson has switched over to Johnson and is impressed with the performance. Again, there are sacrificies. Dan fishes the Missouri River system a lot and went to the Johnson because it seemed best suited for his Yar-Craft. Still, on those occasions when Dan needs to troll down to a crawl, his Johnson doesn't fill the bill. To compensate, he makes good use of his electric trolling motor and Boat Brakes.

The key element with any brand of motor is appropriate propping. Whether you like the Mariners like I do or the Johnsons like Dan, you'll find that neither will perform unless it has the right propellor. I always use a stainless steel prop rather than the standard aluminum. SST props have more bite and more durability. Have your dealer help you in selecting the right sized prop for your engine and boat.

There are several other things to keep in mind when narrowing your choices of outfits.

First, don't allow yourself to be swayed by the dealer's sales pitch. Carefully consider everything the dealer tells you, but do not accept his pitch as gospel. Dealers have a vested interest in everything they sell. If, for instance, one company is offering dealer incentives, that company's product may be pushed on you. Or it could be that the dealer is overstocked with one particular line of boat and wants to clean out his inventory. Listen to the dealer, because he's likely to be an expert on boats and motors. But take everything he says with a grain of salt.

Second, don't be overly impressed with cosmetics. Some boat manufacturers spend more time developing eye appeal than performance. If you select a boat that's strong on appearance but lacking in performance, you may have the best looking boat on the bottom of the lake.

Finally, test drive any boat before you write a check. If the dealer doesn't have one rigged up for the water, get the name of someone who owns one and see if you can arrange for a test ride. Pick a day when the lake is turbulent so you can discover how the boat performs in rough water. If it's not possible to actually ride in the boat, at least interview someone who owns one and get his honest opinion.

The hull, or overall performance, of the rig should be your number one priority as you narrow your choices. But this is a major investment. You'll probably own that boat for a long time and will spend many hours inside that rig. So choose a boat that will be functional inside and out.

Look at things like dry storage, rod lockers, roominess, interior layout, seats and pedestals—things that will provide comfort and convenience on the water. Lack of dry storage may not seem like an important factor on the showroom floor, but it can be a real annoyance when you're fishing in a downpour and your sandwich turns into a wet sponge.

The trailer you put under your new rig is also important. You may be tempted to cut corners when it comes to trailers. You're already spending more than your conscience allows, so it's easy to rationalize that it would be wise to save a few bucks on the trailer.

That, friends, is a mistake. You don't need a color-coded trailer with an electric winch, fancy pin-stripping and mag wheels. It looks nice and may bring a few extra dollars when it's time to sell or trade the outfit, but it's not necessary. Be sure that the trailer you choose will provide adequate support for the hull and offers ease of loading and unloading.

Today's drive-on trailers are, in my opinion, a must. Instead of standing up to your belt buckle in ice-cold water trying to coax the boat aboard, you drive right up to the winch stand. Some trailers are made to be driven on, others are not. Ask your dealer for a demonstration before you decide.

With fiberglass boats, you should purchase a bunk and roller trailer because of the extra support bunks offer the hull. An aluminum boat requires only rollers.

## Accessories

There are a handful of other options that fall under the convenience package classification. These options also qualify as budget breakers.

The first thing a dealer will want to add to your outfit will be power trim. We're talking about another $500 or $600 for this little gem. Power trim is not a necessity, but it's something this angler would not be without.

If you've spent much time pulling a 50-horse in and out of the water, you know what an exasperating and back-breaking task it can be. Power trim does the job with the push of a button.

Power trim offers other benefits as well. You'll come out of the hole more quickly with the motor trimmed all the way in, then you can trim it out for maximum performance when running. You can easily adjust the bow to accommodate different loads in all water conditions.

In big waves you can raise the bow accordingly. On calm water, flatten out the ride for maximum speed and fuel economy.

When pulling into or away from a shallow ramp, you can trim the motor out and save on props. Personally, I would not be without power trim. But as I said, it is not a necessity.

How about electric start? I used to own a manual start engine and most of the time had no problem. But with an extremely cold or flooded engine, you can jerk your arm off before she finally cranks over. Electric start isn't really that expensive an item. Without it, your arm may be too tired to cast a ⅛ ounce jig.

If you think these options overextend your budget, wait until you see the list of options waiting on the showroom floor. Some are necessary, others are luxuries. All of them can make you a more efficient angler. The final choice depends on how much money you have to spend on a fishing boat.

— Trolling motors. An electric trolling motor *is a must* for any serious walleye fisherman. Electrics enable you to move super-slow and offer absolute boat control. They are also much quieter, easier on the ears and don't spook the fish like a gas engine will. I have two electrics on my boats, a Minnkota 95 on the transom and a 395 on the bow. I have found the Minnkota to be very reliable, with plenty of power and low battery draw. Electrics provide boat control superior to that of gas engines which, at times, will be an absolute necessity. For actual walleye fishing, I use my electrics much more than my outboards.

— Graphs and flashers. I wouldn't put my boat in the water without a flasher. In fact, I have two Eagle flashers mounted on my boat, a 30' scale in the bow and a 60' scale in the back. A flasher isn't something you look at occasionally, it's a piece of equipment you keep your eyes glued to the entire time you're fishing.

I'm spending your money like crazy, but if you really want to become a more efficient walleye angler, a graph recorder is almost a must. I like the Eagle Mach 1 and the Lowrance X-15B. I've come to rely more and more heavily on my chart recorders. If you have to draw the line somewhere, a graph recorder is not a necessity. But I'd start saving my pennies and add one to the boat as soon as possible.

— Surface temperature gauge. On some bodies of water, the surface temperature can tell you a lot about what to expect from your fishing day. This is especially true in the spring of the year, when the fish are in their pre-spawn, spawn, post-spawn, and transition periods. A reliable performer is the Eagle digital temperature gauge. I have one in all my boats.

— pH Monitor. This is another item I wouldn't be without. A pH Monitor won't result in a good catch every time, but under the majority of conditions it will help you narrow your choices more quickly into a workable pattern.

*Understanding fishing electronics is a must to be a consistent walleye angler. Flashers, graphs, ph Monitors and temperature gauges all have their place.*

— Trolling speed indicator. This is a handy little device that has put a lot of fish in the boat for me. It's most effective when trolling at faster speeds using a crankbait or spinner. It is not considered a necessity, but it is a very good option.

— Boat Brakes. A good sea anchor like the Boat Brake can make the difference between a nice mess of fish and no fish at all. There are certain conditions when no boat, regardless of size, will slow down enough for an effective presentation. How do you slow down in eight-foot waves? I consider Boat Brakes an integral part of my total fishing system.

— Color-C-Lector. With this monitor you can discover the most productive color for different depths, water conditions and light conditions through trial-and-error. Or, you can eliminate possibilities quickly, using a Color-C-Lector. While it cannot be considered essential, I certainly plan to have one on my boat at all times.

— Marine band radio. For walleye fishing, a marine band radio is not a necessity. It could be a life-saver if you get into trouble on the water. And for salmon fishing, monitoring the radio can lead you to hot action. But when fishing for walleye on smaller bodies of water, it's not something you need.

— Oxygen meter. On some lakes, an oxygen meter can really help locate fish. On bigger bodies of water you can locate the thermocline with a good graph. On smaller bodies of water an oxygen meter might not be a bad tool. But it's not vital. As a rule, I don't carry one.

— Extra gas tanks. The amount of gas required on each trip is determined by the size of water you're fishing and how much gas your engine consumes. At times, on truly large expanses of water, you'll need as much as 18 gallons with a 50-horse. On most lakes, a six-gallon tank might last several days.

— Electric winch. Unless you have a really large boat, an electric winch isn't necessary. With a drive-on trailer, you'll never need to pull out more than a foot or two of rope.

— Temperature probe. A probe, like the Fish-N-Temp, will provide a temperature profile of the lake and can really be helpful. Being able to find the thermocline, or stratification, can eliminate unproductive water fast.

— Cigarette lighter. This may seem like a silly option, especially if you don't happen to be a smoker. But there's another application for a cigarette lighter. It provides a convenient plug-in for a spotlight, which is another important option. I haven't had many occasions to use my spotlight, but when it was needed, I sure was glad to have it aboard.

— Anchor. An anchor is an inexpensive item which, even though rarely used, is a necessity. If you only use it once a year, it's worth the minor investment. I have an anchor for both ends of my boat to keep the boat from whipping.

— Marine battery. You may get by cheaper buying a car battery, but I'd strongly suggest that you purchase a quality, deep-cycle marine battery (or two) for your boat. Deep-cycle batteries are designed to be drained down and charged back up. A deep-cycle battery will last a lot longer than a car battery. Gould and Exide make good ones.

— Splash guards. For anyone who does a lot of back-trolling in rough water, you can't get along without splash guards. There are some excellent commercial splash guards on the market, or you can make your own out of a few pieces of angle iron and some rubber mud flaps. Just hang them on the transom and they'll deflect the spray when you're back-trolling, keeping you relatively dry.

— Fire extinguishers and Personal Floatation Devices (PFD). It's just common sense for you to have both in your boat. Accidents can, and do, happen. And I don't want to lose any of my fishing friends.

Options, options, options. The whole works can cost more than a car. What you ultimately spend will depend on how serious you are about fishing and how liberal a budget you have to work with. But make no mistake, quality equipment can help you catch more fish.

# Chapter 6
# Patterns

## The Key to Success

*"If the fish aren't where they're supposed
to be, they're probably someplace else".*
**—Anonymous**

Clyde and Melvin run into each other at the boat landing. Clyde is just pulling out with a nice stringer of fish. Melvin arrived just in time for the evening bite.

"What'd ya catch 'em on?" Melvin wants to know, admiring Clyde's catch.

"Fuzz-E-Grubs", says Clyde.

"Where'd ya catch 'em?" asks Melvin, visions of any easy limit dancing in his head.

"Fox Island," answers his buddy.

You can bet your subscription to *Fishing Facts*, that Melvin will head straight for Fox Island, where he'll spend the rest of the evening dragging a Fuzz-E-Grub. Unfortunately, about 25 other guys had the same idea, and Clyde's hot spot is going to be just another disappointment for Melvin. The easy pickings are done for the day.

Now, if Melvin had a basic understanding of pattern fishing, there's a good chance he could have salvaged the trip. If he'd taken the time to ask Clyde a few pertinent questions about his catch, it might have been possible to duplicate those same conditions in a different section of the lake—one that hasn't been burned by fishing pressure.

In a sense, Melvin is pattern fishing. But he's just scratching the surface asking "what" and "where." Most patterns are more complicated than that.

There is no better way to consistently catch fish, any species of fish, than by taking the time to work out a successful pattern. A discussion of pattern fishing will constitute a major portion of this book.

By now you should understand the basic nature of the walleye and his seasonal movements. You should be familiar with the various types

*If Melvin had a basic understanding of pattern fishing, there's a good chance he could have salvaged the trip.*

of environment, structure, presentation, and equipment. All are fundamental aspects of developing a pattern.

Now it's time to take a closer look at the subject of patterns. Because only with a thorough understanding of how to establish and fine-tune a pattern can you hope to be consistently successful.

## What's a Pattern?

A pattern is, "a reliable sample of traits, acts or other observable features characterizing an individual." If you substitute the word fish for the word individual, you will have a workable definition of a pattern as it pertains to fishing.

Clyde had good fishing on Fox Island. But what observable features on that island were attracting walleye? Were the fish on a rocky point, a clam bed, or working the weedline? Were they hanging in deep water or in shallow water? Were they in boulders, gravel, or sand? Armed with the answers to these and other questions, Melvin might have been able to discern a crude pattern that would have helped him locate active fish on another, similar structure elsewhere in the lake.

Every pattern involves two basic elements—location and presentation. In their hurried exchange, Clyde and Melvin touched on the most basic of these components with "where" and "what." But in most cases, where and what are not enough. Sure, it could be that walleyes were scattered all over Fox Island and were hitting anything that came their way. It could also be that your name appears at the top of a newly found Howard Hughes will. It could be, but it's not likely.

My grandma used to make the best chicken in the world. I couldn't wait to get over to her house on holidays to eat that chicken. Now, it would be a mistake to assume that Grandma just tossed a chicken in the pan and hoped for the best. She had a very complete, very precise, recipe for her chicken. Try as they may, no one was ever quite able to duplicate Grandma's chicken because the old gal never revealed all the ingredients in her recipe. And chances are, it wasn't just the seasonings that made her chicken so special. It was probably little things, like the kind of pan she used, how long the bird was browned, or at what temperature she set the oven.

The same principle holds true with fishing. If just one tiny ingredient in a pattern is missing, it could throw off the whole recipe.

Spring transition is the only calendar period in the walleye's life cycle where a haphazard approach to pattern fishing could possibly yield a few fish. And spring transition is about the only time of year when fishermen enjoy much success. During that period, the walleyes will be loosely scattered on a variety of different structures, mostly shallow, and will be susceptible to a host of presentations. During the remainder of the year, however, your presentation will have to be more exact.

Developing a workable pattern is a lot like putting together a jigsaw puzzle. The first few pieces of the puzzle are always the most difficult. The more pieces that fall into place, the easier it is to finish the job. In fishing, until you manage to catch that first walleye, you're really in the dark. Once you're able to locate an active fish, you will have some of the information you need to finish the job. Thereafter, the pieces of the puzzle will start to fall together for you.

The essence of setting patterns is nothing more than the process of elimination. You eliminate the unproductive and concentrate on the productive.

Your knowledge of the water you've chosen to fish, prevailing weather conditions, water clarity, season, and time of day can all offer clues as to where you should start.

If you've picked a deep, clear body of water, and it's bright and calm, you can safely assume that the fish will either be deep, suspended, or tucked into the weeds. On a shallow, eutrophic lake with questionable oxygen levels, it's a good bet that the fish will be relating to the weeds. On a river, the amount of water being released through a dam could provide valuable information for a starting point.

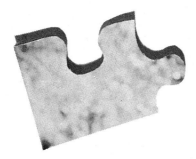

*Setting a pattern . . .*

Weather is a critical aspect of setting a pattern, as we've discussed at length in other chapters. Wind, wave action, sunlight, barometer, and the like, can all affect where the fish will locate and how active they will be.

Changes in weather can alter your pattern. If you're hammering fish at 15 feet with heavy overcast and a good chop, you can expect those fish might move deeper if the clouds blow away and the wind subsides.

An incoming cold front, and a quickly falling barometer, could trigger a feeding binge that will bring the fish in to shallow water. Pay close attention to all the weather conditions as you're setting a pattern, and be prepared to experience some changes in that pattern if the weather changes.

Early in the spring, you may find some walleyes hanging around the gravel shorelines or at the mouths of tributaries, where they spawn. In late fall, you should know that the walleyes will be hanging near the deepest water in the lake and will prefer a rocky bottom.

All of this knowledge will provide shortcuts to setting your basic pattern. Some of the sophisticated electronic gadgetry at your disposal can further hasten your search for active fish.

Taking a temperature profile of the lake, we find the surface water to be 78 degrees with only a slight change all the way to 18 feet. But from 18 to 22 feet, the temperature drops five degrees. We've located the thermocline. While the fish can, and will, penetrate that thermocline, we have established a good starting point in our search for walleyes. We'll work the water above the thermocline.

If we're working a weed-choked, shallow lake, it could be that oxygen levels will be a factor. This can be especially true if there have been several hot, calm days prior to our fishing trip. Oxygen levels throughout the lake can be greatly reduced under these conditions in late summer. And in that event, we'd probably start our search for walleyes either in the weedbeds, which give off life-supporting oxygen, or anyplace where we can find moving water.

We also will depend on our graph recorder to provide some valuable clues. By circling several key structures and watching for baitfish as well as predators, we may discover active fish without ever wetting a line. In the last couple of years, I've come to rely more and more on my Mach 1 graph to locate baitfish and gamefish alike.

With any luck, our equipment will have provided the answer to the first important question we must ask when setting a pattern, "How deep?"

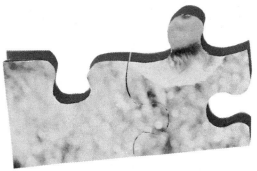

*. . . is something like putting together a jigsaw puzzle . . .*

Our knowledge of the system and the basic nature of the species should offer a clue as to which type of presentation will be most productive. On a clear, deep lake we'll probably start with some variations on the Lindy Rig. In a eutrophic body of water, we may well run a spinner on the outside edge of the weeds or toss a crankbait right into the weeds. However, the approach we would take would depend a lot on the time of year. For example, we probably wouldn't start with a crankbait in early spring, even on a weed-chocked eutrophic lake.

But, there's a whole lot more involved in presentation than just deciding to go with a Lindy Rig, a spinner or a crankbait. First, we must determine what type of live-bait dressing is likely to be most successful. One day that might mean using nightcrawlers, while the next day, fish might decide they want leeches or even minnows.

Keeping in mind our goal of eliminating the unproductive, we'll check all the possibilities before making a final decision. If there are three of us in the boat, we'll have one fishing with a crawler, one with a leech and one with a minnow. We're asking the fish what they want on that particular day.

Color can be a very important part of an overall pattern. With spinners, crankbaits and jigs, color is ultra-important. Remember what we learned in the chapter on color? Fish not only can distinguish between different colors, but also between different shades of the same color. We'll keep changing until we find the color that produces best for that set of conditions.

Speed is yet another vital element. With Lindy Rigs, slow is usually the only speed that will produce many walleyes. With spinners, crankbaits and, yes, even jigs, speed can be very important. In cold water you'll want to just drag a jig over the bottom, in warmer water a speedier retrieve, either swimming or hopping, will usually be more effective.

Action very often will make a world of difference. A jig, dragged over the bottom in July, may not result in a single hit. That same jig, controlled with big, sweeping hops might put several fish in the boat.

The importance of working out different presentations can't be stressed too much. Sometimes the most subtle variations can be the difference between a mess of fish and only one or two fish.

Direction can be an important consideration. Usually, you'll want to present any bait to the fish's mouth, which means trolling or drifting from the direction the fish are facing. This can be determined through trial-and-error. If you're getting lots of action moving east to west but no action, or very little, moving west to east, that should tell you something about how the fish are lying on the structure.

Sometimes, as we discussed earlier, changing directions will trigger a strike. As you get over the top of the school, make a quick about-face and come back at the fish from the other direction. You'd be amazed how many strikes this tactic will evoke.

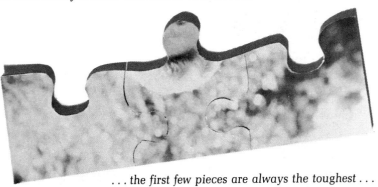

*... the first few pieces are always the toughest ...*

Wind very often plays a critical role in the development of a pattern. A sunken island on the windy side of the lake may be producing lots of nice fish. That island's twin, on the lee side of the lake, may not be holding any active fish because the wind isn't churning up the water. Wind is an important part of the overall pattern and should be given serious consideration as you fit together the pieces of the puzzle.

You may even have to take into account the direction and velocity of the wind on those days prior to your trip. Perhaps a north wind pounded the southern shoreline for several consecutive days, drifting plankton and algae and riling up the water. Even though it's calm the day you're fishing, the water is still much dirtier on the south side of the lake. And that could result in some active fish working the southern structures.

Next, we must establish what types of structures the fish are using. It's not enough to determine that fish are in the weeds. We must take that one step further and learn what kind of weeds. Are the fish tucked into the weeds or working the outside edge of the weeds? Are they working weedbeds adjacent to deep water or weedbeds in shallow water? Is there a mix of two varieties of weeds? What's the bottom content at the base of the weeds?

It's important that you be able to recognize the most obvious elements of a pattern very quickly. From there, you can begin to fine-tune the pattern until you have a complete recipe for the day's outing.

Remember that a pattern can change quickly. Fish working the outside edge of the weedbed, under a heavy overcast, could quickly tuck into the weeds when the clouds burn off. It could be that the fish are blasting an orange floating rig under cloud cover but prefer pink-and-white in bright sunlight.

There will be, in most cases, any number of productive patterns for a given body of water on a particular day. The primary pattern is the most important, but there can also be any number of secondary patterns.

It would be a mistake to think you'll be able to put together two or three productive patterns on each and every outing. It's more likely that you'll be lucky to zero in on one solid pattern in a day's time.

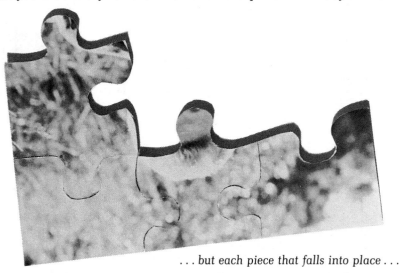

*. . . but each piece that falls into place . . .*

Let's say it's July and we're fishing a mesotrophic lake that's fairly deep and has good water clarity. We find fish up in the cabbage weeds in about 17 feet of water, and they're attacking a Lindy Rig tipped with a jumbo leech.

Upon further investigation, we learn that the only cabbage weeds holding fish are those that are extremely dense. Scattered weeds aren't producing much action. These productive dense weedbeds have gravel beneath them and break off very sharply from the primary breakline, which occurs at 17 feet.

Not every cabbage bed that duplicates those exact conditions is going to be holding fish. But it's a good bet a few other areas in the lake of the same description will produce similar results. That's the nice thing about a good pattern—it can be repeated.

Only under extreme conditions will the primary pattern be the only one that's producing. There could be several secondary patterns. In day-to-day fishing, secondary patterns probably aren't of much importance. But, in a tournament situation, having a handle on several secondary patterns could mean taking home first-place money.

In a tournament, it's likely that a few of the other participants will have figured out the primary pattern. So, get in there and slug it out with all the other boats, getting everything you can.

The ability to go point-hopping and pick a fish or two off several secondary patterns will give you the extra edge that separates the winners from the losers in competition.

Perhaps there are a few fish working a deep rock pile in the middle of the lake, more hanging on the tip of a long, tapering point, and others at the mouth of a tributary where in-flows of fresh water provide oxygen to attract baitfish.

Given enough time to develop patterns, you may well be able to pinpoint several such secondary patterns. None is likely to yield a tubful of fish, but they may provide the few extra bonus fish that'll boost your total over the top at weigh-in time.

There also are big-fish patterns and little-fish patterns. In some cases, a mere change in presentation accounts for a catch of mules as opposed to a catch of bank-runners. I've seen situations on some major reservoir systems where a Lindy Rig would take fish after fish, eating size, while a crankbait, worked over the same ground, would produce something closer to trophy proportions.

A jig tipped with a small fathead might produce lots of decent-sized fish during the fall period, but that same jig in front of a seven-inch redtail might entice a wall-hanger.

A rig-and-leech combination might produce small fish off a shallow rock pile in spring, but a salamander could call up that once-in-a-lifetime trophy. I think you get the point.

Often times I've found bigger fish lying just below small fish, or vice-versa. You may be hammering two to four-pounders in 16-feet of water while a school of six and seven-pounders is lying in 22-feet looking for something to eat.

Timing can also be critical in developing a pattern. When weather conditions remain stable for any length of time, fish become more and more patternable. By the third or fourth day after the passage of the last front, they may become downright predictable. An entire school might move onto a structure at 2:00 and remain there for half an hour before they retreat back to deep water. By paying attention to the time of day, you may be able to set up a schedule. Work Point A from 2:00 to 2:30, move to Point B from 2:30 to 3:00 and so forth.

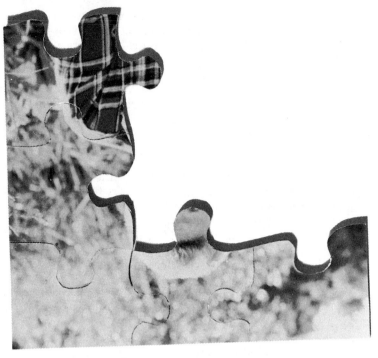

*... makes the job a little easier ...*

Most often it will be a little more complicated than that. The fish might move onto a food shelf at 2:00 one day, 2:30 the next and 3:00 the day after that. Obviously, it will require a little more time and effort to work out the details in that particular instance. I like to study the Solunar periods for this reason. Sometimes they will have an affect on feeding times, particularly in stable weather.

In past years I've noted a phenomena associated with moon phase. I've always believed very strongly that the moon affected the movements of fish. The biggest fish seem to be caught three days before the full moon and three days after the dark of the moon. In fact, records show that the majority of state and world records in all species were caught during these time frames. But I've seen another pattern unfold, one which cannot yet be substantiated with solid evidence. I pass it along as something to consider.

It seems that during the period around the full moon, just before the moon rises in the sky, bigger fish have a tendency to become active. Three days prior to the full phase, the moon will appear well before dark. Following this phase, the moon will appear over the horizon just after dark. I've taken some of my biggest fish during that half hour period just before the moon makes its nightly appearance.

There is more speculation than fact in my observations. But, it's something to keep in mind the next time you're fishing during the full moon phase.

There are other aspects of patterns, some quite obvious and others very obscure. I'll look at both in the coming section on fine-tuning a pattern.

*. . . how deep are the fish . . . ?*

## Fine-Tuning a Pattern

Big Sand is a 200-foot deep, pre-Cambrian lake, located on the Winnipeg River system in Manitoba.

Big Sand has a cisco, whitefish and perch forage base. It's full of rock and contains a ton of nice walleyes. It was the perfect setting for a major international tournament, sponsored by Hart Mallin of Payless Sales in Winnepeg.

My goal in preparing for this—or any—tournament, was to establish at least one primary pattern that I felt would hold up in actual competition. With only one day to pre-fish thousands of acres, I had my work cut out for me. I started by second guessing a pattern I thought would work.

I found big walleyes working cisco off the deep sides of rock humps, just like I'd hoped. Under normal conditions the fish would hold off the deep side of the hump in 30 to 32 feet. In a big wind, they'd herd those cisco right up to the tops of the humps.

Big Sand contains a lot of rock humps. But there were three key features common to all the humps that were holding good fish. First, they were in close proximity to the deepest water in the lake. Second, they contained giant boulders—not big rocks, boulders. And third, the humps topped out at 20 to 25 feet.

In presentation, there were two elements that constituted the basis for my pattern. When holding off the deep edge of the hump, the fish would tuck into the boulders and I'd have to yo-yo a quarter-ounce jig in front of their noses to take any fish. That changed dramatically when the wind came up and the fish moved to the humps. When the fish were "up," I'd have to pick up speed until the jig rode six to eight feet off the bottom. In some cases, I was using my electric motor to move five or six times faster than I normally would.

On the humps, I could take smaller walleyes relating to the bottom. But the bigger fish were riding up as much as eight to ten feet, herding cisco. In fact, a few times I could see cisco being chased right out of the water.

At this point, I felt my pattern was fairly complete. But when competing against some of the toughest guys in walleye fishing, you want to fine-tune your pattern one step beyond the obvious.

Through continued experimentation, I learned that the fish preferred a fluorescent yellow jighead tipped with a leech under dark conditions. When it was bright, they seemed to hit better on a raw, or unpainted jig. That little piece of information, I hoped, would put an extra fish or two on my stringer.

Scouting revealed another peculiarity about the way these fish were moving. When spooked, the fish would move down and away from the structure, suspending in deep water. I could follow them easily with my graph. I hoped that tidbit of information would also yield some bonus fish.

I'm certain there were other refinements I could have made in that pattern, but time is always a limiting factor in fishing, especially with only one day to scout. Besides, I had two days of competition to build on the pattern.

During the opening day, I put all the information I'd collected to good use. I took my share of fish early before the boat traffic spooked the fish. Most boats stayed on the hump, apparently hoping the fish would come back and be active. No one else knew where they went after they were chased off. I did. Following the school out to deep water enabled me to milk some bonus fish, and they put me well into the money after the first day.

On the second day of the tournament the wind changed direction. The rock hump that had been producing turned out only a few fish, then died. With heavy traffic on calm water, the fish were forced out to deep water where they developed a serious case of lock-jaw.

Having a solid pattern, one that I could duplicate on other sections of the lake, really helped to pay some handsome dividends. I needed a bunch of fish and I needed them in a hurry. But it was obvious this particular spot had kicked out its last walleye for awhile.

I headed to the windy side of the lake and ran the shoreline looking for a set of conditions similar to the area I'd been fishing. The fifth hump I encountered was a carbon copy of the first. It topped out at 20 feet, had a stairstep at 32 feet, was loaded with giant boulders and dropped off into deep, deep water. And best of all, there were four-foot rollers breaking over the top.

In the 40 minutes of fishing time I had to devote to this particular spot, I put 28 pounds of fish in the boat—enough to finish in second place.

I had a fairly precise pattern going in that tournament. But that's what it takes to get the job done. Had one ingredient been missing, I might not have finished nearly so high. Had I been able to polish that pattern another degree or two, I might have won.

It's one thing to find a pattern. It's quite another to fine-tune that pattern to 75 to 90 percent reliability. Paying attention to the most minute details often spells the difference between a successful pattern and a so-so pattern. For instance, had I not noticed the change in color preferences between light and dark conditions, it would have cost me two or three nice fish. And losing two or three of those fish would have dropped me out of the top ten.

Obviously, time can be a limiting factor when developing a pattern. Just how much time you devote to working out the fine details is a matter of judgement. Once you feel you've compiled enough information for a successful outing, you've accomplished what you set out to do. Still, you should study every possible feature and do as much experimenting as possible.

When you're sitting over a school of fish and the action is fast and furious, it's easy to become lax and just haul 'em in. But, when that spot goes sour, you're going to want to move to another area and catch more fish. Selecting a second productive site will only be possible if you've collected as much information about the first as possible.

On the other hand, you have to be able to distinguish between meaningful information and worthless information. For example, the fact that an island holding fish breaks off into the deepest water in the lake can be very significant. The fact that there's a reed bank 100 yards down the shoreline could be, but probably isn't, of any consequence. And the type of trees growing around the nearest cabin is not worth considering—usually.

Location and presentation are the key elements in building a pattern. Timing, weather conditions, and fishing pressure are also essential considerations.

Deciding which of these is most important in a given situation, is the challenge of pattern fishing. A fisherman, like a writer, begins each day with a blank page. Every observation must be dutifully recorded until the page is full. Then begins the process of editing. Some of the information collected will be meaningless, some of it will provide the clues necessary to build a pattern. Think of yourself as a writer, sifting through all the details to create the story line. Following are some of the items that should be weighed when fine-tuning a pattern.

First, there's depth. Depth can be divided into two categories. Obviously, it's important to determine the actual depth the fish are using. Second, there's the depth of water adjacent to the structure to be fished. In the case of the Minaki tournament, close proximity to the deepest water in the lake was of ultimate importance. Big Sand is full of rock humps, but only those with the immediacy of deep water were holding bigger fish.

A complete pattern may include several depths. The fish will be working one depth as they approach the structure, another depth when they become active and still another when they retreat into deep water.

Another consideration in fine-tuning patterns is the type of structure to be fished. You could be dealing with points, islands, bars, humps, weedlines, flats, backwater areas, wingdams or any of a hundred different structural configurations.

For purposes of this discussion, let's deal first with a point, one of the more common types of structures.

Should you locate a school of active fish on a point, you'll want to know several things about that point. You'll want to discover if it's a long point, a short point, or an average-sized point. You'll want to determine where the fish are lying in relation to the point—on the top, on the side or off the tip.

Ask yourself what features about this point make it different from other points? Why is this particular point attracting and holding fish? If there is rock on the point, try to determine the size of the rock. In some cases the fish will be relating to giant boulders, some of them the size of small automobiles. In other cases, rocks the size of basketballs will attract the fish. In another instance, baseball-sized rocks may be scattered over a gravel bed. Or, gravel may be surrounded by a muck bottom, or a muck bottom with emerging weed growth.

Note the weed growth around the point. Is it a thick weed growth or is it sparse? What kind of weeds are you dealing with? Walleyes

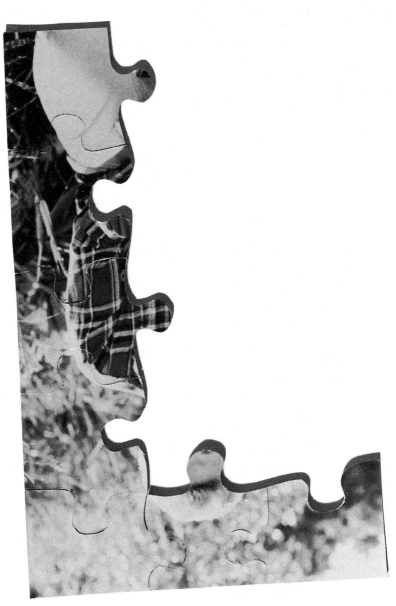

*. . . what type of structure are they working . . . ?*

have an affinity for cabbage weed. But they could be relating to coontail. Or, the weeds could be a mixture of cabbage and coontail. You may even find walleye relating to sand grass or reeds.

Study the edge of the point for a stairstep ledge, rock piles and the like. Consider the angle of the sun. If there is a stairstep, the walleyes may be lying on the shaded side of the point. If that's the case, you may see them moving as the sun rises in the sky. In the spring of the year, I've seen walleyes avoiding the shade. In cool water, rocks will absorb the sun's rays and serve as a radiator to attract baitfish which, in turn, attract walleyes.

Check for inside turns, secondary points, hooks, or outcroppings that may serve as holding areas for active fish. Fish may be on the shallow side of the point or on the deep side of the point.

Under ideal conditions, several schools of fish may be working the same point. Discover which structural feature is holding the bigger fish and which is attracting small fish as quickly as possible.

Wind direction can be of critical importance. Is the wind hitting the point directly, is it coming in at an angle, or is the point located on the calm side of the lake? I've seen several instances where the fish were relating to wind-swept points but were actually lying behind the points in a protected area. The wave action was acting like current, washing food towards the fish. But the fish were hiding around the corner in a slack-water area.

Wind, sun and current will all affect the position of fish on a structure, and that's an important consideration. Weather may also dictate fish movement on a structure, and that's another concept you should try to understand.

Now, let's look at islands, one of my favorite walleye structures. One of the most vital aspects of an island is the depth at which it tops out. You may be hitting good fish on an island that tops out at 18 feet. When the action slows, you move to another, almost identical island, but no fish are present. The only difference between this island and the first is that this one tops out at 23 feet.

On the major reservoir systems, which experience constant water level fluctuations, a different situation occurs. One year an island will produce an abundance of walleyes. The next year, with another five feet of water over the top of that same island, not a single fish will be produced.

Determine if the island is connected to a point by a saddle. The presence of a saddle gives the fish options that wouldn't exist on an island without a saddle. A saddle provides the fish with an option to work the island if conditions dictate, or to move back to the point by way of the connecting saddle. The saddle serves as a bridge that links point fish and island fish. I'm not implying that only islands with saddles attract walleyes. But the availability of a saddle is another feature to consider in developing a pattern.

In some waters, especially in major rivers and reservoirs, trees and stumps will be an important feature in a pattern. Believe it or not,

*. . . what's the bottom content . . . ?*

*. . . the availability of deep water . . . ?*

tumbleweeds that blew into the lake the previous fall will hold spring-time walleyes on some of the bigger reservoirs.

We can't possibly outline all the structural elements that may be vital to a pattern. There simply are too many variables. The final interpretation rests with the fisherman. The most obvious and the most fundamental pattern components include depth, access to deep water, bottom configuration, bottom content, weed growth or lack of it and weather conditions. There are other, more subtle factors that, in some cases, will be of prime importance. The more observant you are, the more easily you will establish these obscure factors.

Seasonal changes have a big impact on which factors are most important in setting your pattern. For instance, early in the year when the water is so cold that fish are inactive, water temperature is about the most critical factor of all. You're then looking for any water warmer than the majority of the cold water. At times like this, I'll rely on my Surface Temp gauge more than my graph. Differences of a degree or two can be critical in determining when and where walleyes will get active.

During the summer months I'll not worry so much about temperature as about such things as structure, the forage base, water clarity and the prevailing weather conditions. Temperature, if important now, has its main impact by the way the thermocline sets a lower limit to where walleyes will feel comfortable.

The weather factor is obviously important, yet its effects have not been completely figured out by any fisherman I've ever known. Changing weather sometimes improves your fishing and sometimes hurts it. In my experience, the 12 hour period prior to the passing of a major cold front can produce unbelievable action—but not always. The impact of a front depends on the weather that preceded it, the weather that will follow behind it, and the overall magnitude of the change.

One thing I'm sure of—the best fishing is brought about by periods of stable weather when the barometer isn't going up and down and when it's a joy to be out on the water. You certainly don't have to have nasty weather to catch walleyes, though we've often heard that.

But weather is just one of the elements that make up a pattern, and not an element you can do much about. Concentrate on defining the key aspects of any piece of structure that gives you good fishing. Don't think of it as a single "spot" but as a *type of place* that is holding active fish. If you do a good job of figuring out what is most important about that spot, you're on your way to finding other spots like it. That's pattern fishing, and it's the only way to catch fish consistently.

While you're recording your observations about the most important locational patterns, don't forget to experiment with presentation.

The first, and most obvious, element of presentation is the family of lures used to produce fish. Very basically, the possibilities include rigs, jigs, spinners and crankbaits.

Let's assume that on a particular lake it becomes obvious that rigs are going to produce the most fish. You should immediately start experimenting with variations on a rig pattern.

Included among these variations might be length of snell, live-bait dressing, color (in the case of a floating rig), line size and the size of live bait.

Of these considerations, live-bait dressing is probably the most crucial. If the fish want crawlers, you'll be wasting your time fishing a leech or minnow. If they want large minnows, as is often true in the fall, you may not take a walleye using three-inch fatheads.

When using floating rigs, experiment with depth by moving the float closer to and further away from the hook. And don't get locked into one color. Black may produce a stringerful of fish while orange results in only a modest catch.

I discussed presentation variables at length in a previous portion of this book, so there's really no sense repeating myself here. The important thing is that you not underestimate the importance of changing your presentation to meet the needs of fish on a given day.

Speed, direction, action and color are all factors to be explored. Maybe the fish want a yellow jig tipped with a small fathead and they want it moved rather quickly in long, sweeping hops. If you're slowly dragging a green jig, tipped with a leech along the bottom, you'll think you're fishing the Dead Sea.

Establishing the proper presentation is strictly a matter of experimentation and observation. If you try enough different combinations and pay close attention to what's happening, a solid presentation will often times become quite obvious.

For example, I was trolling a spinner along the outside edge of a weedbank on a shallow, off-colored carp lake. I was taking a few fish off the face of the weeds, only the action was anything but fast.

While making a turn to go back down the weedline, my partner stuck a really nice walleye. Was it a fluke? I decided that, since his line was on the outside when we made the turn and thus momentarily picked up speed, perhaps speed was the critical factor here. Sure enough, by running through the same area, half again as fast as we'd been moving, we started catching fish consistently. And the fish were a lot nicer than those we'd been catching.

In this case, speed was the main ingredient in the recipe. Once I'd found the right speed, it was easy to determine the rest of the pattern. Blade size, color and live bait all came into focus quickly once I found the right speed.

On another day, it might be blade size that makes the difference. Or blade color. Speed might be of secondary importance. That's the way it is with patterns. There will be one or two elements of primary importance and several factors of secondary importance. Fine-tuning can be relatively simple once you discover the primary factors.

But, as I said earlier, it's easy to get lazy once you find something that catches fish. If a crankbait is catching a few fish, why mess around with anything else? Why experiment with different styles or crankbaits? Why change colors? Why alter boat speed? You're catching fish, so why fool around?

*. . . what type of lure do they want . . . ?*

Well, it could be that going to a different style of crankbait and altering speed will not only take more fish, but will result in bigger fish to boot.

The point is, you'll never know unless you try. It only takes a few seconds to cut off what you're using and tie on something different. Once you get a sniff of a workable pattern, you should imagine yourself a detective who's narrowed his list of suspects to a handful. Now's the time to get serious. You should be going through your tackle box so fast that sparks are flying.

*. . . what color . . . ?*

Perhaps I can further illustrate the concept of a good pattern with a series of examples. When discussing these examples, I won't attempt to outline the entire pattern. I'll concentrate only on the one or two features that made each so unusual.

## The Every-Other-Day Pattern

Following is one of the most off-the-wall patterns I've ever been confronted with, but recognizing it helped me attain a strong finish in a tournament.

During my pre-fishing, I ran into some good concentrations of fish. I had half a dozen good schools of walleyes pegged and was having trouble trying to decide where I should open the tournament.

I decided on a long point that had been producing the best-sized fish during our scouting. This spot had been so productive that I left it alone the day before the tournament.

Right out of the chute I headed for the point and immediately started catching nice fish. Staying away the day before seemed to have paid off because there wasn't another tournament boat in sight most of the morning. But, by late morning a group of non-tournament fishermen moved in and within an hour most of the action had stopped.

Next, I moved to several areas that had been hot the day before. Nothing. I stopped and thoroughly fished six or seven such spots without turning a single fish.

That evening, I pored through my memory bank looking for some sort of logical pattern to the fish activity. I visited with a few of my friends who had fared poorly. They all had the same complaint: "We killed 'em yesterday, but they were gone today." Since there had been no change in weather for several days, the slow activity simply didn't make any sense. It almost seemed that different areas were productive on an every-other-day basis. And that was a situation I'd never before encountered.

I had a hunch. Armed only with a notion, I decided that on Sunday I'd only fish areas that had been good on Friday. If my every-other-day theory was correct, Saturday's hot spot would be devoid of fish.

Now, don't think for a second that it isn't tough to turn your back on a spot that put you in tenth place after the first day. I knew that several of the teams ahead of mine would falter the second day, and that we could probably move into the top five with a performance similar to that of opening day. But we ignored the point that had been so productive on Saturday and went back to the spot that had been poor the first day.

Sure enough, we'd taken a nice limit of fish by noon and spent the rest of the day high-grading until we took a stringer that boosted us all the way to second place. What's even more interesting is that the point that had been so active on Saturday didn't produce a fish on Sunday. Not one.

... *what live bait dressing* ... ?

## The Pressure Pattern

When you get into a big bite, there's a good chance that other fishermen will show up to help you catch some fish. Let's face it, a lot of anglers don't look for structure, they look for a crowd of boats. On most of the more popular waters in the country, excessive fishing pressure is the rule rather than the exception.

*... pretty soon the pieces start falling into place and ...*

I was confronted with this situation one fall while fishing a large reservoir that had been producing some big, big walleyes. The fish were hanging on a long (more than a mile) shelf that dumped into the main river channel at 100 feet.

Easily the most productive spot along the entire length of the shelf was a hard-bottomed, gradually tapering point on the west tip. I started the day working that point and quickly put several walleyes in the live well.

But each time I pulled out the net, it was like waving a red flag in front of an angry bull, and before long I had two dozen boats on my hot spot.

Since it was a calm day, the fish were easily spooked and none of us enjoyed much success. In most cases, fish that are driven off a structure by heavy traffic will retreat into deep water. But in this case, the walleyes had another option. They could also move laterally along the mile-long shelf to one of several secondary sub-structures.

The fish had been active in 20 feet, so I followed that contour along the shelf until I came to a small rock pile. There I caught a ten-pound, four-ounce walleye. Further down the shelf was a little hook which produced another big fish, this one about nine pounds.

By staying out of the traffic I was able to catch several nice walleyes while the area that should have been holding fish produced a big zero for all those other boats.


### The Sun Pattern

Working the outside edge of a weedline with a jig-and-leech combination was producing some decent walleyes for me. It was a dark day and the fish were really popping.

Every once in a while there would be a break in the cloud cover and the action would stop. I assumed that with a bright sky, the fish either retreated into deep water or tucked into the weeds. I tried both areas, but couldn't locate any fish.

The sun appeared intermittently and the fish continued to bite and retreat. I simply couldn't locate them when the sun was out.

Finally, it occurred to me that the change in light conditions might affect the way those fish were perceiving color. Sure enough, by switching to a different colored jig when the light changed I was able to continue to catch fish along the edge of the weedline. They hadn't moved at all, they just required a different presentation.


### The 2:00 Feed

Timing can be a very important part of any pattern. Once, while preparing for a tournament, I got into a nice mess of fish on a tiny sunken island.

Visiting with some of the local guides, I was surprised to hear the island had been inactive for weeks. No one had been catching any fish there. Yet, I'd managed to take fish two days in a row. In fact, it was the only place on the whole lake that had produced fish in mid-afternoon.

*. . . you've established a pattern for . . .*

That little island was so good to me in practice that I decided to open the tournament there. After about an hour, I was convinced that the guides were right. I hadn't had so much as a bite.

I worked a number of other areas until something occured to me. The first two days I'd fished that island at exactly 2:00. By the time the light went on in my head, it was nearly 2:00, so I headed straight for the island. I caught several nice fish.

For some unknown reason, the walleyes had been moving up on that island from 2:00 to 2:30 each day. And by hitting that spot at 2:00 each afternoon I milked enough bonus fish to win the tournament.


## The Underneath Pattern

Everyone knows that Lake Erie's walleyes suspend and herd smelt and alewives. The best way to catch walleyes in Erie is to toss a weight-forward spinner and bring it back through the school.

Gary Roach likes to break tradition. And his ingenuity really paid off in a major tournament on Erie. There were lots and lots of fish being caught by casting and counting down a weight-forward spinner. The fish seemed to come out of a mold—all the same size.

Gary knew that in order to win the tournament he'd have to devise a way to snag a few bigger fish. To accomplish this, he rigged up a Red Devil spinner behind a heavy bottom cruiser and worked underneath the main school, right on the bottom in 25 feet. And there, under those heavy concentrations of smaller fish, lay some bigger fish. Those bigger walleyes enabled Gary and his team to win the tournament and $25,000 in prizes.

If I sat and thought about it long enough, I could probably come up with a thousand pattern stories. Every successful outing has a pattern and just about every pattern is unique.

Usually, the pattern consists primarily of one or two key features. Find those primary elements and you've won half the battle. After that, it's a matter of examining every possible detail until that pattern is fine-tuned.

Establishing a pattern requires the versatility to try different approaches and a mind sharp enough to see the obvious, even when it's not so obvious. The fish will provide little clues. You just have to be alert enough to pick up on those clues.

Patterns are the essence of walleye fishing. Rest assured, there will be days when you simply won't discern any kind of pattern. It's not that you aren't smart enough. As the late Vince Lombardi used to comment on his Green Bay Packers, "We never lost a game, we just ran out of time." Setting a pattern is time-consuming, and often there won't be enough hours in a day to get the job done. But it sure is fun trying.

*. . . success!*

# Chapter 7
# Specific Patterns

## What Works on Your Water?

*"The ignorant man marvels at the
exceptional; the wise man marvels at the
common; the greatest wonder of all is the
regularity of nature."*
**—George Dond Boardman**

An old guide's trick is to check the stomach contents of any walleye he catches. Finding out what fish are feeding on today, can tell you a lot about where you might find them tomorrow. Imagine my surprise when, while cleaning a mess of walleyes, I found their stomachs full of wood chips.

Now, there's a forage base you don't often run across . . . wood chips. But, believe it or not, the presence of those wood chips put me onto a dynamite walleye pattern.

I was on a popular Midwest reservoir, fishing the edge of the old river channel in 15 to 18 feet with spinners. It was spring, right in the middle of the transition period. While I was taking few fish, the action was anything but fast and furious. I was putting in long days for only a handful of walleyes. That's not uncommon during the transition period, when walleyes are often scattered and tough to pattern.

This particular reservoir was rising fast, following a snowy winter and a wet spring. The rising water freed a lot of logs that had been high-and-dry on the shoreline for several years and were now floating everywhere. It was a boater's nightmare.

As the wind changed, that floating forest shifted from one side of the reservoir to the other, stacking against the shoreline for several days at a time.

Finding wood chips in the stomachs of walleyes suggested that perhaps those fish were spending some time right up under the timber in the shallows. The fish I was catching had moved down to the first break, but the majority of the active fish were working the shallows under floating logs. All that debris was holding a lot of minnows, which I was also finding in the fish stomachs.

It was worth a try. Next day I moved closer to the shore and experimented with spinners and shallow-running minnow baits, using the electric motor to move as close to the logjam as possible. Boy, did my luck change. I started smacking fish consistently, only a few feet from the breakline I'd been fishing the day before.

That's the way it is with patterns, sometimes. Clues can come from the most unusual places. The key is putting those clues to work so you can solve the puzzle as quickly as possible. It's called listening to the fish.

This chapter will address specific patterns, patterns that have produced fish in the past. I'll include patterns for rivers, reservoirs, and each of the three different types of natural lakes. I'll categorize them according to the seasons.

Remember, it's up to you to set the parameters of a pattern. I can't possibly tell you exactly, detail for detail, what pattern is going to be effective on a given day. These examples can only be described as guidelines.

I'd suggest that whenever you're out to set a pattern, don't waste a lot of time working any one spot. What you're seeking is active, aggressive fish. Once you get an indication that an area is holding walleyes, you can begin the process of refining the pattern using the information we discussed in the last chapter.

These are patterns you can anticipate on lakes you fish regularly. But, don't expect everything to fall into place as described here. There are far too many variables involved for that. Simply look for the basic pattern I'll be outlining and take it from there. Fine-tuning the pattern until it's productive will be your job.

## Spawn Patterns

For purposes of discussion, I will include three seasonal periods under one heading. I'll be talking about pre-spawn and post-spawn walleye patterns.

In many sections of the country, fishing is closed during the pre-spawn and spawning periods. The fishing season begins while the fish are still post-spawn. But in areas that allow year-round fishing, it may be possible to capitalize on some of the following patterns.

## Rip-Rap Walleyes

On many of the country's man-made reservoirs, fishing season is open year-round. Catching walleyes during the spawn is tough, but this is one pattern that makes it possible.

I first encountered this pattern on the Missouri River system near Chamberlain, South Dakota, but it works equally well anywhere rip-rap exists. Rip-rap is a very large rock used for bank stabilization along the faces of dams or where highways or railroads intersect a reservoir. Rip-rap also serves as an ideal place for walleye spawning activity, and, in some cases, is the most ideal spawning habitat in the entire area.

It stands to reason that you're going to have a lot of walleye activity in these areas around spawning time. The fish will move in when the water warms to the lower 40s and could be around until the water pushes past 50 degrees.

But, you don't catch walleyes that are spawning, right? Wrong. Males are actually quite easy to catch during the spawn and, occasionally, you'll even take some bigger females.

The best fishing occurs at night when walleye move into a couple feet of water to carry out the courtship ritual. You can take them during daylight hours as well, but it will be necessary to drop down deeper during the day. And your chances of taking a big fish get slimmer.

Since rip-rap areas are basically structureless, this is a simple way to fish. You just run the boat parallel to the rip-rap and as close as you can safely get to the rocks. The best bait is a floating, minnow-type lure like the Lindy Baitfish or Cordell's Redfin.

Color choices will vary from blue and black to blaze orange strawberry blonde. As a rule, the darker colors are best, but you'll have to experiment.

Since the boat will be moving along in extremely shallow water (three to five feet), you may figure you'll take every fish out of the country. But that isn't necessarily the case. You will want to long-line the fish, running 75 to 125 feet of line behind the boat. And using a long (six to seven-foot) rod will help you stay a little further from the shore. As the boat passes over, the fish may scatter. But they'll quickly return and will be back in position by the time your lure comes along. Actually, these spawning fish are pretty bold and don't spook all that easily.

The first time I saw this pattern being practiced, I was absolutely amazed. Bob Propst, a well known angler from Nebraska who guides on the Missouri River, was fishing down the rip-rap along the interstate highway crossing near Chamberlain. He was running in just a few feet of water using his outboard engine. And to top it off, he had a big old camping lantern sitting next to him, lighting the area with a spotlight effect.

I'd always believed that if you sneezed or lit a cigarette near water that shallow, every fish in the country would high-tail it to deep water and not return for hours. But Bobby was hammering fish right and left. He took an easy limit in just a few hours.

As I said, most of the fish will be males. But occasionally a six or seven-pound female falls for this tactic.

Speed can be a critical consideration in this type of fishing. If the walleyes are spawning, or getting ready to spawn, we're talking about cold water. The fish will move into the rip-rap areas early and will probably still be around when the water warms to the lower 50s. In cold water, the fish's metabolism is low and they're not about to chase down a fast-moving bait. You'll want to move as slowly as possible, perhaps using an electric trolling motor when the water's calm.

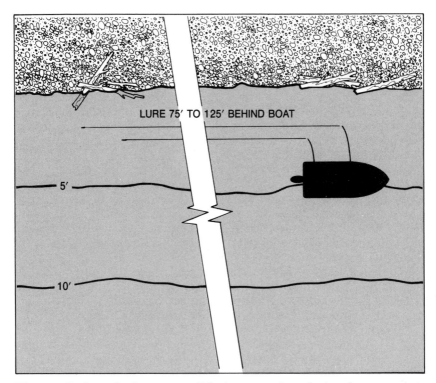

**Figure 1.** Perhaps the best way to fish rip-rap sections during the spawn is to troll parallel to the bank with a minnowbait. With this method you can catch smaller, more aggressive males, and an occasional big female.

## Dragging the Channel

Here's another pattern that works extremely well for pre-spawn walleyes, this one for rivers.

Remember that river fish are constantly on the move, particularly around spawning time. It's not unusual for walleyes to make several false spawning runs during late winter, running all the way to the dam before turning around and heading back downstream.

There are two things I look for when seeking pre-spawn river walleyes. One is an S-curve in the river channel and the other is a large food shelf adjacent to the channel.

You may find fish lying right in the channel in 20 to 30 feet of water and right off the edge of that large food shelf. Or, they may be concentrated around an S-curve in the channel.

I'm talking about the period prior to the actual spawn—February and March—in the northern tier of states. These fish are actively feeding to build up as much strength as possible for the spawning ordeal. At this time, the water temperature is 34 to 38 degrees. So, while the fish are feeding, they're not "chasing," and a slow presentation is called for.

In some areas, you can use a Boat Brake to slow down your drift speed. In moving water, you'll want to use the electric motor to slip the current, holding boat speed to a crawl.

By far, the best lure for this kind of fishing is a jig-and-minnow combination, like the Fuzz-E-Grub. I've had some of my best luck with hot yellow-green and brown-orange, but color preferences will change depending on water clarity and light conditions. It's imperative that you drag the jig along the bottom.

I can't emphasize this point enough. I recall a trip Wayne Ecklund and I made on the Mississippi River a number of years back. We located an S-curve in the river and a sandbar in the middle of the channel. The walleyes were stacked on that sandbar in 12 to 14 feet of water. As the current hit the leading edge of the bar, it boiled over the top, creating a slack-water area over the surface. This provided an ideal food shelf for hungry walleyes.

We took a limit of walleyes, ranging from 4½ to nine pounds, on that chilly March afternoon. I was catching most of the fish by just dragging my jig across the bottom. Wayne was putting a little action on his jig and wasn't having much luck, at least with big fish.

I wasn't about to reveal my secret, but Wayne figured it out when he put his rod down to light a cigar. It was breezy and he had trouble getting that stogy going. Obviously, with his rod stationary, the jig was just dragging along on the bottom. That's when he caught his first big fish of the day—a nine-pounder.

Keep in mind that when you're fishing lethargic walleyes, you aren't likely to experience any violent hits. Often as not, it will just feel like

**Figure 2.** *"Dragging" a jig is a good way to catch slow, negative walleyes. The slow, methodical action indicates the jig is an easy meal that takes little effort to capture.*

your jig fell into a cup of molasses it will feel heavy. If you suspect your jig may have fallen into a walleye's mouth, put a slight pressure on the fish by raising the rod tip, then set the hook with a quick snap of the wrists.

Once in a while you'll pull in a weed. But, you'll be surprised how often it'll turn out to be a walleye. Remember, the key to this pre-spawn pattern is s-l-o-w.

## Shield Lake Spawners

I discovered this pattern years ago fishing a Canadian Shield lake while the walleyes were actually in the spawn.

I was looking for large gravel or sandy flats, typical spots where the walleyes would spawn. But I wasn't finding the walleyes on the spawning grounds. Oh, I suspect the little males were up there most of the day. But the bigger fish were hanging on rock piles, just below the edge of the flat.

It's important to note that I didn't find walleyes all along the edge of the flat, only in specific areas. Through trial-and-error, I learned that those sections of the edge that contained good concentrations of bigger rock were holding most of the fish. That was the first important consideration, finding the fish. Equally important was the presentation I used to catch those fish.

The walleyes seemed to want a swimming jig, one moving steadily along with no hops or jumps. And since the water temperature was 46 degrees, they wanted the jig to be swimming along very slowly. But that was a tricky assignment, because they were lying just below the edge of the drop-off. With a straight swimming retrieve, the jig would slide right over the tops of the fish and they'd ignore it.

This kind of fishing requires a good sense of feel, a sensitive graphite or boron rod and a lot of concentration. I'd swim the jig along, letting it touch bottom every once in a while. It was important to know where the jig was in relation to the bottom at all times. As soon as I could

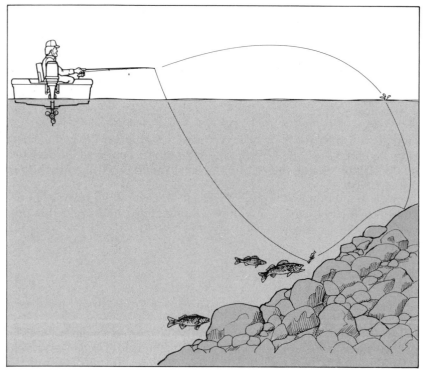

**Figure 3.** At times you may find walleyes sitting over rock drop offs. In this case, a swimming retrieve is very productive.

no longer feel the bottom, I'd assume it was at the edge and would let it fall down the face of the rocks. The moment it hit a rock, I'd flick my rod tip and start that jig swimming again.

The fish would gently pick up that jig and swim with it for a few feet. You couldn't detect a strike, there was just pressure on the line. As they started to swim off, I'd tighten up on the rod tip and snap set the hook.

The keys to this pattern were first finding the *exact* location of the fish and, second, maintaining the perfect swimming action on that jig.

## Spring Transition Patterns

For most folks, spring transition is a tough time to catch walleyes, as mentioned at the outset of this chapter. Fish tend to be scattered at this time of year, making it seem difficult to set any kind of pattern. You'll take one fish here, one fish there. The action tends to be inconsistent, at least in the classic type of areas.

Ironically, spring transition is when some anglers enjoy their highest degree of success. I suspect that's because other fishermen employ a random approach to walleye hunting. Rather than seeking out a specific pattern, they just troll around, bumping into fish every once in a while.

Actually, catching transition fish isn't all that difficult if you understand what the fish are doing and how they're relating to the environment. Fish can be using extremely shallow water during the transition period. They'll be up in the shallows because insect hatches are coming off, perch fry are becoming available, and emerging weed growths attract small minnows. The water's warmer in the shallows, as well. Light penetration isn't as much of a factor because the angle of the sun's rays is fairly indirect during this time of year.

## Wading and Casting

About the only equipment needed for this kind of fishing is a rod and reel, chest waders, and a small selection of floating minnow lures. Well, some warm clothes, a thermos of hot coffee and a little flashlight you can strap around your head won't hurt, either.

The beauty of this pattern is that it can produce some of the biggest fish of the year. I can't tell you how many eight, nine and ten-pounders I've seen caught using this simple procedure.

First of all, I should qualify myself somewhat. While this tactic is liable to work in just about any type of water, it seems to be most productive on older, natural lakes (eutrophic or late-stage meso-trophic). While I've heard it works on other bodies of water, the older, silted lakes seem to be best suited for this kind of fishing.

The best results will be obtained at night. While I'd be the first to agree there are better things to do at night, this is a great way to cash in on some trophy walleye opportunities.

Several sections of the lake are likely to produce big fish. One would be a large mud flat with emerging weed growth. These flats will draw a literal smorgasbord of food items for the walleyes, particularly may-flies, caddisflies and other invertebrates.

I usually like to arrive about dusk so I can get my bearings while there's still a bit of daylight left. Armed only with rod and reel, a few lures tucked into my waders and a stringer tied to my waist, I'll wade out until the water reaches my belt. Wading should be done as quietly as possible. Big fish are easily spooked, and if you're sloshing through the water and making commotion, those monster walleyes are going to leave the country.

Once in position, start fan-casting with the surface plug, like a Cordell Redfin, Rebel floating minnow, Lindy Baitfish or Whopper Stopper Hellcat. Rapalas aren't preferred by most of the died-in-the-wool wading fishermen because the lure is too light to get adequate casting distance. However, some anglers drill out Raps, inserting split shot for extra weight. Strawberry blonde, blue and shiner are three of the more productive colors.

At times, I've had my best luck retrieving the lure just under the surface. At other times, I'll add a small split shot about 18 inches in front of the lip to give the lure a bit more depth. How deep the fish want the lure will vary from night to night.

After standing and casting from one spot for 15 or 20 minutes, you'll want to move to a different spot. Again, be careful to move very slowly and quietly to avoid spooking any fish that are swimming in the immediate vicinity.

The retrieve is an important aspect of this kind of fishing and may require variations from one night to the next. You can experiment with a slow retrieve, a faster retrieve, a straight swimming retrieve and a stop and-go action. Sometimes, letting the lure sit on the surface until all the ripples have disappeared before beginning the retrieve will prompt a strike. Other times a big walleye will grab that bait right off the surface the instant it hits the water.

Structurally, there are many options. Mud flats have produced a lot of nice fish, but rocky points also attract transition walleyes. The water's still cool, maybe 55 to 60 degrees, and the rock absorbs and holds heat from the sun, which in turn, attracts minnows in the evening.

Any time you can find current there's a good chance walleyes are nearby. This might include a neck-down area between two lakes or an incoming river or stream. Emerging weed growth adjacent to the moving water makes such a spot even more attractive to the fish.

Timing remains a major mystery. I've seen nights when the primary movement occurred just at dusk and for the first half-hour after dark. On other nights, the fish won't move into the shallows until one or two in the morning. And, of course, some nights they don't show up at all.

The darker nights seem to be more productive than moonlit nights. I've not had a great deal of success under a full moon, but have really produced in the dark of the moon or on cloudy nights.

Night fishing is anything but a treat. A simple backlash is cause for a nervous breakdown, and the slap of a beaver tail at close range is enough to give you a heart attack. A big fish splashing water in your face from point-blank range might necessitate taking your waders to the cleaners. But, it's a great way to catch walleyes—big walleyes—during the often difficult transition period.

**Figure 4.** Under the cloak of darkness, big walleyes often cruise the shallows in search of food. Armed with waders, rod and reel, plus a selection of floating minnowbaits, you can often catch some of your biggest walleyes of the year.

## Cranking the Rock Piles

After the spawn is completed, walleyes will head in several different directions. Some will be working muck bays, some will be cruising soft-bottomed food shelves with emerging vegetation, and others will linger around the spawning grounds.

A few fish will head for shallow rock humps. There's nothing consistent about this particular pattern except that you can, on occasion, tie into some really dandy walleyes. Not a lot of fish mind you, but some biggies.

I prefer shallow rock humps with big, boulder-sized rocks. And I prefer them to be in fairly close proximity to shore. They don't necessarily have to be tied to the shoreline, but they should be fairly close.

This pattern works on natural lakes, either eutrophic or mesotrophic in nature. I've not enjoyed much success with it on oligotrophic lakes or reservoirs.

The rocks, if they're close enough to the surface, absorb heat from the sun like a solar panel. The warmth attracts minnows and you know the rest. A few scattered weeds growing up between the rocks can be a real bonus.

A wind coming into the rock pile can be advantageous, although I've enjoyed some nice catches on hot, calm days. Remember, the angle of the sun's rays is not as direct at this time of year so the fish can be quite shallow. The direction of the wind will have a lot to do with how the fish locate. Usually they'll be working the windy side of the rock pile.

You might think the best way to approach such a spot would be with a jig or a Lindy Rig. I have taken some fish with rigs off the bottom. But, by far, the best catches have been with crankbaits.

Crankbaits, like Lindy's Snipe, Bagley's Small Fry and Lindy's Shadlings, have been excellent producers. Towards evening, when the fish move shallower, the surface minnow lures take over as the number one producer.

It's best to slowly circle the rock pile using your electronic motor to avoid spooking the fish. Cast right up to the edge of the rocks—I prefer a stout baitcasting outfit with a fast tip—and retrieve right down the side of the rock pile.

The keys to this pattern are big rocks and a hump that tops out anywhere from two to ten feet and is in fairly close proximity to shore. Humps way out in the middle of the lake aren't nearly as productive.

You might not catch a lot of fish with this pattern, but you can take some good-sized walleyes in the middle of the day.

**Figure 5.** *Shallow rock piles and reefs attract spawning baitfish and, in return, hungry walleyes. You can effectively work these areas with an electric trolling motor, casting as you move.*

## Emerging Weed Growths

On many mesotrophic and oligotrophic lakes, emerging weed growths will attract a good percentage of the active walleyes. But not just any weed growth.

I've had my best luck on shallow points and flats gradually tapering to deeper water. In fact, that's what I'm looking for. I don't necessarily want something that's close to super deep water. Instead, I'm looking for shallow weed growths in two to ten feet of water with six to 15 feet of water around it. The shallower weedbeds will turn on first with water temperatures ranging from 58 to 66 degrees. Deeper weeds will turn on later in the period.

My favorite presentation is a jig tipped with a leech, but I've also done well on a jig-and-minnow combination, a floating jighead and a Lindy Rig. You'll want to fish slowly, moving quietly through the shallows using your electric trolling motor. Quick movements will tend to spook the fish while a slow, deliberate retrieve will not. You're looking for small clumps of weeds that might attract a school of minnows. You can enjoy excellent success right in the middle of the day, even in very shallow water.

The best jig colors seem to be yellow and brown-orange. I'll tip that jig with a minnow in cooler water and start experimenting with leeches as the water warms to the upper 50s. Once the water tops 60 degrees, crawlers come into their own.

Cabbage weed and coontail produce the most activity. Weeds can be anywhere from two inches to a foot and a half in height on a sand or an organic substrate.

**Figure 6.** Even though walleyes are generally thought of as a deep water fish, they often locate themselves in shallow emerging weed beds to feed on the abundant forage. A great way to take weed walleyes is with a jig and leech.

This is a rather loose pattern. Fitting the particulars into the puzzle is a day-to-day task. One day the most productive area may be adjacent to a large bay. The next day it could be where current enters the lake. Bottom content could change from all sand to all muck, but will more likely be a mixture of the two. Each of these features is going to make a difference. You'll have to look for the features that are important as you fine-tune the pattern.

The important thing is that you recognize that the fish can be moving in shallow water, working around sparse weed clumps.

## Beaver Huts

*Beaver huts?* Wait a minute, is Winkelman pulling our leg here?

Actually, beaver huts have produced some truly incredible catches of walleyes for me, including many from 8 to over 12 pounds.

This particular pattern is best on oligotrophic lakes, although I've had similar results on meso lakes, assuming conditions are right.

Beaver huts are attractive to baitfish in several ways. First, the brush provides protective cover for schools of minnows. Shiner minnows will move into these areas in clouds. Second, the timber absorbs and holds warmth. Consider also the fact that the back bays where these huts are located warm much faster than the main lake, and you've got the makings for a dynamite walleye spot—at least for a week or so.

Actually, walleyes can be using beaver huts all year long. But in spring the movement in and out of the bays occurs rather quickly and isn't long in duration. I anticipate the movements in one of two ways. First, I use my surface temperature gauge to seek 58 to 62 degree water in the bays. Second, there's a chartreuse pollen that comes off the trees at that time of year. This pollen lies on the surface of the water, turning the lake green and blocking out the sun's rays. These two biological signs tell me it's time to hit the beaver huts.

Beaver huts that occur where a river enters the main lake are prime spots to check. I'd suggest that if you can find a bunch of huts, you could establish a milk run and hit them all. The fish will move in and out a few times a day and you'll want to be there when they arrive. Movement is fairly predictable, so you'll want to try and time them.

The most important single factor in finding a good hut to fish is a sizeable food shelf near that hut. The shelf can be three to four feet in depth in the immediate vicinity of the hut with a gradual tapering to 6 to 10 feet. A quick drop from the edge of the hut might attract fish later in the year, but not during the transition period. Some sand can be an important ingredient, but is not always necessary.

The best presentation is a brown-orange or hot yellow Fuzz-E-Grub tipped with a minnow or sometimes a leech. The action you impart to that jig depends on the activity level of the fish and the amount of brush and debris along the food shelf. If there's too much debris, I'll swim and hop that jig to keep it from getting tangled. If the bottom is fairly clean, a straight swimming motion seems to work best. However, the more active the fish, the more action you'll want to put on that jig.

A good indication that walleyes are working the beaver huts is the presence of white suckers. If you can see a school of suckers swimming around the dam, there's a very good chance the walleyes aren't far away. In fact, on occasion you'll even find smaller walleyes swimming right with the suckers.

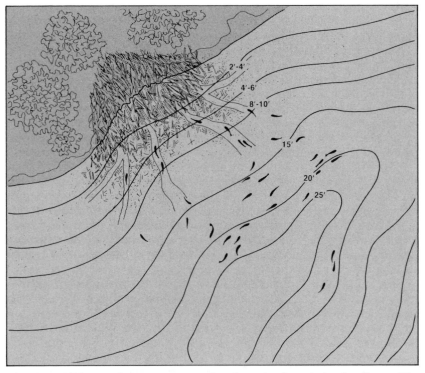

**Figure 7.** All beaver huts are not equal, at least in the minds of walleyes. The best huts are those with adjacent deep water where the walleyes can retreat to rest.

Move around very quietly, using your electric trolling motor. Using a pair of polaroid sunglasses, you may actually be able to see the fish swimming around in the shallows. When they're this shallow, the fish are easily spooked.

I've taken a lot of really nice fish with this pattern on Pre-Cambrian lakes. The key is picking the time when the walleyes move into the bays for this brief feeding foray.

## Summer

Summer is one of the best times to consistently catch walleyes. Distinct patterns are much easier to set because the lake has settled and the fish are schooled and making predictable movements.

The warm water temperatures of summer increase the walleye's metabolism and those fish are feeding more often and more intensely. This is the growing season for walleyes and all species of fish. They're more active and more aggressive.

There will usually be a number of patterns that might work during the summer period, some at the same time. However, you might find only one, maybe two, big-fish patterns.

Because the water is warm, faster speeds will often produce better catches, especially late in the summer.

The key to catching summertime walleyes is finding them. There are many considerations that affect fish location during summer. The angle of the sun's rays is more direct during the summer months, which means on clear lakes the fish may be forced to much deeper water. Oxygen levels can become depleted in some bodies of water, which forces the fish into the weeds.

Pinpoint location becomes important in summer. Earlier, during the transition period, the fish may have been scattered. In summer, they tend to be bunched up, and a random approach to location simply won't yield many big stringers. But warm water is an excellent time to catch big walleyes.

## Prairie Lake Weeds

On many of the older, highly fertile lakes, oxygen depletion forces fish out of what deep water exists and into the weedbeds along about late July.

These lakes generally produce a lot of fish in spring and fall and can be extraordinary ice fisheries. But anglers typically have a difficult time finding warm-weather walleyes.

Until recently, the best presentation was thought to be working the outside edge of the weeds with a spinner or small crankbait. Indeed, that presentation produces some fish. But when the lake really stagnates with several days of hot, calm weather, the only fish working the outside edge of the weeds will be "cigars."

In recent years, anglers have discovered a better way to fish highly eutrophic bodies of water during the summer months. They're going right up into the densest weed growth and yanking big fish on crankbaits or even spinnerbaits.

Why, you may ask, are walleyes up in shallow weed growths acting like largemouth bass? Well, when you think about it, they really don't have any options. Walleyes are not, in most cases, natural to these lakes. Because of siltation, alkalinity and other factors that inhibit spawning, such lakes must usually be stocked.

Since these lakes do not offer a natural environment for the fish, walleyes are forced to act like bass. It's simply a question of the options that are available to the fish. Aside from any current coming into the lake, the only area with adequate oxygen and forage is the weeds. So the walleyes move into the weeds and act just like bass.

The problem with this pattern is that there's an awful lot of weeds in these nutrient-rich bodies of water and only a handful of them will be holding fish. As with any pattern, it's best to hit and run, looking for a section of weeds that has attracted and is holding fish. The key may be the type of weeds, density of growth, bottom content or any number of factors.

Pay attention to those sections of the lake exposed to the sun first. As the sun climbs into the sky, photosynthesis will occur, giving off oxygen and changing the pH of the water. The sections of the lake exposed to the early day sun might turn on first, with the rest of the lake picking up at mid-day.

Perhaps, the most effective presentation I've found is to cast a crankbait into pockets or openings in the weeds. Don't restrict yourself to deep weedlines here. The fish will be up in two or three feet of water at times.

This can be a very frustrating way to fish. You're apt to catch something on every cast. Usually it will be weeds. Spinnerbaits catch an awful lot of fish under these conditions and weight-forward spinners are another good choice of lures.

The beauty of this pattern is the size of fish you'll encounter tucked into the vegetation. While a trolling pass along the outside edge of the weeds might produce some 1½ and two-pound fish, casting plugs or spinnerbaits into the weeds can account for some four, five and six-pounders. Some of the biggest fish of the season are now being caught on this weed pattern, where summertime once meant under-sized fish.

**Figure 8.** *Weedy, prairie lakes can hold their fair share of walleyes. But the thick weeds can make presentation difficult. Casting a shallow running crankbait or spinnerbait into weed pockets is perhaps the best method for these lakes.*

### Reservoir Mud Lines

Many of the more productive reservoir systems in the country were carved out of nutrient-rich farmland. For this reason, they have remarkable carrying capacities and can hold some exceptional walleyes, both in numbers and in size.

While these systems contain lots of rock, sand, gravel, shale and scoria, they also are comprised of a great deal of clay. Should the wind blow for any length of time out of one direction, the soft-bottom will become agitated creating a mud line. And these mud lines are a great place to search for walleyes.

Under the protective umbrella of dirty water, the walleyes can move into the oxygenated shallows to feed on insects, grubs, minnows and other food stuffs that are normally out of their reach. It's not uncommon to find large groups of fish working in just a foot or two of water, totally unaware that a bright sun is beating down on the surface.

Not just any mudline is going to produce fish. But several conditions will prove to be fish magnets. I'm going to deal with soft-bottomed food shelves. I'm not referring to a flat here, but a large, rounded point with a gradual taper on at least two sides. It helps if the shelf is adjacent to deep water on at least one side. What you're looking for is a large shelf with four to ten feet of water, a soft bottom, a gradual taper on two or three sides and a quick drop to deep water on at least one side.

Trolling or casting a spinner over the tops of these shelves is an excellent way to catch walleyes. Because of the turbidity of the water, I prefer large blades (No. 4, 5 or 6 in Colorado) in orange or fluorescent red. It's been my experience that fluorescent red is the most visible color under these conditions, and that experience is backed up by Dr. Loren Hill's color research.

The longer the mud line has been there, the further up the fish will move. After several hours, active walleyes might be prowling in just a few feet of water.

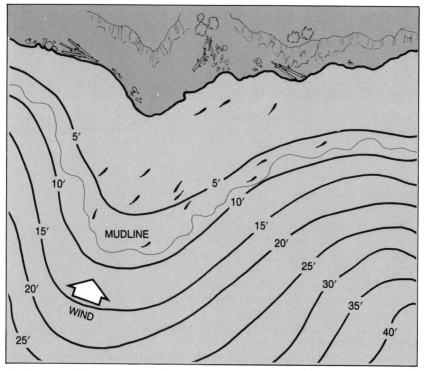

**Figure 9.** Mudlines are often used as underwater highways by walleyes. Under the cover of the suspended particles, walleyes move into the shallows in search of food.

When they move that shallow, you'll want to cease trolling and cast a weight-forward spinner like a Tom's Walleye Lure tipped with a nightcrawler, dragging it over the top of the shelf with an erratic, jerking motion. Crankbaits can also produce good walleyes under these conditions.

Crawlers are almost always the best live-bait dressing for spinners and weight-forward spinners, but leeches can, at times, be excellent.

Should the mud line coincide with a drop-off or breakline, you might want to troll right along the water color breakline, that is the edge between clean and dirty water. You'll encounter that situation shortly after the mud line begins to form and the fish are still fairly deep. Once the mud line has set up, it will likely cover the entire shelf, at which time the fish will move right up on top and become active.

The stronger the wind, the more active the fish will become. And the larger the food shelf, the more walleyes will move up to feed.


## Sallies

Salamanders catch big fish. In the mid 70s, I discovered a late spring/early salamander pattern that's pure dynamite.

This pattern seems to work best on mesotrophic, or medium-fertility lakes with fairly good water quality, rock and gravel. What you're looking for structurally are points or sunken islands with rock and/or gravel that comes off a major flat. Close proximity to a big flat with ample weed growth is all-important.

Depending on water clarity, the fish could be anywhere from 15 to 35 feet deep. The more distinct the structure of these points or islands the better the possibility that they'll be holding some big fish. And make no mistake, this is a big-fish pattern. You won't take many fish under five pounds on a salamander. For that matter, you won't take many fish, period. You might work all day for one or two strikes. But usually, you can call them ten-pound bites whether you land them or not.

I prefer structures that drop into deep, deep water. They seem to hold most of the bigger fish.

I like sallies in the four to seven inch range with gills. The gilled variety won't have to be brought up repeatedly for air.

I'll fish a salamander behind a regular Lindy Rig sinker to which I'll attach a No. 5 Kahle hook on a three or four foot snell. Before heading out, I'll take a paper punch and knock out a bunch of tabs from the plastic lid of a coffee can. These tabs will be used to hold the sallie in place. Force one tab on the hook, then hook the slamander through the lips from the bottom side. Then push the second tab on the hook. When you squeeze the two tabs together, they'll hold the sallie in place so it swims straight through the water.

You're not likely to get many hits when fishing a salamander, but you won't have much trouble knowing when you do get one. Walleyes generally hit like a freight train. As a rule, they'll hit the sallie from the side, then swim off to slowly turn it in their mouth before swallowing it head-first.

You should always follow the fish with the boat, feeding out line until it has had time to get the bait turned around. Position the boat directly over the top of the fish before setting the hook. I prefer a heavy spinning rod for this kind of fishing with eight or ten-pound Stren. If I'm fishing in heavy rocks, I'll go with 12-pound line.

Finding the structural element that's holding fish is the key to this pattern. And that can be time-consuming, because fishing with sallies is anything but fast. You're dealing with big fish, and one or two hits per day is the norm. Then too, I've had days where I took double limits that averaged better than nine-pounds.

Look for tiny hooks, points, knobs, anything that would be classified as a mini-structure. Work that salamander slowly through each of these mini-structures, concentrating on the rocky edges.

It's a great way to take a trophy walleye, if you have the patience to be a true trophy hunter.

**Figure 10.** Fishing deep drop-offs with salamanders, or "water dogs" as they are sometimes called, is strictly a big fish pattern. You may only have one, two, or three bites in a day. But what bites they'll be!

## Night Pattern for Big Fish

On natural lakes that receive intense fishing pressure or have ultra-clear water, big walleyes can be tough. Some suspend, some use very deep water and others are locked into the dense vegetation during daylight hours. These big, big fish won't become active until after dark, when boating pressure ceases to be a factor and light penetration subsides.

There are several features to look for in this particular big-fish pattern. First, you want to seek out dense growths of cabbage and coontail weeds. Some of the really big fish will be tucked into the heaviest weed growths in the lake during daylight hours. Second, it is best to find an area which offers reasonably quick access to deep water.

Your lure should be a very big (No. 4 to No. 7 Colorado) spinner blade in chartreuse or orange with a bunch of beads, a treble hook and a gob of crawler on the back. This type of spinner isn't available commercially, you'll have to make it yourself. Don't use any weight, just connect the snell to your line with a swivel.

**Figure 11.** During lowlight periods, walleyes in weeds will often rise up above the weed tops to feed. A spinner/crawler combination longlined over the weed tops is a dynamite pattern.

You're going to be fishing over the tops of the weeds on the outside edge of the weedbed. Look for an area where there's a foot or two of open water between the tops of the weeds and the surface.

Those big walleyes will move up and out of the weeds at dark. Maybe they're up there just playing, but more likely they're going to be cruising the tops of the weedbeds looking for a big meal.

Obviously, you're going to have to move very quietly using your electric trolling motor. Let out a lot of line, up to 150 feet. The walleyes may spook as the boat passes overhead, but will be back in position by the time your bait comes along.

I've found it best to fish quite slowly, just letting that blade flop along right under the surface. Always vary the speed, letting the fish tell you which speed they prefer on that particular night.

Along the edge of the weedline you'll encounter points and inside turns. It's been my experience that the inside turns will hold more big fish. It's important to watch your flasher and be able to follow the edge of the weeds, working your bait into those inside turns.

On certain types of lakes, this pattern is not only a good way to catch fish, it's the only way to take a trophy fish during the summer months.

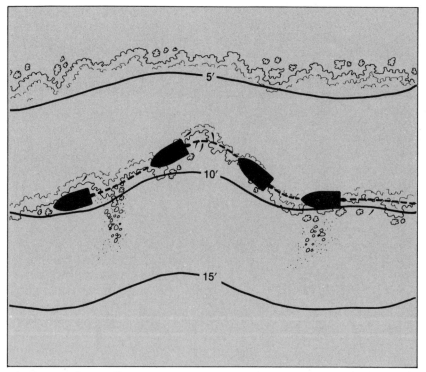

**Figure 12.** When trolling the edge of a weed bed, concentrate on irregularities in the weedline. Small weed fingers, points, and inside turns are great hotspots.

## Crankbaits on Rivers

On many of the major river systems across the country, there's no better way to catch a big walleye than trolling a crankbait *against* the current.

I know that goes against the grain of everything you've ever read or learned about river fishing. The best presentation is supposed to be a bait or lure moving with the current rather than against it. But believe me, this tactic works.

Look for a large, shallow, rocky food shelf. The bigger the food shelf the better the chances that it will be holding any numbers of fish. By shallow, I mean expanses of water 7 to 15 feet with a gradual taper to deep water. The rocks are important because they offer protection from the current.

The bigger the rock the better. Very large boulders are by far the best. The fish can tuck behind these boulders and hang out of the current, waiting for an easy meal to wash by. Incidentally, a food shelf that's out of the current won't be likely to hold many, if any, big fish.

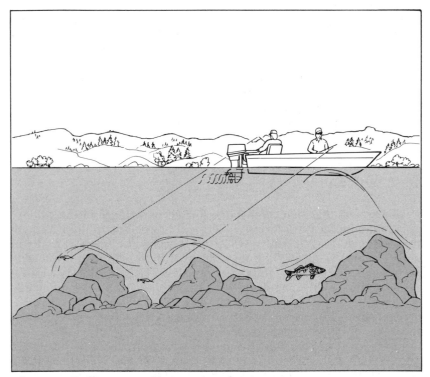

**Figure 13.** Trolling a crankbait against the river current may seem wrong to many river fishing experts. But past experience, and some heavy results, shows it definitely works.

I've had my best luck with a Lindy Shadling. The color will vary according to water clarity. But color does make a difference and it's important to experiment with different colors and shades of crankbaits.

Let out just enough line so you can still feel the vibrations from the crankbait and so the lure is occasionally bumping the bottom. If you lose touch with the plug, reel in just enough line so you can feel the bait wiggle. I prefer a fairly stiff rod with a very fast tip. The soft tip allows you to better feel the vibrations from the crankbaits. Using fairly light line, eight or ten-pound, will allow that crankbait to attain its maximum depth and to swim with an uninhibited action.

Vary trolling speed as you move over the shelf. Short bursts of speed often trigger a strike. At times, I'll drop the rod tip back and then pull it forward with a quick jerk, making that plug dig and dive for a split second. Sometimes that sudden movement will catch the eye of a waiting walleye.

The biggest fish will usually be working the upstream side of any such food shelf with the smaller fish hanging downstream. But that's not a hard-and-fast rule. I have taken some good fish in the middle and downstream portions of a shelf as well.

If the current is strong enough, it may be necessary to attach a Rubbercore sinker about 18 to 24 inches in front of the lip of the plug. You want that lure working as close to the bottom as possible.

On the back side of big boulders there will be an eddy, or slack-water area, where the water is boiling over the tops of the rocks. When your plug hits these sections of dead water, you'll lose all sensation from the bottom, momentarily. It will almost feel like your Shadling fell off. When the plug climbs out and hits the current again—that's when the fish will usually strike.

This pattern has produced some sensational catches on walleyes—big walleyes—in river systems all across the country.


## Weed Pattern

As I've mentioned several times, a good percentage of the walleye population on medium-fertility lakes will be relating to the weedbeds during the summer months. Once the thermocline sets up in July or early August, a lot of the forage fish will be forced into the weeds. Weeds give off oxygen through the process of photosynthesis while at the same time offering protection for baitfish like minnows and perch. Weeds also offer a shield from the sun's rays.

There are many patterns that will work in the weeds. This happens to be one of my personal favorites.

I look for the weedbeds that have ample growths of both cabbage and coontail. Cabbage and coontail are the two weed types that attract the most walleyes. Bigger food shelves tend to be much more productive than smaller ones. A quick drop to deep water on the outside edge of the weeds seems to be another important consideration.

What I'm looking for with this pattern is a weedline breakline, in other words, an area where a clump of coontail joins a growth of cabbage. The best depth seems to be from 10 to 15 feet. A sand or gravel bottom at the base of the weeds or a pocket in the weeds, with some rock, can really serve as fish magnets.

The toughest part of the equation is working in and out of the base of the weeds without constantly snagging vegetation. I prefer a short, stiff rod with enough backbone so I can rip the jig free, but with a soft enough tip so I have maximum sensitivity to be able to distinguish weeds from fish.

My favorite jig for this kind of fishing is a ¼-ounce Lindy Flatfoot, which has a standup head. Instead of tipping that jig with live bait, I like to use an Uncle Josh ripple rind enhanced with a good scent product. The ripple rind is a lot tougher than plastic or live bait and won't be constantly tearing off when you tangle up with the weeds.

I'll let that jig settle to the bottom, then give it a quick snap. As the jig falls back to the bottom, the ripple rind will give off an enticing action that walleyes find hard to resist. If you hang up in the weeds,

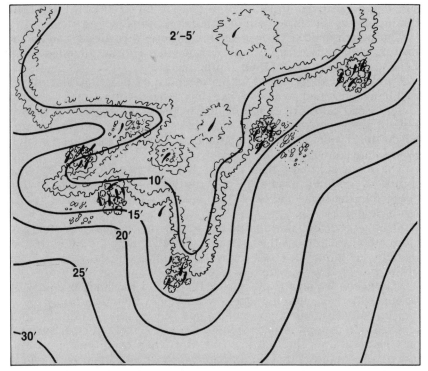

**Figure 14.** "Weed breaklines" are areas where one type of aquatic vegetation border another, such as coontail clumps merging with cabbage weeds. One of these breaklines in about 10 or 15 feet of water, along with a few rocks or gravel runs, can pull in walleyes like a magnet.

that same quick snap will usually tear the jig free and you can allow it to settle back down to the bottom.

Obviously, it's best to use an electric trolling motor and work very slowly for this kind of fishing. As you're cleaning the water, try working the shady side of the weeds first, then try the sunny side. The best action usually occurs during the low-light periods.


## Boulder Walleyes

Canadian Shield lakes, by their very nature, contain a lot of rocks and boulders. Under certain conditions, the walleyes will become active and cruise the boulder-strewn sunken islands aggressively, herding ciscoes or small whitefish.

On hot, calm days, the walleyes will tuck right into the cracks and crevices between the boulders. Randomly bouncing a bait over the tops of the rocks isn't enough to produce fish. You'll have to get right down in there and coax them out.

First, let's look at the types of structures likely to hold these lethargic fish. Favored locations are points or sunken islands with big boulders. The depth can range from 20, to as deep as 40 or 50 feet. Light conditions and water clarity will be the determining factors.

The most important aspect of this pattern is realizing you're not dealing with active fish. These walleyes have to be force-fed, they have to be coaxed out of their hiding places.

I prefer a small jig tipped with a leech or, on occasion, an inflated nightcrawler. I may go all the way down to a 1/16th ounce jig if the water's dead calm. An eighth or quarter may be necessary if there's a slight chop. Obviously, to get a jig that small to the bottom requires a light line. I generally use six-pound clear Stren but have been known to use four-pound.

The rod should be a light to very light 5½ foot boron or graphite jigging stick. You'll need a lot of sensitivity not only to avoid being snagged in the rocks constantly, but also to detect the often light hits by these finicky fish.

Fishing vertically, positioning the boat with the electric motor, pay close attention to what the jig is doing at all times. Try to work that jig right down into the cracks between the rocks and dangle it in front of the walleye's nose, tempting it to feed.

Should the walleye really smack the jig, set the hook instantly. If he sucks the bait, put on a little pressure, and then drill him.

This pattern is effective under a specific weather condition—hot and calm. In choppy water, walleyes are more likely to be active and moving around on the tops of rocks. But when conditions are calm, you'll have to crawl that jig around the rocks and literally dangle it in front of the walleye's nose.

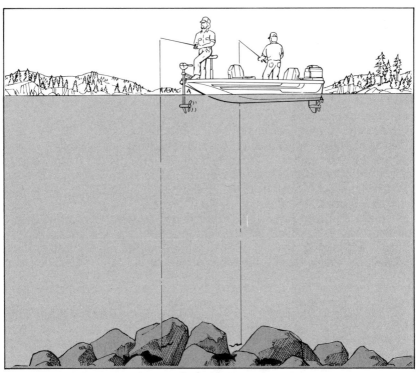

**Figure 15.** *On hot, calm days, walleyes will often tuck down between rocks to seek shade. You generally can't coax these fish out with haphazard retrieves. You've got to put your offering right on their noses.*

## Tailwater Walleyes

Most of the country's major river systems today contain hydroelectric dams that generate power. Depending on water levels up and downstream from the dams, strong flows tend to move fish upstream while reduced flows push them downstream. It seems to be the fish's nature to move upstream when lots of water is moving through the system. I suspect the fish have learned over the years that high flows mean food will be coming through the turbines.

During extended periods of strong flows, literally every predator for miles will stack into the tailwaters, below the dam, to feed on the smorgasbord of forage being ground up and coming through the dam.

You can catch some nice walleyes during the daytime hours, but by far the best fishing will occur after dark. There are basically two presentations that have proven to be effective under these conditions.

One is drifting with the current, bouncing a minnow-type lure off the bottom. In strong current, you'll need a two-ounce egg sinker to get down. Behind that sinker run a four or five-foot leader with a Baitfish, Rapala, Cordell Redfin or any of the popular floating minnow lures.

Usually, I just drift at a rapid speed. If that doesn't produce, try slipping, a tactic described in the "boat control" section of the presentation chapter. Slipping will slow your drift down.

Snags are an ever-present nuisance in tailrace waters, but you can avoid being hung up constantly by bouncing that heavy sinker off the bottom. Lift the rod tip as soon as you feel the bottom, then drop it back until you again contact the bottom. The bait will be swimming downstream, backwards in the heavy current, moving right toward the fish's mouth.

Usually, the best presentation is the downstream drift, which immitates stunned baitfish. But you can often milk a few bonus fish by running a crankbait against the current along the edge of the rip-rap that usually exists along both sides of the chute.

**Figure 16.** *After dark, predatory fish of all kinds move below hydroelectric dams to feed on the dead and stunned minnows that run through the turbines. Trolling a weighted minnowbait along the bottom will produce walleyes, and several other bonus species.*

# Fall

Fall is big-fish time. Late in the season, after the turnover, is perhaps the best time of year to catch a trophy walleye. Big females are actively feeding, putting on a layer of fat to see them through the lean times ahead.

During the actual turnover, fishing can be tough. However, there are patterns that will work throughout the fall season. Actually, I could break down the fall season into several categories—turnover, early fall and late fall.

You should keep some important points in mind when heading out on a fall trip. First, big fish like big baits—a fact that was never more true than prior to ice-up. The water's cooling down rapidly and those fish won't expend a great deal of energy on a snack. They want something substantial.

Second, since the water is cooling off, the fish are slowing down metabolically. They won't chase a meal. They want something easy, and they want lots of it. They'll simply burn off too many calories chasing a meal. It's a losing proposition. So the angler must resort to a very slow presentation.

There's one other thing to keep in mind during fall fishing. The lake has turned over oxygen levels and water temperatures are pretty much constant throughout the lake. You'll likely find the pH to be steady from top to bottom. The fish can be just about anywhere. I've caught fall walleyes in two feet of water and I've caught them in over 80 feet. Sometimes, on the same day.

As a general rule, if you can establish a depth pattern, it will hold as long as the conditions are unchanged. But during fall, you might possibly establish several solid depth patterns in the same day.

While walleyes can be unpredictable, I've uncovered several patterns that will work for various types of waters with some consistency. As is true with all patterns, small refinements make a difference. And those refinements are something you'll have to discover on a day-to-day basis, specifically for the lake you're fishing.

## Turnover Pattern

As the lake is turning over, fishing can be tough. At times, it can be downright impossible. There's really nothing to hang your hat on during the turnover. The fish seem to be disoriented, out of sorts. I have, however, found at least one pattern that can ease the pain of the turnover blues.

The process of photosynthesis gives off oxygen, attracting walleyes to the weeds. But as those weeds die and decompose in fall, oxygen is consumed. At the same time, carbon dioxide, which can actually kill fish, is given off. Obviously, the fish are going to be forced out of the weeds while all this is taking place.

During the first few days of this decomposition process, the fish will still be hanging fairly close to the weedbeds, maybe five to ten feet below the deep edge of the weedline.

If there's one area that seems to hold more fish than any other, it's the steeper breaks below the weed growths. Don't expect to find anything resembling a concentration of fish, because this probably isn't going to happen. The fish will be scattered. However, the sharper breaks seem to attract more fish than the slow tapers. These fish have just evacuated their summer environment and they seem to be confused. You'll find one walleye here, one there, and probably some largemouth bass in the same areas.

The key to a turnover pattern is finding how far below the weedline the walleyes are locating. It could be as close as five feet or it could be a great deal deeper. If there's a point coming off shore, the fish usually will be holding on the inside turn of that piont rather than on the tip.

My most productive presentation has always been a rig and night-crawler fished very slowly. It's as if the walleyes are so disoriented they don't know whether they want to eat or not. You almost have to spoon-feed them.

It's not fast action, but it's the best way I've found to get some walleyes for the frying pan during the turnover period.

**Figure 17.** During the transition period, walleyes are generally scattered and disoriented. This makes for spotty fishing at best. But you can convince a few fish to bite by working a live bait rigged tipped with a crawler along weedlines.

## Frog Run Walleyes

On many of the more fertile lakes, eutrophic or late mesotrophic in type, there are frog runs in the fall. And I've found that a certain percentage of the walleye population will be chasing frogs.

Sometimes, it's possible to locate the marshes experiencing an invasion of frogs just by driving around and watching for frogs hopping across the road. A better way is to walk the shoreline around bays, looking for concentrations of the little critters.

At night the walleye will swim to the marshes to chase frogs. If there's a little current moving through the marsh, you can get into some superb action anchoring and casting towards shore.

During the day, I look for the deep-water sections of the lake that are adjacent to frog-infested marshes. In the case where there's a gradual taper from the shoreline, those fish might have to move a considerable distance to find deep water. But most fish will be holding in deeper water during the day.

I like to use a plain Lindy Rig with a No. 4 hook instead of the standard No. 6 or No. 8 hook. In some cases, it may be necessary to go with a weedless hook. I'll hook the frog lightly through the lips and work the bait with a pumping action similar to what the frogs natural movement would be.

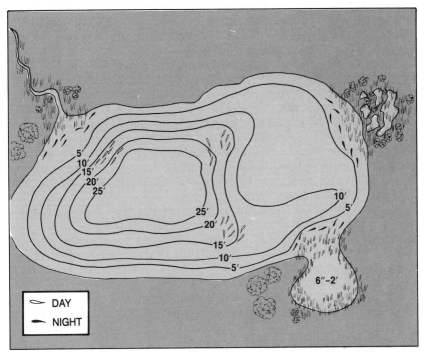

*Figure 18.* Walleyes are opportunistic feeders that take advantage of any feeding opportunities that come their way. The fall frog run is a good example. The key is to fish areas with soft bottoms where frogs return to hibernate.

259

When a walleye hits a frog, it's like hooking up with the south end of a northbound 18-wheeler. If you're using very large frogs you may have to feed some line until the fish gets the bait turned around in its mouth. But with big fish, this usually won't be necessary.

The frog run is one fall pattern that produces a lot of big walleyes.

## Reservoir Pattern

If you've read this far, you probably know that reservoirs have the capacity to produce some giant walleyes. And there's no better time to catch those big lunkers than in the fall.

Reservoirs can be huge bodies of water, so pinpointing walleye location can be a real challenge, even for the experienced walleye hunter. But I've found one pattern that's almost sure-fire.

Keep in mind that reservoir walleyes are, by nature, river fish. They are very nomadic. The section of water you're fishing could be devoid of walleyes. You may have to cover a lot of water to get to the fish, but once you do this pattern is sensational.

The key to locating fall walleyes in reservoirs is finding bends in the old river channel. Walleyes follow the river channel on their upstream and downstream migrations. Anywhere the channel bends towards shore and actually touches shoreline structure is an excellent place to begin your search for fall walleyes.

The point where the channel meets the shoreline and the point where it swings away are both going to hold fish. The section of water in between those two points also has the capacity to attract and hold good fish. Often as not, there'll be a bay at one end or the other. If there's a point coming off the bay and hitting the river channel, you'll want to cover that section of water thoroughly.

As you're drifting or trolling along the shoreline, keep a sharp eye out for tiny hooks or points that exist along the contour you're fishing. These hooks and points, no matter how small, serve as mini-structures and will hold the biggest fish.

As we discussed earlier, the key factors in presentation are speed and size of bait. You'll want to fish slowly, simply because of the fish's slowed down metabolism. I like to fish big (six to ten-inch) suckers, redtails or shiners, whatever is available, behind a Fuzz-E Grub jig. Color can vary from day to day, but we've enjoyed our most consistent catches with hot yellow.

An ultra-sensitive graphite or boron jigging stick, a high-quality spinning reel and premium eight or ten-pound monofilament line are vital equipment for this kind of fishing. You don't want to risk a once-in-a-lifetime trophy on faulty equipment. I like jigs that are ⅜ ounce for fishing 20 feet or deeper, and will go with a ¼ ounce for more shallow fish. Make sure the hooks are razor sharp.

With a bait that size, you may have to feed the line after the hit. In some cases, you'll have to feed out a lot of line until the fish gets the bait turned around and well into its mouth. Another option is using a stinger hook buried just behind the dorsal fin of the bait. I prefer not to use stinger hooks unless it's absolutely necessary.

If the fish moves off too far, it may be necessary to chase it with the boat, getting yourself directly over the top of the big walleye before attempting to set the hook. Line stretch can keep you from hooking the big fish.

Boat control is an essential part of fall fishing. Some of the most productive times are nice weather days with a stiff wind. A big wind tends to push baitfish against the steep-walled cliffs along shore, and that attracts lots of active walleyes. But maintaining the proper speed in a wind can be difficult. I like to use Boat Brakes (sea anchors) when making a controlled drift along a windy shoreline.

A Lindy Rig tipped with the same giant bait can also account for some jumbo fall walleyes on reservoirs, especially in the early fall season. In late fall, you just can't beat a jig.

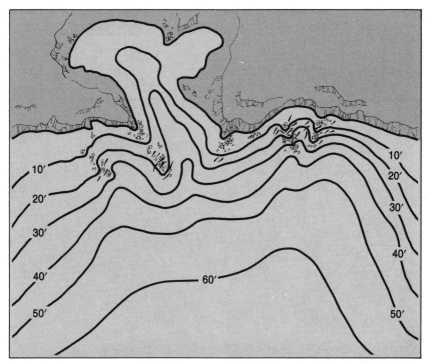

**Figure 19.** As walleyes make their fall migrations, they'll hold over in bends in the old river channel especially where it meets the shoreline. The key to catching them is to use jigs tipped with large minnows.

## Cisco Runs

On many of the medium-fertility lakes which have a fall-spawning forage base, like cisco or tullibee, you'll have a lot of walleyes hanging around the spawning grounds looking for an easy meal.

Cisco and tullibee spawn on big flats in four to ten feet of water with a gravel bottom. You'll want to find a fairly large flat that drops off into the deepest water available. You're looking for those steep, steep breaks coming off the spawning flats. A hook or point with scattered rock or boulders on the edge will attract a lot of walleyes.

During the day, the walleyes will be lying just off the break, in anywhere from 15 to 75 feet of water. Towards evening they'll move up on top of the flats to actively chase the spawning baitfish.

My favorite bait is a four to eight-inch redtail on a Lindy Rig. A salamander behind a rig has also turned some trophy walleyes under these conditions. And a jig redtail combination has its moments as well.

The keys to this pattern are first, finding concentrations of active fish. Don't hang around in one spot for very long. Cover a lot of water until you encounter fish.

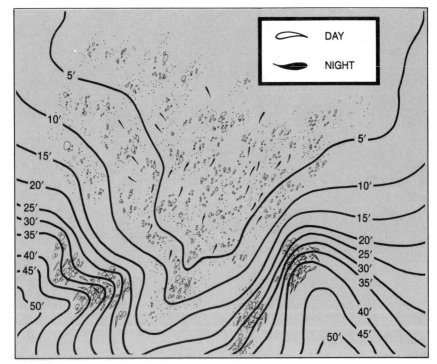

**Figure 20.** As fall spawning cisco and tullibee move up on shallow flats to spawn, walleyes often feed on them heavily. The best flats are those adjacent to deep water.

Once you locate some fish, fine-tune your pattern. The next most important thing to seek out are the irregularities (mini-structures) that exist along the structure. Some smaller fish may be scattered loosely along the sharp breaks, but most of the trophy fish will be relating to some kind of mini-structure.

The best hours for fishing are from nine to five, which is good, because it can get pretty chilly after dark. The absolute best fishing occurs during the afternoon.

These patterns are all fairly loose. I didn't break them down any further because the ultimate fine-tuning is up to the angler. The specifics of exact color, size, action, depth, speed, bottom content, structure, mini-structure and the like will vary from day to day and from one body of water to the next.

These patterns are merely guidelines that should, in most cases, get you close to where the action is. What you do from that point on, is up to you.

# Chapter 8
# Wrap-up

## What Did We Miss?

*"I wish him a rainy evening to read this discourse, and that the East wind may never blow when he goes fishing".*
**—Izaak Walton, 1577**

### Fishing a Strange Lake

In my travels, I rarely get the opportunity to fish where I have the "home field advantage."

Whether I'm fishing a tournament or filming a television show, a great majority of my time is spent on strange water. I'm not looking for sympathy here, but fishing a strange lake can be tough. I have to try to figure out in a day or two what the locals have spent years learning.

With the pressures of a tournament or a promotion, or when the television cameras are rolling, I've got to find some fish. My reputation is on the line, it's my livelihood.

Most fishermen won't find themselves under that kind of pressure to produce fish. But the weekend angler does have a real problem when it comes to selecting and fishing an unfamiliar body of water. The dilemma comes into focus each year when vacation plans are being made.

Booking a vacation is a two-sided coin. First and foremost, you want to select an area with beautiful beaches and ample recreational facilities for your family to enjoy. Second (maybe first in your mind), is finding a lake that will produce some fast walleye action, or maybe a couple of real horse walleyes.

Unfortunately, the two don't always go hand-in-hand. The more heavily developed areas don't always offer exceptional fishing. And the lakes that afford prime fishing don't often have the kind of facilities to satisfy a family's needs.

The good news is that most of the popular resort regions, like those in the upper midwest, are usually located right in the heart of lake country. It's not at all uncommon to have 100 lakes within easy driving distance of your base.

So you make reservations and the trip is planned. *Whoa.* If you expect to cash in on some fast fishing, the job has just begun. There's a lot of ground work to be accomplished between now and the day you start packing the wagon for two weeks of R & R. If you wait until arriving to start tending to your fishing needs, it could be too late.

An important part of fishing any strange lake is first selecting the right lakes. And that should happen before you leave home.

First, you'll want to compile as much information about the area as possible. You can begin by getting in touch with the state's department of natural resources or game and fish. Write to the information officer and ask for any guidance he can provide about the immediate area you intend to fish. Ask about the availability of lake maps and where they can be obtained.

Next, contact the local chamber of commerce or resort association. There are two pieces of information you'll want to check out. First, are there any fishing tournaments held in the area? Any lake that hosts a fishing tournament is usually going to have a fairly strong walleye population and, thus, would be a good bet for your fishing trip. Lakes with marginal walleye populations rarely, if ever, are selected as tournament sites.

Second, see if there are any local fishing contests. These contests are fairly common throughout the resort belt. And often the sponsors publish a book listing all the nice catches recorded the previous year. By studying such a book, you may find that one or two lakes produced a lot of nice fish during the time you plan to spend vacationing. That would be a pretty good indicator that those lakes will be productive during your stay.

Next, subscribe to any local outdoor publications. If possible, ask to purchase a year's worth of back issues. You'd be surprised how much you can learn about an area just by poring over these publications. You'll see which lakes in the area you plan to visit were producing fish the previous year. Often, you can even find out what the fish were caught on. You'll get insight into the area that you couldn't possibly obtain from any other source.

What you're trying to accomplish here, is to compile as much information as possible about the area you plan to visit. That way, when you leave home, you won't be coming in as a stranger. By the time you arrive, you should feel like you're going home.

By reading papers, studying contest results and visiting with DNR officials, you should be able to narrow your list of choices to half a dozen lakes. If at all possible, obtain hydrographic maps of each body of water, so you can begin studying them well in advance of your trip.

With the knowledge of lake types and fishing tactics you've gained through reading this book, you should be able to predict, to some extent, where the active fish will be in each of body of water before you leave home.

One word of caution here—select several different *types* of lakes. If you're narrowing your choices to half a dozen bodies of water, pick three mesotrophic lakes, two eutrophic lakes and maybe one river. Why do you want such a diversity of lake types?

Well, it could be that weather conditions during your stay simply won't be conducive to fishing one particular body of water. Maybe a series of cold fronts will chase each other through the region during your stay. In that event, you'd probably want to shy away from the mesotrophic lakes and concentrate on the prairie lakes and a river. On the other hand, weather conditions could be stable, which would make the meso lake the number one producer. The point is, you'll want to have some options available.

It could be that the weather will be stable for several consecutive days and the walleyes will be suicidal, 100 yards from the dock in

*Fishing's fun . . . even when the walleyes aren't trophy sized.*

front of your cabin. But then a severe cold front moves through, knocking the fishing on its heels. No problem. You simply move to an off-colored body of water or river, each of which is less affected by weather conditions, and start over.

Once you arrive at your vacation spot, you'll want to immediately contact several people. First, see a conservation officer (game warden) or fisheries biologist. In some areas, fisheries personnel are stationed close by. And no one knows more about the population dynamics of individual lakes than the local biologist.

Some of the things you'll want to find out concern the overall fish population and forage base in the lake you intend to fish. Is it a naturally producing walleye lake or is it a stocked lake? Are there lots of fish or only a few, bigger fish? Stocked lakes often have excellent walleye populations and those fish are, as a rule, easier to catch. But the average size will run smaller than those in a naturally producing lake. A biologist or game warden can fill in a lot of blanks about what to expect once you get on the water.

Next, you'll want to talk to the owner of a bait shop. Now here's a spot where you've really got to be careful. Remember, this guy talks to dozens of fishermen every day, and every one wants to know where he can catch a bunch of fish. Put yourself in his shoes. If you had a lake that was producing some nice fish, would you send hundreds of tourists out to rape your honey hole? Not a chance.

But if you play your cards right, you may be able to milk some valuable information out of this guy. I may get into some trouble with bait shop owners about this, but there are two good ways to obtain information from a tight-lipped local.

First, flash a little cash. Make it obvious that you intend to spend some money on this trip, but only if you can find some fish. Don't tell him you're booked into the resort down the road for a week or two. If he knows that, he's got a captive audience. He knows you'll be around for a specified length of time and will drop some cash in his store whether you're catching fish or not. Give the impression you're either going to catch some fish or head down the road. He doesn't want to see a hot customer disappear and might just give you some good information.

Second, don't walk into the store like a novice on his only fishing trip of the year. Talk as intelligently as possible about fishing. Give him the impression that you're conservation minded—nobody likes meat hogs. Bait dealers and guides are bombarded with novices five months a year and aren't likely to send the average weekender anyplace where the fish are going. But if he suspects you're a skilled fisherman and care about nature, he might just take you under his wing.

That doesn't mean you should walk into the store wearing a jacket held together by patches. Your overall attitude about fishing and the basic knowledge you have of the sport are what will convince him that you know your stuff.

Not all baitshop owners are closed-mouthed. A few are more than willing to give you all the straight information they can. There's a good chance that, while you're on vacation, these guys are going to be into some kind of action. But only that tight little clique of local fishermen is going to know about it.

You can, if you play your cards right, be included in that clique. But only by gaining their confidence will they include you in the group. You'll have to convince them that you're a good fisherman and a conservationist and, most important, someone who will keep their secret in strictest confidence.

Now, let's get down to the subject at hand—fishing a strange lake. You've got half a dozen choices and weather conditions should dictate which body of water you choose for your initial outing.

As we mentioned earlier, if the weather has been stable for several days, that larger, clear-water lake with prominent weed growth could be producing some dandy walleye. If a cold front just moved through the area, you'll be better off working that more fertile, off-colored lake or a river.

Forget about the "you should have been here yesterday" story you're going to hear. And don't be misled by reports that a certain lake was really hot within the last few days. You could be on a wild goose chase if you worry about lakes that were hot last week.

Your only hope is to find a body of water that's producing now. Fish caught by the guys in cabin number six last weekend may not do you any good.

Based on weather conditions and time of year, select a body of water for your first outing. After wasting the better part of a day picking the bait dealer's brain, you're probably a little impatient to wet a line. Don't get overly anxious. Spend some time getting a feel for the lake before you actually go fishing.

In your frequent checks at the bait shop, you may see a guide or two coming in with some nice catches of fish. If that happens, it might not be a bad idea to hire a guide for one or two trips. A good guide will not only take you to a productive lake, he'll also show you the most productive tactics for that particular area. If you're really determined to make this a successful fishing trip, hiring a guide can be a worthwhile investment.

Oh, it may sting your pride a bit to think you have to hire a guide. But listen folks, one of the advantages I have as a professional fisherman travelling around the country filming my *Good Fishing* television series, is that I get to share a boat with some of the top hands in each area of the country. I think I've compiled a fair amount of walleye savvy over the years, but I'm never too old or too experienced to learn. There's always a new trick to be picked up. I'm not the least bit afraid to expose myself to anything new, and you shouldn't be either.

If you decide to tackle the lake on your own, purchase a map and spend some time studying the contours and marking the more likely fish-holding areas. But remember that maps show only part of the

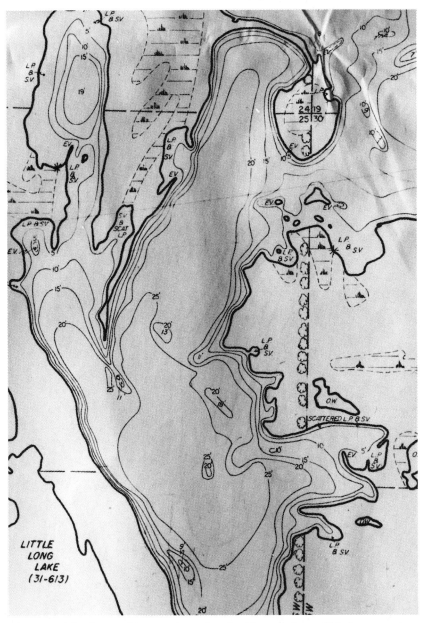

***Figure 1.*** A hydrographic map is an invaluable tool that will help you get on fish holding structure in no time at all.

picture. I have yet to see a lake map that included all of the best structures. In fact, the best spots usually don't appear. You'll have to find those for yourself.

Using the map as a guide, make a few preliminary trips around the lake to familiarize yourself with the system. Once you get your bearings, start looking for particulars.

Begin by finding the primary breakline, the depth at which the first sharp drop in the bottom occurs. Let's say on this lake the primary breakline is at 19 feet. You run the entire lake at 19 feet, looking for points, hooks, bars and the like. Each time you encounter such a structure, carefully mark it on your map for future reference.

Once you've run the entire shoreline, you'll want to explore the main body of the lake. This is relatively simple with a smaller lake and a real time-consuming chore on a big lake.

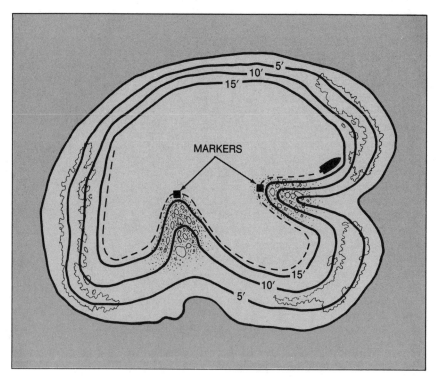

**Figure 2.** Start your search for fish holding structures by running the first distinct breakline and marking points and sharp inside turns.

If the lake is a few hundred acres, you can quickly check it out by running a criss-cross pattern and watching your depth-finder. A quality flasher will allow you to run the lake at full throttle and still find every slight change in bottom content. Should you run across an island or bar in the middle of the lake, carefully mark the outline on your map. I'd suggest using marker buoys so you can develop a clear mental picture of exactly what's down there. And, by all means, record all shoreline markings so you can easily relocate the structure later when it's time to actually start fishing.

On a big lake, something with a few thousand acres or more, it's best to divide the lake into sections. Look at each section as an individual lake. If the lake is very large, you may have to limit yourself to one or two sections each day. Don't hurry through this process—mid-lake structures likely will hold a lot of walleyes and you'll want to check them out as thoroughly as possible.

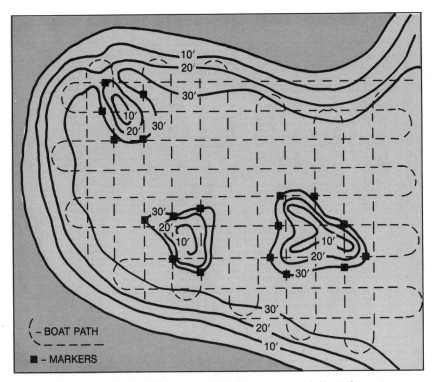

**Figure 3.** You can find midlake structures by running a lake with a criss-cross pattern, marking structures as you go.

*Babe and Bud Riser, editor and publisher of **Walleye Magazine**, worked out a successful pattern and caught this beautiful stringer of walleyes.*

If you have the equipment, you'll want to run temperature and pH profiles of the water. In the shallow eutrophic lakes, you may even want to check oxygen levels.

Make elaborate notes to yourself on the map. What's the bottom content? Is it rock, gravel or sand? What kind of weeds are growing on the bottom, coontail or cabbage? Are the weeds thick or sparse? What is the water color? What kind of baitfish can you spot in the shallows?

By now, you should be developing a mental picture of the lake. Working out the shoreline areas was easy, plotting the mid-lake structures takes a bit more time. But the few hours you've devoted to this learning process is well worth the effort. There's nothing more frustrating than to spend a week of hard fishing on a body of water only to learn that while you were striking out, someone else was slaughtering big fish on an unmapped island.

If you work hard enough at it, you can know as much about a lake in half a day's time as most of the locals know about it.

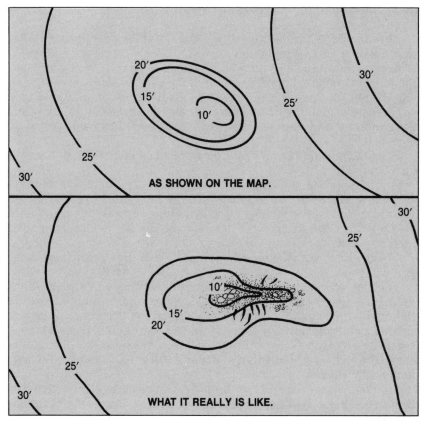

**Figure 4.** Hydrographic maps are great for locating structures, but are often incomplete. Check each structure thoroughly for overlooked "mini-structures."

If you're fishing a eutrophic lake, you'll encounter different scouting options. Some lakes tend to be dishpans, and often as not the fish will be relating to the weed growth. Look for the largest food shelves with the best-looking weed growths.

Oxygen, or lack of it, may be a problem on such a lake, especially in July and August. That's one reason the fish will be relating to the weeds. They also may be hanging around any moving water. If rivers or streams feed the lake, the point of conjunction is an excellent place to begin your search for walleyes.

You can also study the bottom for slight changes in content. On prairie lakes a small gravel bed surrounded by muck or a clam bed on a large sand flat will often attract fish.

On rivers and reservoirs, you'll be able to limit your choices by "reading water".

On a river, look for tell-tale surface boils that indicate an underwater obstruction of some sort. A large boulder, rock pile or sandbar under the surface serves as a current break for active walleyes. Look for inside and outside turns into the river channel, eddies, backwater areas ... anything that might hold fish. Don't stop and fish each one as you come to it, but develop an overall picture of a given stretch of river.

Develop the picture in your mind, looking at the overall river rather than just one or two particular spots.

Reservoirs can be easy to read. On most reservoirs, you can locate the old river channel just by watching the shoreline. Those steep cut-banks indicate the old river channel, gradually sloping hills suggest shallow water. Follow the channel, looking for bends or points where the shoreline and channel intersect. Check out bays and points on bays.

The final question is, how long do you fish each spot? That's a tricky question, at best.

Since you're dealing with an unknown quantity, you'll want to move as quickly as possible from one area to the next until a pattern begins to unfold. You can accomplish this by fishing several different depths at the same time. That's only possible, of course, if you have more than one fisherman in the boat.

Change lures with each pass, giving the fish the opportunity to tell you what they want.

The size of the structure will dictate how long you should spend there. On a very small sunken island, it may be possible to work it thoroughly in 10 or 15 minutes. With a large bar that contains several smaller points, some weeds, rock fingers and the like, it may take as much as an hour. Stick with it until you're confident that you've covered every possible section of the structure that could conceivably hold any walleyes.

But don't waste time, either. Initially, you're looking for active fish. Once you find active fish, you can begin the process of setting and fine-tuning your pattern.

Regardless of what kind of water you plan to fish, you'll be money ahead by taking the time to learn it thoroughly *before* you put a bait in the water. Believe me, I know how anxious you are to start fishing. But the extra effort spent learning everything you can about the lake you'll be fishing will pay big dividends in the long run.

## Trophy Hunting

Trophy. Whopper. Lunker. Brute. Mule. Horse. Wall-hanger.

Whatever you want to call it, there's nothing like catching a big walleye. For most fishermen, catching a ten-pound walleye is a dream, a bonus they hope will come their way once before they die. For the serious student of walleye fishing, catching a trophy is more than a dream, it's an obsession.

And why not? Catching a ten-pounder is the ultimate challenge in walleye fishing. Those ten-pounders are rare, no matter what body of water you fish. And getting one of those bruisers in the bottom of the net requires a lot of skill and experience. There's a bit of well deserved pride that goes with landing a ten-pounder.

*Another walleye comes to the net.*

275

## SELECTED STATE RECORDS

| State | Weight | Angler | Year | Where Caught |
|---|---|---|---|---|
| Arkansas | 22-11 | Al Nelson | 1982 | Greer's Ferry |
| Colorado | 16-8 | Julius Steuer | 1973 | Cherry Creek Reservoir |
| Kentucky | 21-8 | Abe Black | 1958 | Lake Cumberland |
| Michigan | 17-3 | Ray Fradley | 1951 | Pine River |
| Minnesota | 17-8 | LeRoy Chiovitte | 1979 | Seagull River |
| Missouri | 20-0 | John Vaholek | 1961 | St. Francis River |
| Nebraska | 16-2 | Herbert Cutshall | 1971 | Lake McConaughy |
| New York | 15-3 | Blanche Baker | 1952 | Chemung River |
| North Dakota | 15-12 | B. Chapman | 1959 | Wood Lake |
| Ohio | 15-1¼ | Steven Slowinski | 1980 | Maumee River |
| Oregon | 17-9½ | Peter Klick | 1984 | Columbia River |
| Pennsylvania | 17-9 | Mike Holly | 1980 | Kinzua Lake |
| South Dakota | 15-3 | George Heyde | 1979 | Missouri River |
| Tennessee | *25-0 | Mabry Harper | 1960 | Old Hickory |
| Virginia | 22-8 | Roy Barrett | 1973 | New River |
| Washington | 16-15 | | 1977 | Columbia River |
| West Virginia | 16-19 | E. C. Cox | 1967 | New River |
| Wisconsin | 18-0 | Tony Brothers | 1933 | High Lake |

* Indicates world record

## IGFA LINE-CLASS RECORDS

| Line Class | Weight | Angler | Date | Place |
|---|---|---|---|---|
| 1 kg (2 lb) | 4.70 kg (10-6) | Thomas Bitting | April 18, 1984 | Branched Oak (Neb) |
| 2 kg (4 lb) | 8.27 kg (18-4) | Mark Wallace | March 14, 1983 | Red River (Ark) |
| 4 kg (8 lb) | 8.75 kg (19-5) | Erma Windorff | March 2, 1982 | Greer's Ferry (Ark) |
| 6 kg (12 lb) | 10.29 kg (22-11) | Al Nelson | March 14, 1982 | Greer's Ferry (Ark) |
| 8 kg (16 lb) | 8.27 kg (18-4) | Howard Brierly | January 12, 1982 | Greer's Ferry (Ark) |
| 10 kg (20 lb) | 6.86 kg (15-2) | Dan Nelson | July 16, 1984 | Columbia River (Ore) |

I remember the first ten-pounder I ever put in the boat. It took years to bag my first one. But during the 1983 season, I caught 56 walleyes, each over eight pounds, one over 13 and three more over 11 pounds. Why the sudden land-slide of trophies?

Simple. Over the years I have learned to put myself in the right place, at the right time. And that, friends,is the biggest secret to catching a trophy fish of any species. Being in the right place at the right time.

Granted, a lot of big walleyes are caught by accident. Some folks are just plain lucky. I, however, have never fallen into that category. I've had to work for everything. If it was raining ten-pound walleyes, I'd get hit with a carp. And I think most fishermen are the same way. Perhaps 99 percent of the walleye enthusiasts in the country will never experience the thrill of landing a ten-pounder.

Still, there are a select group of anglers who consistently take fish in the eight, nine and ten-pound class, even bigger. And in just about every case, he's a guy who understands *when* and *where* to pursue trophy walleyes.

Maybe your favorite lake is an old (eutrophic) body of water that's weed choked and short on oxygen during the summer months. The lake produces lots of two and three-pounders and, at times, some five and six-pounders. You figure it's only a matter of time until you tie into a ten-pounder. You are wrong.

Chances are the body of water you're knocking yourself out over contains some ten-pounders, but certainly not in numbers great enough to make the odds of taking a trophy.

Not only must the lake contain a good population of trophy fish, but it also must have a reputation for producing lots of big fish. Maybe the Department of Natural Resources personnel in your area claims a particular body of water is literally teeming with big fish. That's fine, but if the environmental conditions aren't right, the lake may not yield more than one or two big fish a season. Unless you're the kind of person who always leaves Las Vegas with more money than he came with, you're wasting your time on such a lake.

Once you find a lake that produces lots of big fish, the next step is to time your trip accordingly, putting odds in your favor. On most bodies of water, big fish are caught more easily during certain times of year. Sure, they can be caught year-round. But if a big fish is your objective, it really helps to be on the water during those few times a year when the big fish are popping.

The last rule is that you must be fishing for big fish. You see, big fish are not the same as smaller fish. Presentations that work on two, three and four-pounders won't necessarily produce any nine, ten and 11-pounders. Big fish are different, and you'll be more successful if you tailor your presentation specifically for trophies.

Big fish, for instance, have more of a tendency to adhere to mini-structure. Your smaller fish may scatter randomly over the tops and edges of a particular structure. Your presentation can be slightly off and you'll still manage to catch some fish. But those big fish are special sort of creature. They're going to come up and tuck into a little hook, lie on a tiny stairstep or work around that one large boulder. A scattergun approach to working structure may produce some smaller fish, but you'll have to be right on the money if you want to fool a trophy.

Big fish are more affected by pH, light and oxygen levels and have a more sensitive sense of smell. Because their eyes are larger and more light sensitive, they are apt to hang back a little deeper than the rest, lying in the shadows. And a highly developed olfactory system enables them to detect the little foreign odors that younger fish might ignore. Then too, they certainly don't have to worry as much about predation as the smaller fish.

Yup, you have to do everything right to catch a trophy.

As we discussed earlier, fish tend to school by age classes. The longer a year-class group of walleyes has been in the system, the smaller it becomes. A school of three-pounders may contain 150 fish. Because of its number, the fish in that school are more competitive and more aggressive. By the time a fish reaches its eighth or tenth year, attrition has trimmed the school's numbers to a very few. These fish have reached the top of the food chain and no longer find it necessary to be highly competitive. They feed when they want and eat what they want, where they want.

Remember, too, that big fish didn't get that way be being stupid or careless. I'm not saying they have a higher degree of intelligence. But their survival skills have been honed to a fine edge by time and experience. They are, by nature, more easily spooked than smaller fish. And here's where a lot of fishermen get into trouble. I'd say that the majority of trophy fish I've hooked over the years were caught on the first pass over a structure. If several boats have made trolling passes over the area, there's a distinct possibility that the big fish have long since retreated to deeper water.

If I'm going to fish a structure I believe is holding trophy walleyes, I'll shut down the big engine long before arriving on the spot and sneak in using the electric trolling motor or idling the big engine. I don't want that lunker to know I'm around until it feels the sting of my hook in its lip.

Another common mistake made by would-be trophy-hunters is choice of equipment.

I'd wager that 75 percent (maybe as high as 90 percent) of the trophy walleyes hooked each year are lost because of faulty equipment. I've stressed the importance of using fresh line, tying a strong knot, sharpening hooks and fishing with the best rod and reel your budget can afford. Perhaps you didn't take me seriously because each year you land lots and lots of smaller walleyes without following my suggestions.

Gary Roach, one of the country's top anglers, hoists a 13-pound walleye.

Each season, as I travel the country talking and listening to avid anglers, I hear literally hundreds of fish stories. Usually they're about "the one that got away." Once you have that big fish hooked, the most important consideration is how well your tackle system is going to hold up. One weak link, and that monster is going to be free. It'll probably wind up dying of old age.

A fray at the end of the line might hold up under the pressure of an average-sized fish, but it'll fail every time under the weight of a trophy. A bargain-basement reel with a crude drag system will suffice for smaller fish, the first strong run by a trophy and the line is apt to break. That tiny little landing net has plenty of room for a three-pounder, but try to fit a 12-pounder inside.

Then, too, a lot of anglers panic when they tie into their first trophy fish. I guess there's nothing wrong with that. If you don't get excited about fighting a lunker, you should take up another sport. But try to keep your cool, even if your insides are break-dancing all over your body. The angler and the net man should be talking back and forth, planning their course of attack.

Be prepared for several things when you hook a fish that feels like a big rock. First, the chances are very good that fish is going to make a dash for the security of deep water.

If your line happens to be on the shallow side of the boat, move around to the other side at your first convenience. Eventually that fish will head straight out, and if it pulls your line under the boat, that can lead to some real problems.

Get that trolling motor or anchor rope out of the water. Don't give that monster a place to hang you up. Get the big motor up, too, unless the wind is blowing the boat toward shore. Keep someone on the motor at all times, ready to shut it down if the line gets anywhere near the prop.

Let the fish wear itself out down deep. Never try to horse a big fish. With 35 feet of line out, you have a lot of room for error. Should that trophy make a sudden run and your drag sticks momentarily, there may be enough stretch in the line to compensate. Better yet, learn to backreel.

Keep the rod tip high and maintain constant pressure on that fish. Never, never allow the fish any slack. All it needs is a split second with slack line and it'll spit the hook. With the rod tip high—I mean way over your head—you have more room for error. Should the fish make a sudden, unexpected run, you can drop the rod towards the water without putting too much pressure on the line.

Bring the fish to the boat as quickly as possible. Play it out thoroughly, but don't waste too much time. The longer that fish is in the water, the better the chance it's going to find a way to get free. Don't attempt to net a trophy until it's ready to be netted. The angler should lead the fish gently towards the net, head-first. By this time the fish should be on its side and thoroughly exhausted. Never chase the fish with the net, trying to take it from behind.

*Trophies like this are possible if you understand the habits of big fish.*

Most important, stay cool. One moment of panic may cost you a trophy. The longer you can keep your composure, the better the chances you'll get the fish to the taxidermist. You can faint *after* the fish is safely in the boat. Until then, keep your wits about you.

One more thing about trophy walleyes. To catch more than one, you've got to be fishing for them. Big fish require patience and special tactics.

Only rarely will the tactics that produce average walleyes put a monster in the boat. Usually, you'll have to be fishing specifically for lunkers.

At certain times of year, a salamander trolled off the edge of a rocky, submerged island, is an excellent way to catch a monster. Bear in mind that with a big old sally on the end of your line, you won't be turning many twos and three-pounders. Now, if everyone around you is pulling in smaller fish by the bucketful with leeches or minnows, the temptation will be to go with the flow. But if it's a trophy you're after, stick with the bigger baits.

The same is true in fall. A jig tipped with an over-sized shiner or chub (six to ten-inches) is a good bet to produce a wall-hanger. But, again, if everyone around you is pulling in three and four-pounders using small fatheads, it's going to be tough to pursue a trophy.

On some reservoirs where spinners are the number one producer, the big-fish enthusiasts use over-sized blades. We're talking No. 4, 5 or even 6 in the Colorados and 6 and 7 in the Indiana style. Big blades catch bigger fish. They might not catch as many fish, but they'll consistently produce bigger fish.

I know of some huge walleyes that have been caught trolling musky baits, like Lindy's Giant Shad. In several cases these baits are being trolled for suspended fish. That big old bait calls those walleyes from a long way down. I expect musky baits will be part of a revolutionary trophy pattern in the years ahead. My research staff is working on polishing this method right now.

Crankbaits like the Shadling turn a lot of over-sized fish. Again, a crankbait may not result in a large stringer of fish, although at times they certainly can. But if trophies are your goal, dragging a crankbait may be the answer.

There are a few things to remember once you do catch that trophy. I haven't seen the experienced fisherman yet who didn't take one look at his first big walleye and envision that fish hanging over the mantle. If you intend to have the fish mounted, there are several precautions that should be taken.

Never, never cut into that fish. Take it to the taxidermist whole. Handle that fish as carefully as possible. If you want to snap some pictures (and who wouldn't), go ahead. But don't beat the fish around any more than is necessary. Missing scales and broken fins are two of the toughest things any taxidermist must deal with.

If possible, put the fish on ice right away. If it's in the live well all afternoon, it's going to come out looking like Tex Cobb after going 15 rounds with Larry Holmes.

Once you're off the water, carefully wrap the fish in a large garbage bag. Tuck each fin against the body and secure it with masking tape. You may even want to place pieces of cardboard over the tail to keep it from being damaged. Lay the fish out flat in the freezer or take it directly to the taxidermist.

You'll want that fish to hang on your wall for many years. Select a quality taxidermist. A good professional will cost a little more money, but it's well worth the investment. Check his work. If his walleyes resemble chinook salmon, better find another taxidermist.

There are several things to look for. Is the lateral line straight? If the lateral line looks like a mountain highway, the guy isn't a quality taxidermist. Is the skin around the head of the fish shrinking? If it is, the guy probably hurries his work and doesn't give the fish ample opportunity to dry. Find someone else.

Does his paint job look natural? If the belly looks like it was done by a house-painter, you want a different taxidermist. A good taxidermist can repair damage to fins and the tail. If the dorsal fin looks like the fish went through a blender, you're not dealing with a competent taxidermist.

I know you're anxious to put that fish on the wall. But a good taxidermist probably won't have it done for a month or two—sometimes as long as six months to a year. Beware the taxidermist who promises the fish will be done a week from Tuesday.

Remember, I said catching big fish was mostly a matter of being in the right place at the right time. If you're not afraid to travel in pursuit of your trophy, you may want to consider booking a trip somewhere in the country (or Canada) where you'll have an excellent opportunity to catch big fish. No body of water guarantees a ten-pounder, not even for the most experienced of anglers. But, there are a few lakes, rivers and streams that have a tradition of turning out trophies. What follows is a list of some of the better trophy waters around the country, including the best time of year to fish and more successful tactics for turning in big fish.

### Columbia River

I can't think of a better place to catch a ten-pound walleye than the Columbia River in Washington and Oregon.

In two extended trips in 1983 and 1984, Dan Nelson and Gary Roach put *23 walleyes over ten pounds* in their boats! The biggest was Dan's 15-pound, 2-ounce lunker—one of the finest walleyes caught in recent years. At least five more of those fish were better than 13 pounds.

The Columbia has an excellent population of big fish. According to rumor (and what's trophy fishing without tantalizing rumors?), a walleye exceeding the current world record of 25 pounds was "rolled up" by a fisheries electro-shocking crew in 1983. Fish from 17 to 19 pounds show up in test nets with amazing frequency. The state records in both

Washington and Oregon are now over 17 pounds, with both fish coming from the Columbia.

There just isn't any other place in this country or Canada where a good fisherman is so likely to catch a ten-pounder. Commercial fishing by Indians threatens the fishery, but for right now the Columbia is *the* trophy hunter's preferred hunting grounds.

## Lake Sakakawea

Of the six mainstream reservoirs on the Missouri River system, North Dakota's Lake Sakakawea is the top producer of trophy walleyes.

*Dan Nelson (left) and Dave Jenson had never seen the stretch of water that produced this dandy stringer of walleyes. But as you can see, they worked out a fish-catching pattern.*

Like the Columbia, Sakakawea's future as a trophy fishery is uncertain. Prime spawning conditions for several consecutive years back in the 1970s resulted in several huge year classes of fish. Those fish have survived in good numbers and have been providing some incredible trophy fishing in recent years.

Strong year classes, coupled with a thriving forage base of rainbow smelt, make Sakakawea one of the top spots in the country to catch a wall-hanger.

Surprisingly, one of the best times to fish Sakakawea is July. Because of mountain runoff that enters the lake via Montana's Fort Peck reservoir, Sakakawea warms slowly. Depending on water levels and the amount of runoff, the walleyes usually go on a feeding binge beginning about the 4th of July. During this spree, hundreds of eight to 12-pound walleyes will be harvested.

The best presentation is a leech, nightcrawler or minnow speed-trolled behind a big-blade spinner. The fish are usually fairly shallow at this time of year, seldom going deeper than 15 feet, and often found in four to seven feet. Crankbaits can also produce some excellent catches.

Fall is another good time to fish Sak. The fall run can last anywhere from a few weeks to several months. Fuzz-E-Grub jigs tipped with big baits produce most of the trophy fish in fall.

## Lake Oahe

Below Sakakawea lies Lake Oahe, which runs all the way to Pierre, S.D. Oahe was, at one time, a top producer of big fish. And I expect that during the next few years it will once again be one of the country's hot spots.

Several strong year classes of fish are fast approaching trophy proportions and within a few short years the system promises to explode. With normal water levels, the best fishing will occur in the Mobridge-to-Gettysburg area. With high water, look for the fish to move upstream from Pollack (S.D.) and Fort Yates (N.D.).

Oahe tends to be most productive during the latter part of May and all through June. It's not a trophy fishery right now, but keep an eye on it. The future is extremely bright.

## Gull Lake

This is one of my personal favorites because it lies just a few minutes from my home in Brainerd, Minnesota.

Gull doesn't kick out big fish as consistently as the first three bodies of water I mentioned, but it has the capacity to produce a lot of hawgs in a short period of time.

Gary Roach took one of the heaviest stringers of walleyes I've ever seen off Gull just a few years back. His two-man limit for two days of fishing *averaged* ten pounds. And his first day's catch averaged an incredible 12 pounds.

Even though Gull Lake lies in the heart of tourist country and receives a lot of fishing pressure, it continues to produce trophy walleyes, perhaps a couple of hundred a year over eight pounds.

The best time to fish Gull lake is from Memorial weekend through the first part of June. The best depth depends a lot on conditions, and could run anywhere from 18 to 40 feet.

A rig and a leech or nightcrawler and sometimes a jig and leech combination seem to be most effective, but some real dandies have fallen for a salamander.

Look for quick drop-offs and rock breaks, prominent points or sand and gravel with clam beds.

Gull is one of those rare heavily developed trophy lakes. It has several luxurious resorts, which means you can combine a family outing and a trophy hunt. It's a beautiful lake located in the midst of some of the most beautiful country on earth.


## Lake Saganaga

Located on the Minnesota-Ontario border, Saganaga has produced some of the most remarkable catches of trophy walleyes of any body of water in the country. The biggest fish I know of was caught in 1979 on Sag and held the Minnesota state record at 17-8.

A 7,800 acre lake, Saganaga is a typical Canadian Shield lake that yields hundreds of trophy walleyes each season. Located on the Seagull River, Sag yielded three walleyes over 12 pounds to one fisherman on one outing—his first fishing trip ever!!! Talk about being born lucky!

The best times to fish are from the opener through June and early July. As with other typical Canadian Shield lakes, the fish can be doing a lot of different things, depending on when you visit the 135-foot deep body of water.


## Sturgeon Bay

Located off Lake Michigan near the town of Sturgeon Bay in Wisconsin, this fishery offers not only good trophy walleyes but a real diversity of tactics and structures to be fished.

Crankbaits probably produce most of the top action during July and August, but rigs and jigs also take their share of lunkers.

There are all types of structures to be considered. And they'll be teeming with everything from big walleyes to jumbo salmon. A fun trip.

## Saginaw Bay

Michigan's Saginaw Bay, located off Lake Huron, is making a strong comeback as a walleye fishery.

The spring fishery has traditionally been tops, with a jig-and-minnow combination accounting for a lot of fish around the mouths of the Themes and Rifle rivers. Because it has fairly stained water, Saginaw Bay has the capacity to produce a lot of big fish all through July. Crankbaits worked in three to 12 feet of water produce the best summertime catches.

The more activity that takes place on this Michigan hot spot, the more new big walleye patterns are being discovered.

*Babe lands a Saginaw Bay walleye as the television camera crew capture the action on film.*

## Lake Simcoe

Located in southwestern Ontario, Lake Simcoe is only about an hour's drive west and north of Toronto.

One of the biggest stringers of walleyes ever caught came out of Simcoe. That stringer included a couple of 12 and 16-pounders and one 17 and one 18-pounder. Every year walleyes over 20 pounds are netted from this Shield lake.

May and June sees huge walleyes caught with regularity. In May, the best tactic is to work off points with a jig and a leech.

In June, the fish will suspend to feed on cisco and tullibee. A lot of monsters are caught on crankbaits in ten to 12 feet of water over anywhere from 30 to 100 feet of water.

I've talked before about suspended walleyes. As more anglers experiment with the suspension factor and uncover the secrets of catching suspended fish, I expect to see some mind boggling catches coming from Lake Simcoe.

### Georgian Bay

Located on the Canadian side of Lake Huron, Georgian Bay produces some exceptional walleye fishing.

There are any number of rivers dumping into the bay. Among the best are the French, the Key and the Pickerel.

May and June are good times to visit Georgian Bay with minnow bait proving to be the most productive lure. Late fall also sees many lunkers boated. Trolling big Raps just under the surface turns a lot of suspended fish, both night and day.

### Pipestone Lake

An hour's drive north of International Falls, Minnesota, this Ontario Lake is one of my favorites. It's not only a beautiful body of water, but it contains some huge walleyes along with great musky and smallmouth fishing.

Depending on weather conditions, the fishing usually picks up around Memorial Day and becomes fairly consistent during June and July.

The biggest walleye I know of from Pipestone weighed 19 pounds. I've observed bigger fish and have caught a lot of ten to 13-pounders.

Like most Canadian Shield lakes, Pipestone has a lot of pattern possibilities.

I've had my best luck with a jig-and-leech combination, but a floating rig has also fooled some wise old walleyes.

Early in the year the fish will be fairly shallow, but by July they'll have moved down to 30 to 35 feet.

A trip to Pipestone has become a regular annual event for the Winkelman family, and we've never yet been disappointed.

*Jimmy Hayes of Pipestone Lodge hoists a beautiful stringer of walleyes and bonus smallmouth bass.*

## Oak Orchard Creek

Located on Lake Ontario, not far from Rochester and Syracuse, Oak Orchard Creek is another body of water where walleyes are doing a lot of suspending. Fall is the best time to fish here.

I know of any number of ten to 12-pounders caught from 70 to 80 feet by salmon fishermen. Why are the walleyes down there? Forage, of course. They're feeding on smelt and shad. They're deep and suspended, and that makes for some tricky fishing. Late summer and fall are prime times.

## Lake Erie

Most of Lake Erie, particularly the Western Basin, is noted for numbers of fish rather than size. It's not uncommon to catch a couple hundred walleyes a day casting to suspended fish. But Lake Erie also has some trophies for those willing to move out and go deep.

Downrigger fishermen around Barcelona Harbor and Dunn Creek Harbor have been hitting a lot of seven to 12 pound fish using Finsel Spoons and fishing 60 to 100 feet of water. And I mean a lot of big fish. More suspended walleyes, more food for thought. August and September are usually best.

Another big-fish area on Lake Erie is just off Buffalo, New York, where, again, you will encounter suspended fish. This section of water is most productive during the fall period when fish suspend five to ten feet under the surface over 30 to 40 feet of water.

Drifting and casting a weight forward spinner has produced a tremendous number of seven to ten-pound walleyes.

As long as we're still in that region of the country, how about the Sandusky and Maumee rivers in Ohio? The spring spawning run which occurs in March and April, provides the best opportunity to tie into a record fish. A jig-and-minnow combination takes a lot of fish, but shore fishermen also enjoy a great deal of success during the spring season.

Several state records have been caught on these rivers, including the current Ohio standard of just over 15 pounds caught in 1980.

## Arkansas

There's no better place in the world to look for a *world record walleye* than several of the big reservoirs located in Arkansas.

If you had to bet on one body of water that will produce the next world record, it would have to be Greer's Ferry. The current state record of 22-11 came out of Greer's Ferry in 1982, and each spring literally dozens of walleyes topping 17 pounds are caught.

Most of the huge fish are caught during the spawning run, which occurs in late February and early March. The best area would be one of the three branches of the Little Red River.

Greer's Ferry is a 31,000 acre impoundment with a maximum depth of 200 feet and clear water. It's best known for its bass and crappie fishing, but also contains a limited number of monster walleyes.

Another good bet in Arkansas is Bull Shoals. This 45,000 acre reservoir also contains some very big walleyes, perhaps some up to 20 pounds. But, again, it's a spring shot.

No one has really figured out how to catch walleyes from either of these reservoirs during the summer months. A good bet is that the fish are suspending.

Neither of these bodies of water has a strong walleye population, just a few very, very big fish. And with all the pressure on those fish during the spawning run, your chances of catching a monster are not terrific. On the other hand, if you're the lucky sort, there's no better place to catch a fish weighing 15, 17 or even 20 pounds.

*A big stringer of big fish. Understanding the system and putting together a fish-catching pattern resulted in this catch.*

## Merritt Reservoir

Nebraska's number one walleye lake used to be McConaughy. Mac used to kick out an incredible number of ten-pound walleyes. But a forage imbalance brought about by the introduction of stripers temporarily brought the Platte River impoundment to its knees. Fisheries personnel are working to rectify the situation and Big Mac promises to be a top walleye producer again in the near future.

But for right now, the best water in Nebraska is Merritt Reservoir, located in the central part of the state just below the South Dakota border.

A 2,800 acre lake, Merritt produces a lot of ten-pound plus fish in May and June. Jigs fished fairly deep off prominent points produce the best action during this time.

## Glen Elder

The folks in Kansas are pretty excited about their rapidly developing walleye fisheries. And why not? They may have some of the best walleye fishing in the country down there.

Glen Elder is probably the best of the state's many reservoirs. A 12,000 acre impoundment, Glen Elder has strong year classes of fish in the two to three-pound range but has been producing a lot of ten-pounders lately. And I look for it to get better as time goes on.

May and June offer the best fishing. Look for walleyes suspended in the brush feeding on shad. Yo-yoing a jig in that brush is a dynamite way to get those bruisers out.

## Winnipeg River

Back north, the Winnipeg River is an excellent bet for a ten-pound walleye. The area around Pine Falls, a couple of hours east of Winnipeg, offers some of the best fishing during the fall period.

A jig-and-minnow fished around 20 feet is the top producer.

Another great place to catch jumbo walleyes is the Red River just north of the city of Winnipeg. September, October and November are the most productive months.

## Mille Lacs

Do you wonder why I live where I do? As close as Gull Lake is on one side of my house, Mille Lacs is on the other. And Mille Lacs is one of the country's foremost walleye factories.

Mille Lacs holds lots of big fish. It isn't the best place in the country to catch a ten-pounder, but you can put a lot of fish in the boat that will be pushing that magic mark and there's always the possibility of a ten-pounder.

Some of the best fishing occurs at night in August and September, casting crankbaits in two to eight feet on reefs or islands. Those same areas will produce a lot of fish during the daytime hours in a big wind. The best tactic is using a slip bobber tipped with a leech.

Mille Lacs is a big (115,000 acres), shallow body of water that can really get ornery in a wind. But when the waves are rolling, that's the best time to be chasing trophy walleyes.

## Attitude

I was guiding a gentlemen to walleyes. Well, actually I wasn't guiding. I've tried to get away from that. What this fellow wanted was an on-the-water course in fishing. And since he was willing to meet my price, I agreed to conduct a three-day seminar under actual fishing conditions.

This gentleman, whom I refer to as the "Tooth Fairy" because he was a lovable fellow who happened to be a dentist, assured me that catching fish was not his primary concern. He wanted to learn how to catch fish. He had an intense desire to learn more about the sport.

The first two days were devoted to studying depth finders, boat control, equipment, presentation and structure. Since there was no emphasis on catching fish, we didn't necessarily hit the spots that were producing a lot of walleyes, opting instead for areas that afforded the best conditions for teaching.

When we returned to the ramp after the second day, several other boats showed up with healthy stringers of fish. We had caught only a few, smaller fish. It was obvious that the Tooth Fairy was disappointed and really wanted to put his lessons to practice by tying into some big walleyes. So, I decided we'd spend day number three trying to fill the live well.

After several hours of point-hopping, we ran across a sunken island that was loaded with active fish. But by this time the Tooth Fairy had lost his intensity. He had become convinced we weren't going to catch any fish.

A few passes over this island produced several beautiful walleyes, five and six-pounders. But the Tooth Fairy hadn't caught anything. And I knew that in his frame of mind, he wasn't going to. This called for drastic action.

Since I was catching quite a few fish, I offered him my lucky rod and reel to which was attached my lucky lure. I hoped this offering would perk up his spirits long enough to finally put a fish in the boat.

It worked. For the duration of that pass he was alert and attentive. And sure enough, he managed to tie into a nice fish. After that he got hot and before long we were approaching a limit of walleyes. He closed out the day with a beauty that was pushing eight pounds. It was the most successful trip of his life.

What turned a dismal trip into a roaring success? A change in attitude. Plain and simple. Just a slight adjustment in his attitude helped the Tooth Fairy catch fish.

Veteran guides know the importance of attitude. Many's the time a guide would run the boat over a shallow, rocky shelf or through a snag area just so his clients could feel something tugging on the end of their line. The guide knew there were no fish there. He just wanted to get the client's attention long enough to get him believing there was a chance of catching fish.

Why is attitude important? There are two schools of thought on this. First, and very obviously, you're going to catch more fish when you're alert and poised. It's a rare walleye that commits suicide on your hook. It happens, but not very often.

If you don't believe you're going to catch fish, your mind wanders and you're not ready to react to that subtle bump from the other end of the line. By the time you wake up and react, the fish is gone.

It's the same if you're working a piece of structure. Maybe you know the fish are holding at 19 feet. If you're not glued to your depth-finder and studying every inch of that contour, you can easily spend more time in 25 feet than you do in 19 feet. You might miss that rock ledge on the tip of the point, you might not see the school of baitfish on the flasher or that big fish suspended just off the edge of the weeds.

If you don't believe you'll catch fish, chances are you won't. You don't fish well if you're not attentive.

Fishing is like any other endeavor. Would you want a doctor to perform delicate surgery on your body if he wasn't giving the operation 100 percent of his attention? Would you want a lawyer to defend you if his mind was someplace else? Would you trust your car to a mechanic who was more interested in his own problems than he was in repairing your vehicle?

There's not a walleye under 9 pounds on this stringer. Babe was obviously tickled over this mess of fish.

Fishing requires the same kind of intensity. Athletes go into slumps when something in their lives breaks their concentration. And the slump worsens when they stop believing they're going to hit a home run or complete a pass.

Football, baseball, law, medicine, fishing . . . life . . . all require 100 percent devotion to duty if the participant hopes to be successful.

There's another, less obvious aspect of attitude that goes beyond mere alertness. It's almost as if you can *will* fish to bite. No, I'm not probing into the supernatural here. But I strongly believe there's something to it.

I personally have gone out on days when I wasn't in the right frame of mind, and it showed in my overall success. I fished the same, went through all the motions, but just couldn't get into much action.

It's almost as if you're sending an electrical current down that line. When you start believing you're going to catch fish, the fish start biting. If you get down on yourself, the fish disappear.

Before you dismiss such talk as sheer lunacy, think about other activities. Have you ever gotten hot at the poker or blackjack tables? Ever get on a streak where you just *knew* you were going to win? When someone gets hot in a card game, the best thing his opponent can do is to slow the game down and wait until the fellow cools off.

Fishing can be the same way. I've seen guys working a section of water that was literally teeming with fish. They were using the same baits or lures and making basically the same presentation as every one else in the vicinity. But they weren't catching fish while others were.

I've been in the boat with guys who couldn't catch any fish, even though everyone around them was having a field day. In some cases it might have to do with the equipment they're using, lack of intensity, a foreign odor on their hands or whatever. But sometimes, I'm convinced, it's simply that they don't *believe* they're going to catch fish.

You gotta believe. It's almost like magic when you start believing the fish are going to bite. You're giving off good vibrations. Without those "vibes," you simply aren't going to catch many fish. With them, you may fill the boat.

I can even take that one step further. Some people believe they are going to catch big fish. They can be in the same boat with a couple of anglers, and nine times out of ten they'll catch the biggest fish. It's like they're telegraphing a message through the water to those big fish down there.

One of the best ways I know to improve your attitude about fishing is to enter a tournament. I enjoy and believe in competitive fishing. Even though I don't have time to fish for money any more, I think the experience of fishing in competition will probably make a better angler of anyone who tries it. Some folks thrive on competition. To be a top contender, you'll force yourself to concentrate harder and maintain a positive attitude about your chances of catching more fish.

*Releasing fish is a great conservation practice. This is one big female that will live to drop her eggs again. You don't have to release all the fish you catch ... keep a few for eating. But throw back a few as well, especially those prime females in the 4 to 7-pound range.*

For one thing, you learn a lot about intensity in a tournament. You can slough off in your day-to-day fishing, when you don't have to be versatile and cover a lot of water. But in a tournament, things are different. Your name is up there on the board and pride will force you to be the best fisherman you can. You want to do well because your ego is on the line. So is your partner's.

So from the shotgun start to the final weigh-in, you give it your best shot. And you learn, through experience, that putting forth a little extra effort can pay big dividends.

There's another thing about tournament fishing. When we go out for a Saturday afternoon and get skunked, it's easy to rationalize "the fish weren't biting today." But in a tournament, that excuse gets tossed out the door when the top 20 teams all come in with nice stringers. The fish *were* biting. You just didn't figure out what was necessary to catch them.

Often as not, some of the winners will share information with you. After the tournament is over, that is. You can learn from your mistakes, see what the other guy did and gain some valuable experience.

Don't go into your first tournament with the idea of taking home a trophy or lots of cash. Go into a tournament with the idea of learning a lot about fishing and learning something about yourself as a fisherman and about your intensity level.

Intensity is something you have to work at every second you're on the water. I don't mean you have to bang your head against the wall of the bait shop, like an NFL linebacker getting psyched up for a big game. And you don't have to close yourself off from your fishing companions to the point where you're no fun to fish with.

But you should gear yourself up to being alert. Look for the little signs along the way that will help you establish a pattern. Sometimes success is as close as the tip of your nose, but you miss the clues because you're not paying attention.

If you're more concerned about drinking beer or concentrating on your problems, things just won't fall into place on the water. There's a time and a place for everything. And if you want to be a successful fisherman, you should devote as much of your attention to fishing as possible during the time you're on the water.

Think of yourself as a hunter. Be aggressive and seek out fish. Don't sit and wait for the fish to come to you.

You must be willing to practice versatility. Maybe those walleyes just don't want a jig today. Maybe they're looking for something else. With the proper attitude, you'll be able to switch presentations all day long until you find the right one. But if you really don't believe you're going to catch fish, retying lures can become a useless drudgery.

Nor will you feel like running from spot to spot trying to fine-tune a locational pattern. You'll make it through the first couple of spots, but then your intensity will begin to wane and you'll find yourself spending an hour on a point that simply isn't holding any fish. It's just holding you, because you're getting lazy or losing confidence.

I like to relate fishing to waterfowl hunting. Most successful waterfowl hunters build elaborate blinds or pits, set out an impressive set of decoys and employ a good call. They wait until just the right moment before jumping up and firing their gun.

What would you think about a waterfowler who sat on a hillside, firing three rounds into the air every five minutes, hoping a duck would fly into his shot pattern? Obviously, that kind of hunter wouldn't be very successful. Do you fish like that?

It's a laughable thought. Yet that's the way a lot of folks fish for walleyes. They anchor their boat on a spot that produced walleyes a month earlier, toss out a line and wait for a fish to come along and bite their bait.

*Attitude can make the difference between a fishless day and this beautiful sight.*

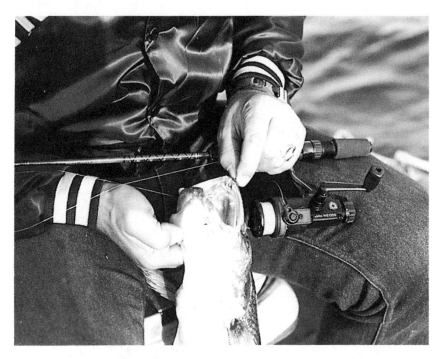

*The reward for the aggressive fisherman.*

The aggressive fisherman doesn't wait for walleyes to come to him. He goes out and tests water, trying to establish some sort of locational pattern. He's constantly changing lures, looking for the best possible presentation for the conditions.

His approach is that of a hunter, stalking fish. He knows he's going to find and catch fish. He takes pride when he's met the challenge and learns from those days when nature chooses to humble him. But above all, he respects what nature is giving him and appreciates his right to participate in one of the grandest sports on earth. And that, to me, is what fishing is all about.

Hey, good fishing!

## The "Facts of Fishing" Video Library

The **Facts of Fishing Video Library** is the only video tape series that teaches a *complete system* for catching fish. Each fantastic tape outlines a specific area of fishing and features a complete understanding of the methods and techniques for successful angling. 18 Unique and exciting titles to choose from. $39.95 each

*VT01*—**Walleye I**—Waging War on Weed Walleyes, Suspended Walleye of Lake Erie, Beaver House Walleye, Deadliest Method for Trophy Walleye, Minnow Madness for Walleye, Trophy Walleye of Lake Sakakawea

*VT02*—**Largemouth Bass I**—Cattail Bass, Bullrush Bassin' Tactics, Coping with Cold Fronts, The Fall Bonanza, Lily Pad Bucketmouths, Understanding Weedline Bass

*VT03*—**Great Lakes Salmon and Trout**—Kings of the Great Lakes, Chinook Stocking Builds Fishery, Early Season Lake Trout Secrets, Ski for Steelhead and Lake Trout, Fall Run Pink Salmon

*VT04*—**Smallmouth Bass I**—Early Season Tactics, Cranking Summer Smallies, Fall Run River Smallmouth, Autumn's Bronze Bombshells, Smallmouth Bassin—Great Lakes Style

*VT05*—**Walleye II**—Bill Binkelman—A Fishing Legend, The Great Lakes Walleye Breakthrough, Creating a Walleye Bonanza, Dr. Loren Hill—pH & the Walleye, A Unique Pattern for Big "Weed Walleyes," Porkin' Out Walleyes—A Totally New System, Walleye Secrets from Around the World

*VT06*—**Largemouth Bass II**—Bass & Rice—A Unique Combination, Dr. Loren Hill On pH & Bass Fishing, Bustin' Bass Off the "Flats," Flippin for Timber Bass, Boat Dock Bassin', Frog Run Bassin', Jig & Pig Bassin'

*VT07*—**Panfish I**—White Bass—The Silver Scrapper, EZ Summer Crappies, Whitefish...Panfish of the North, Small Pond Panfish, Deep Water Slab Crappies, ABCs of Ice Fishing

*VT08*—**Northern Pike I**—Fight'n Pike of Manitoba, Trophy Pike Tackle, Monster Northerns of Recluse Lake, Reindeer Lake—BIG Water, BIG Pike

*VT19*—**Jig Fishing**—Jigs—The All-Around Lure, Jigs & Walleyes...a Natural, Jiggin' Leeches, Jigs...Crappie Magic, Quiver Jigs & Smallmouth Bass, Jigs & Crawlers for Walleyes

*VT20*—**Northern Pike II**—Bucktail Spinnerbait Secrets, Jerkbait Pike Trolling Tactics, Trophy Lake—Trophy Pike

*VT21*—**Smallmouth Bass II**—Jig & Leech Smallies, Smallmouth Gold, Minnowbait Tactics, St. Clair Smallmouth, Spinnerbait Smallmouth

*VT22*—**Live Bait Rigging**—Back to Bobbers, Floater Rigs, One Deadly System, The Crawler "Hauler"?, Time Tested—The Lindy Rig

*VT23*—**The Basics of Fishing**—A Beginners Guide To..., How to Get Started, Basic Tackle, Basic Skills, Fish and Their World, Babe's Pattern Fishing Principles

*VT24*—**Fishing—The Electronic Age**—In the Beginning, Sonar...Which One For You, Big Water Electronics, Battery Maintenance, Electronic Accessories, Future Electronics

*VT25*—**Atlantic Salmon: A New Brunswick Angling Tradition**—In the Canadian province of New Brunswick, there is an angling tradition so important it borders on religious. Fly-fishing for the acrobatic, immense atlantic salmon is a sport handed down to today's anglers by the fanatic, gentlemen casters of the past.

*VT26*—**Canoe Country Fishing: Angling in the Quetico-Boundary Waters**—Come fish a place where there are no motors, no sounds except those made by animals and the wind. The experience of wilderness is the same as it was when this expansive natural garden served as the water highways of the rugged voyagers.

Babe Winkelman gives you everything you need to know to make such a trip yourself. Through leading authorities, you learn: how to plan; why it is best (and less expensive) to work through an outfitter; how to paddle and portage a canoe; how to select a camp site; and, of course, Babe himself teaches you how to fish the scrappy smallmouth bass and abundant walleye.

*VT27*—**Fishing Ontario: It's Incredible!**—Ontario! The name alone conjures up images. Lakes, crystal clear and rimmed with rock and pine. Fish as long as your arm. The lonely cry of the loon. Join Babe Winkelman as he catches fish from one of his favorite places on earth. He feels the pulse of this world, capable of giving up numbers of huge fish. It is a fragile yet bountiful environment and this is a tape you will love. Species featured are walleye, lake trout, northern pike, and brook trout.

*VT28*—**Understanding Walleye**—The name is simple, but the subject a constant source of fascination and frustration for anglers throughout North America. Learn the complete story of this fish from the man who built an international reputation for catching them! Babe Winkelman lays a foundation of knowledge that is a basis for future walleye videos to come. This is the angler's encyclopedia of walleye information from seasonal movements and the basic biology of the species to, most of all, tips and secrets for catching them under all conditions. If you only have one walleye video, this is the one to have!

## Babe Winkelman's "Fishing Secrets"

Babe introduces a sizzling new video series titled, *Fishing Secrets.* Each action-packed video is crammed with facts, tips and fishing's best-kept secrets. *Fishing Secrets,* at a very affordable price, contains the type of "inside" information anglers are looking for from a man they know they can trust...except with their secrets! Approx. 50 min. each. $19.95

*VT100*—**Land of the Midnight Sun: Saskatchewan Fly-In Fishing**—The rugged beauty of a wilderness land untamed by man comes to life as Babe Winkelman offers a special journey into the heart of fishing's dream land. Explosive and awe-inspiring segments on northern pike, arctic grayling, and lake trout.

*VT101*—**Water Wolves of the North: A Northern Pike Spectacular**—Babe Winkelman entertains and teaches viewers everywhere to catch savage northern pike. Contains thrilling non-stop action footage of some of the largest pike ever captured on video.

*VT102*—**Wilderness Walleyes: The Lure of Ontario**—In a home video destined to be a scenic and educational classic, Babe Winkelman teaches four separate modern approaches to finding and catching the fish he built his reputation on: the walleye. Spectacular underwater footage.

*VT103*—**"Summer Heat" Bass: No Sweat!**—Most fishermen have trouble catching bass in midsummer. Babe Winkelman teaches his time-tested methods for catching big bass, in a variety of locations, during the scorching days of summer.

*VT104*—**The Great Lake Erie: A Fishing Success Story**—Babe Winkelman shows you more than one way to catch walleye and smallmouth bass from Lake Erie and tells the amazing story of the lake's comeback from environmental disaster.

*VT105*—**Trophy Time: Fall Fishing Bonanza**—The crisp weather of fall stirs the biggest lunkers into action and Babe Winkelman shows how to be in the right place at the right time. Take this personally guided hunt for those rod-busting brutes of autumn! Features walleye, bass, and crappie.

*VT106*—**Land of 100,000 Lakes: Manitoba Magic**—Come fish the land where legends are born, with legendary fisherman Babe Winkelman. Yes, Manitoba is a huge land of huge fish. If you love fishing, or ever plan to visit the *Land of 100,000 Lakes*, let Babe show you what the legends are all about.

*VT107*—**Cold Water — Hot Action: Ice Fishing Fever**—Ice fishing has undergone a recent revolution in techniques and knowledge unlike anything in the history of the sport. Today's winter fisherman is more mobile and scientific in his approach. Get the inside scoop on today's tactics for catching fish through the ice from Babe Winkelman, a true northern son.

*VT108*—**Fishing the Canadian Shield: The Ultimate Experience**—Babe Winkelman has long been considered *the* expert on fishing the bountiful yet fragile lakes of the Canadian Shield. Join Babe as he experiences a fishing smorgasbord in the rugged, pristine waters of Ontario. Catch smallmouth bass and stop for shore lunch, and then watch as one of Babe's fishing partners hooks a big surprise he didn't quite bargain for!

*VT109*—**Bronzebacks of the North: Smallmouth Spectacular**—Built like a bullet and muscled like a prize fighter, the smallmouth bass is everything you are looking for in a gamefish. Join Babe Winkelman on a tour of the scenic, unspoiled waters "smallies" inhabit. He will share a complete system for catching these bronzed acrobats.

*VT110*—**Spring Fishing: The Cure For Cabin Fever**—After a winter of dreaming, the first day spent fishing on open water is a time to savor. Join Babe Winkelman in a celebration of spring in the north country. Unleash a winter of pent-up energy with this entertaining and fact-filled video guaranteed to cure your cabin fever at any time of the year!

*VT111*—**Big Water Bounty: Great Lakes Fishing Made Easy**—The huge, sprawling Great Lakes are home to a breed of fish that is used to its freedom. These fish wage a battle they don't intend to lose, in some of the most spectacular fight scenes ever! Babe Winkelman, the man everyone seeks for angling advice, shows you there is fantastic Big Water fishing within easy reach of the average angler.

*VT112*—**Family Fishing Fun: Sharing the Good Times**—This tape will help the entire family learn about fishing together. Babe Winkelman, despite his busy schedule as a professional fishing educator, knows the value of quality time with his wife and four daughters. Join the Winkelman family on a houseboat trip where they find a renewed appreciation for the traditional values that make fishing the most universal and endearing lifetime sport of all.

*VT113*—**Fishing the Flow: Wonders of the River**—The flowing peacefulness of a river draws the heart and soul of a fisherman deeply into its grasp. Babe Winkelman is at home in the ever-changing world of river fishing. In the style that has drawn him an enormous following, Babe shares his secrets for catching fish from the river's currents.

*VT114*—**Great Plains Reservoirs: Fishing Midwestern Impoundments**—Some of the most fabled names in fishing history belong to a group of relative newcomers: the flood-control reservoirs. Let Babe Winkelman unravel the secrets to catching walleye and bass in a world where river fish have become lake fish. Or have they?

# THE LIBRARY OF FISHING KNOWLEDGE
## COMPREHENSIVE GUIDE SERIES

Babe Winkelman, America's most renown fishing educator, brings you the highly acclaimed **Comprehensive Guide Series.** These are without question the most authoritative books on freshwater fishing ever produced.

Each book contains concise, detailed information put together into a total system for understanding, finding, and catching more and bigger fish...a system that's guaranteed to improve anyone's fishing results! $11.95 each.

**Largemouth Bass Patterns**—Not just another "ho-hum" bass book. Babe uses detailed diagrams and photos to explain his "pattern system" and revolutionary approaches to bass fishing. Absolutely the last word on largemouth bass! 256 pages.   BK04

**Jig and Live Bait Fishing Secrets**—The basic fundamentals of jig fishing and live bait rigging are covered in Babe's easy-to-understand style. But this book goes well beyond, into the tips and secrets that can help you become a master fisherman. 268 pages.   BK06

**The Strictly Fish Cookbook**—Not just another cookbook—this book includes illustrated "how-to's" on cleaning, filleting, and preparing. Includes smoking, pickling, canning, grilling, and other unconventional cooking methods. 256 pages.   BK05

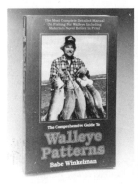 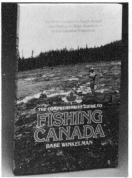 

**Walleye Patterns**—This finicky, highly prized critter is Babe's specialty. His unusual methods and patterns are explained in detail. Includes valuable material never before in print. 304 pages of solid walleye knowledge.   BK02

**Fishing Canada**—The angler's roadmap that unlocks the mysteries of the vast Canadian wilderness. Babe shares his secrets and information on all major species. This book is a MUST if you're planning to fish "God's Country." 230 pages.   BK01

### COMPREHENSIVE GUIDE SERIES GIFT PACK
A new six-volume set of the entire **Comprehensive Guide Series.** $71.70 retail. Sixpk

**"Good Fishing" Audio Cassette Series**—Four 1-hour tapes feature Babe answering some tough questions about catching panfish, bass, walleye, northerns and muskies. Babe explains how his "pattern method" works throughout the seasons. This one-of-a-kind item is the perfect companion at home, in the car, or even on the water. $24.95.　　　　CT01

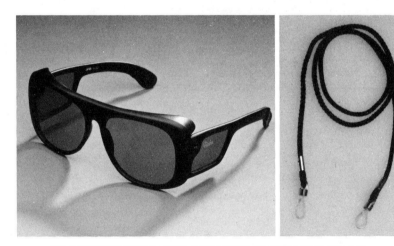

## BABE WINKELMAN'S "FISHERMAN'S FAVORITE"
## POLARIZED SUNGLASSES

See what you've been missing with Babe's **"Fisherman's Favorite"** polarized sunglasses, now in two sizes: large (regular) and new medium size for ladies or smaller men. Both styles feature high quality *glass* lenses in two colors, gray and amber. Floatable case included. $19.95

SG01-A: regular size, amber　　　SG03-A: medium size, amber
SG01-G: regular size, gray　　　　SG03-G: medium size, gray

Keep sunglasses handy and secure with Babe's new **Sunglass Lanyard**, worn comfortably around the neck. Nylon 24" cord with plastic retainers slide directly on bow of glasses and cinch down tight. $1.49 retail.　　　　SG05

### "Good Fishing" Team Hat

Comes with patch sewn on. Black front with silver mesh back. Quality hats made in U.S.A. Adjustable size fits all.                    $5.95

### Patch

"Good Fishing" embroidered patch.                    $1.50

### Decal

Fade-resistant "Good Fishing" Research Team emblem printed black on silver polyester. Water-resistant adhesive. 5½" high x 5" wide.                    $1.00

### Tankard

12 oz. capacity insulated tankard with wide non-tip base. Handsome black trim with "research team" emblem printed in silver.                    Each $3.95
Set of 6 $19.95

*For complete details and ordering information, for all of
Babe's products, send for a free catalog:*

**Babe Winkelman Productions, Inc.**
P.O. Box 407
Brainerd, MN 56401
or call: (218) 829-1144